# EMPLOYMENT POLICIES IN THE SOVIET UNION AND EASTERN EUROPE

*Also by Jan Adam*

WAGE, PRICE AND TAXATION POLICY IN CZECHOSLOVAKIA 1948–1970,
WAGE CONTROL AND INFLATION IN THE SOVIET BLOC COUNTRIES
EMPLOYMENT AND WAGE POLICIES IN POLAND, HUNGARY AND
CZECHOSLOVAKIA SINCE 1950

# Employment Policies in the Soviet Union and Eastern Europe

*Second Revised Edition*

Edited by
## Jan Adam
*Professor of Economics*
*University of Calgary, Alberta, Canada*

St. Martin's Press　　　New York

First edition 1982
Second edition 1987

Published in the United States of America

Printed in Hong Kong

ISBN 0–312–24463–0

Library of Congress Cataloging-in-Publication Data
Main entry under title:
Employment policies in the Soviet Union and Eastern
Europe.
Includes bibliographical references and index.
1. Manpower policy—Soviet Union—Addresses,
essays, lectures.   2. Manpower policy—Europe,
Eastern—Addresses, essays, lectures.   I. Adam, Jan,
1920–
HD5796.E47   1986        331.11′0947        85–25192
ISBN 0–312–24463–0

# Contents

# List of Tables and Figures

## TABLES

# Acknowledgements

The studies in this volume were presented and discussed at a Symposium held at the University of Calgary on 27–29 November 1980. On behalf of the authors, including myself, I would like to express my gratitude to the discussants – Professors A. Abouchar (U. of Toronto), H. Betz (U. of Calgary), M. Bornstein (Michigan U.), R. Carston (Carleton U.), H. Flakierski (York U.), D. Granick (U. of Wisconsin), G. Grossman (U. of California), R. Hutchings (England), B. Korda (U. of Alberta), C. McMillan (Carleton U.), I. Moravcik (U. of Alberta), S. Peitchinis (U. of Calgary), P. Sokolowski (Hessen State College) and R. Stuart (Rutgers U.) – for their valuable comments which helped improve the final version of the studies. Of course, the sole responsibility for any remaining errors is the authors'.

I am obliged to all those institutions whose financial contributions enabled the Symposium to be held. I would like to express my appreciation to the Social Sciences and Humanities Research Council of Canada, Ottawa; the University Research Policy and Grants Committee of the University of Calgary; the Social Sciences Faculty and Department of Economics. I would like to thank especially Professor D. McLachlan, Chairman of the Department of Economics, and Professor H. Betz, Dean of the Faculty of Social Sciences, who, due to their help and encouragement, share in the credit for holding the Symposium. I also wish to record my gratitude to the support staff of the Department of Economics, particularly to Mrs S. Langan who helped to organize the Symposium.

Finally, I would like to express thanks to Mmes. B. Blackman and M. Hess for improving the English of some of the studies and to Mmes. P. Langan, M. Samuels, M. Blount, and M. Huber for their care in typing the final version of the studies.

*Calgary, May 1981*          JAN ADAM

# Abbreviations

For space reasons only full references to books, regardless of the language in which they are published, are listed. References to periodical and newspaper articles are listed without titles unless they are published in English. The following abbreviations are used:

(a) For countries:

| | |
|---|---|
| CSR | Czech Lands |
| CSSR | Czechoslovak Socialist Republic |
| FRG | Federal Republic of Germany |
| GDR | German Democratic Republic |
| SSR | Slovakia |

(b) For national statistical yearbooks:

| | |
|---|---|
| *NK* | *Narodnoe khoziaistvo SSSR* (Soviet) |
| *RS* | *Rocznik statystyczny* (Polish) |
| *SE* | *Statisztikai Évkönyv* (Hungarian) |
| *SRC* | *Statistická ročenka ČSSR* (Czechoslovak) |
| *SJD* | *Statistisches Jahrbuch der DDR* (East German) |

(c) For miscellaneous matters:

| | |
|---|---|
| CMEA | Council for Mutual Economic Assistance (Comecon) |
| JEC | Publications of Joint Economic Committee of the USA Congress, ed. by J. Hardt |
| RFER | Radio Free Europe |

# Notes on the Contributors

**Jan Adam**, the editor, is Professor of Economics at the University of Calgary, Canada. Born in Czechoslovakia, he received his doctorate and candidacy of economic sciences from Charles University, Prague, where he was Dozent up to 1968. He is, *inter alia*, the author of *Wage Control and Inflation in the Soviet Bloc Countries* and *Employment and Wage Policies in Poland, Czechoslovakia and Hungary since 1950*.

**Franz-Lothar Altmann**, Dipl-Vw, is Senior Researcher at the Osteuropa Institut, Munich, and editor of *Osteuropa Wirtchaft* and *Yearbook of East-European Economics*. He is the author of many publications on the Czechoslovak economy, and also co-author of *Die Wirtschaft der ČSSR und Polens* (with J. Keck and D. Keese) and *Die Kompensation im Ost-West Handel* (with H. Clement).

**Zbigniew M. Fallenbuchl** is Professor of Economics at the University of Windsor. Born in Poland, he received his BSc from the University of London; MA from the University of Montreal; PhD from McGill University; and D. honoris causa from Université de Droit, d'Economie et des Sciences d'Aix-Marseille in 1979. He has published extensively on Soviet and East European economics, and particularly on the Polish economy.

**Hans-Erich Gramatzki** is Research Associate at the Osteuropa Institut, Berlin. He received his MA from Kiel University and PhD from Freie Universität Berlin. He specializes primarily in spatial and regional aspects of the Soviet and East European economies. He is, *inter alia*, the author of *Räumliche Aspekte der Sowjetischen Wirtschaftsplanung*.

**Jiri Kosta** is Professor of Economics at the University of Frankfurt, Germany. Born in Czechoslovakia, he is a graduate of Prague School of Economics and received his PhD from the University of Bremen. He has published widely, primarily on Czechoslovakia, planning, labour problems, and codetermination. He is, *inter alia*, the author of *Sozialistische Planwirtschaft* and *Abriss der Sozialökonomischen Entwicklung der Tschechoslowakei, 1945–77*.

**Anna-Jutta Pietsch** is a member of the research staff of the Osteuropa Institut of Munich. She received her Dr. rer. pol. from the University of Munich, and specializes primarily in economic and sociological problems of industrial work in the USSR and has published several articles on this topic.

**David E. Powell** is a Research Fellow at the Russian Research Center, Harvard University. He received his BA degree from Amherst College in 1961, and his PhD in Political Science from Yale University in 1966. He is the author of *Antireligious Propaganda in the Soviet Union*, as well as numerous articles on social, economic and political problems in the USSR.

**Gertrude E. Schroeder**, Professor of Economics at the University of Virginia, received her PhD in economics from Johns Hopkins University. She is the author of numerous articles and contributions to books dealing mainly with economic organization and management, consumer problems, and labour and wages in the Soviet Union. Specifically, she has contributed major articles to a compendia of studies on the Soviet economy published periodically by the US Congress.

**János Timár** is Professor in and Head of the Department of Labour and Education Economics of the Karl Marx University of Economics in Budapest. He specializes primarily in employment and educational aspects of the Hungarian economy. He is the author of many publications in Hungary and abroad. His book *Planning the Labour Force in Hungary* was published in the United States.

**Heinrich Vogel** is the Director of Bundesinstitut für Ostwissenschaftliche und Internationale Studien, Cologne, Germany. He received his MA and PhD in economics from the University of Munich. He has published widely, primarily on the Soviet Union, and is the author, *inter alia*, of *Betrieb und zentrale Planung in der UdSSR* and *Sozialpolitik in der UdSSR*.

# Introduction to the Second Edition

In the four years which have elapsed from the time the first typescript for the first edition was handed over to the publisher many changes have occurred in the five countries under review. Poland has been engulfed in a political and economic crisis and it will require, even according to optimistic views, many years for it to recover. The deceleration of economic growth which started in the second half of the 1970s continued, but in the last two years, some improvement came about. Poland, which suffered a huge decline in economic performance in 1981–3, has managed to reverse the trend in part. In all the countries there was some movement towards economic reforms. Hungary embarked in 1985 on a reform which is in some respects going beyond the objectives of the 1968 reform. Poland is again engaged in efforts to reform the system of management. The reforms in the other three countries do not exceed the framework of the centralized system.

In the light of the development in economic growth, an uninformed reader would expect that labour shortage concerns would disappear and would be replaced by concerns with unemployment. There were such fears in Poland and Hungary (in the other three countries the labour shortages were too profound to bring about a reversal) but they have not materialized. Poland suffers from labour shortages as before. All the factors which brought about labour shortages are still in force, but, at the same time, some provisions have been taken to counter possible unemployment.

This second edition is a revised, updated edition. The extent of updating corresponds to the extent of changes in individual countries in the aspects discussed. Disregarding the new chapters, the chapter on Poland, due to the events mentioned above, is revised the most.

This edition contains two new chapters. One on a new topic, written by David E. Powell, deals with the role of pensioners in coping with labour shortages in the USSR, where the number of working pensioners is still increasing. The new chapter on employment policy in Hungary is written by an insider, János Timár. In contrast to other country studies on employment policy, which concentrate primarily on the present, this study gives a historical analysis of employment policy in Hungary. Since all the countries of the CMEA followed for a long time a more or less identical employment policy, this study will hopefully help the reader to understand employment policy in its historical development.

The authors of Chapter 7 were not in a position to update their study. Gertrude E. Schroeder has been kind enough to undertake this task.

*Calgary, January 1986*                                    JAN ADAM

# Introduction to the First Edition

All the countries of the Soviet bloc suffer from labour shortages to varying degrees. In some countries, however, there are regions where untapped labour resources still exist or where people with certain qualifications have difficulty finding jobs, whereas in other countries the number of people who are able and willing to work and who are not absorbed into the labour force is very small.

Labour shortages have become a serious problem which adversely affects the 'socialist' economies in various ways. They put limits to economic growth; no doubt the present deceleration of economic growth in all the countries is also caused by labour shortages. (It is not an easy task to maintain economic growth by increases in productivity even though various provisions, including incentives, are made.) What is even more important, they have become an obstacle to the continuous process of restructuring the economy in line with technological progress and in response to changing requirements in domestic and foreign markets (the latter being more of a problem in small countries of the socialist camp which are more dependent on foreign trade than in the USSR). A tight labour market unfavourably affects the tendencies to expand the service sector which is undermanned in some branches and thus hampers the effort to increase the standard of living.

Labour shortages are combined with a gross underutilization of labour. This is a fact of life which is generally acknowledged by politicians and economists in the 'socialist' countries. If it were possible to substantially increase the effectiveness of labour utilization by a better organization of the production process and/or by the mechanization of auxiliary production processes and/or by cutting unwarranted losses of working time there would not be a problem of labour shortages.

The socialist countries are confronted with a problem with a known cure which, however, cannot be effectively applied for various reasons. Here, mention will only be made of the political dimension of the cure. To cure the tight labour market effectively would require, among other things, the shutting down of enterprises which produce unsaleable goods, the transfer of labour from non-efficient to more efficient enterprises, the removal of redundant workers and, last but not least, the tightening of labour discipline in all respects. An attempt to solve any of these problems fast and consistently, even if incentives are used, involves political risks which are greater than the politicians are willing to take. It should be borne in mind that in this area Soviet-type authoritarian systems are more vulnerable than Western democracies. Tightening labour discipline beyond a certain point is almost impossible in socialist countries. Workers need some vent for their frustration; if they are not allowed to criticize the system and its representatives, at least they must have some leeway in the work-place. To deprive them of this privilege, even if it were possible – it is doubtful whether Stalinist methods of coercion can still be applied – would be dangerous. In addition, the commitment of communist leaders to full employment (one of the trumps they hold – a trump which it would be very risky to give up) is one of the factors which make it difficult to enforce labour discipline.

Labour shortages are a recent phenomenon and cause great concern to the planners. In order to understand the current economic policies of the socialist countries they must be studied in depth. Unfortunately, no proper attention has been devoted to this problem in the West. The present volume of studies is a modest first step to correct this situation. It is a collective effort which has the advantage that the much-needed research can be speeded up and a greater interest in the problem can be aroused.

The topics of the studies were determined on the basis of a project thought out in advance and then the appropriate authors were selected. Thus, the studies are by no means just the proceedings of a symposium organized around a certain topic.

Labour shortages can be discussed from different angles: theoretical, political, statistical, etc. Among the theoretical questions which cross one's mind when thinking about shortages, the one of great importance, no doubt, is the extent to which this new phenomenon in the labour market means that the countries under review have already achieved full employment. This question is warranted since, as mentioned, shortages are combined with under-utilization of labour. Its significance is enhanced by its potential comparative aspect, by possible comparison with capitalism. However, no attempt has been made to head research in this direction.

The main objective of the present volume of studies is to research the reasons for labour shortages, the policies used to cope with them, and the extent of their success. In addition, the volume examines many other questions which are directly or indirectly connected with the main objective. In order to achieve the first objective the focus of the volume is on country studies. For space and other reasons only the USSR, Poland, the GDR, CSSR and Hungary are discussed.

Socialist country studies on a narrow topic (particularly when there are several, as in this case) are exposed to two contradictory dangers. On the one hand, because the countries are marked by many common systemic features, the studies may be very similar and repetitive. On the other hand, the fact that the studies are written by different scholars may result in great differences in the approach to and the coverage of problems.

No effort has been spared to avoid both extremes. The studies have been coordinated to a certain degree. For this purpose an outline suggesting problems to be covered was given to the authors. The Symposium at which the studies were discussed and commented upon by known scholars also played an important role in the coordination effort.

Yet it was clear from the beginning that it would be impossible and also harmful from the viewpoint of the quality of the studies if an attempt were to be undertaken to confine the intellectual creativity and initiative of the authors within rigid limits. A loose coordination can only be to the benefit of the readers since it gives rise to a richer product with regard to coverage of problems and approaches.

The fact that the countries discussed, though they have common systemic features, are confronted with different degrees of severity of shortages, due to their postwar history, demographic development and concrete economic situation, have also worked against the danger of repetitiveness.

Of course, the reader will make the final judgment on the extent to which the volume has escaped the indicated dangers.

The volume consists of two parts. Part I contains the country studies already mentioned, while Part II is made up of four studies which are in a certain sense supplementary to the first part.

The country studies, though they discuss the same topic in substance, differ in their coverage of the problems and in their approach. For example, G. Schroeder's chapter also covers regional problems, Fallenbuchl's stresses the historical approach, Kosta's deals in detail with the role of the wage system. Altmann's discusses the incentives used to ease the displacement of individual workers and Marrese's tests the hypothesis of labour shortages by an analysis of statistical material.

All five country studies agree that the present labour market situation has been aggravated by the demographic development. Yet the shortages are only relative to the level of productivity; if only the great reserves in labour productivity increases could be utilized the shortages could be overcome.

Adam's study in Part II is comparative; it discusses similarities and differences in the reasons for shortages in four countries, and in their treatment and the extent to which they reflect systemic differences. He comes to the conclusion that the methods used for coping with shortages reflect systemic differences but that there are no noticeable differences in the effectiveness of the methods used.

The chapter by A. Pietsch and H. Vogel discusses the social and educational consequences of displacement by technological progress and their treatment. It is the only study in Part II which is confined to one country, in this case, the USSR, and it is in a sense an extension to G. Schroeder's study. The authors show that the process of displacement is slow compared to the expectations of the Soviet authorities. It is usually combined with loss of earnings for the workers who are affected by it, and this surely makes the process more difficult.

Labour shortages have a regional dimension; the untapped resources are concentrated outside the capitals. Therefore, a study of labour shortages cannot be complete without considering regional aspects. Yet this is a field where only a few studies exist, let alone any comparative ones. H. Gramatzki's study tries to fill this gap. His chapter, which deals with all four East European countries, is conceived more broadly than the focus of our topic is; it also discusses other aspects of regional employment policies.

Labour shortages have not developed simultaneously in all the countries: at a time when some countries were already suffering from shortages, others were plagued by unemployment. It is only natural that the question comes to mind: to what extent has CMEA been involved in bringing about equilibrium in the labour market throughout the socialist camp? T. Vais' study is concerned with the cooperation of CMEA countries in the employment sphere. His finding is that the limited migration between CMEA countries for temporary employment purposes mostly takes place for reasons other than labour market equilibrium.

In a book written by an individual it is expected that the views expressed throughout the book will be consistent. It is difficult to impose such a constraint on a volume of studies unless one wants to limit the free research of the authors. What is important, however, is to make sure that there are no contradictions in the reported facts; and this requirement has received proper attention.

*Calgary, May 1981* JAN ADAM

# Part I

# 1 Managing Labour Shortages in the Soviet Union

## GERTRUDE E. SCHROEDER

## I. INTRODUCTION

In the Soviet-type economy, labour 'shortages' can occur only relative to effective demands that are incorporated in enterprise plans and backed up with funds. In theory, plans in the aggregate are supposed to balance planned demands for labour with available supplies, within an overall policy framework of providing a job for everyone able to work, for work is considered both a 'right' and a duty. If planners' labour force projections are accurate and their expectations about productivity are realized, a general labour shortage would be impossible. Even with overall equilibrium in the labour market, localized shortages and surpluses of labour are conceivable, although they should not occur either, if plans in disaggregated forms were perfect and implementation was in accord with them.

Over the years the Soviet Union has experienced general and localized shortages of labour. Overall shortages have occurred, because economic policies have enforced taut planning, i.e. demands for production have been high relative to resources available and current possibilities for raising productivity. In general, authorities have responded by driving up labour force participation rates, cutting back plan targets, or failing to meet them. Localized shortages have been dealt with through a variety of policies and institutional arrangements. This chapter: (1) describes the labour market in the Soviet Union since the 1970s; (2) assesses the policies and measures used to deal with imbalances; and (3) describes the labour situation that the USSR faces in the next 15 years and considers policies that are being used to deal with it.

3

## II.  THE LABOUR MARKET

### 1.  Supply of labour

The Soviet labour force grew rapidly during the 1970s. Fuelled by annual increments to the population of working age (16–59 for males and 16–54 for females) of about 2 million, the labour force increased by similar numbers.[1]

Growth was somewhat faster during the first half of the decade than during the second half, and by 1978 males made up over half the labour force for the first time since the Second World War. Annual additions to the non-agricultural labour force were even larger, because the agricultural labour force dropped by about half a million persons each year. Both the population of working age and employment expanded much more rapidly in Central Asia and Transcaucasia than in the USSR as a whole, and much less rapidly in the Baltics and the Ukraine.[2]

To facilitate several decades of forced-draft industrialization, labour force participation rates had been raised to near maximum levels. In 1970, 93 per cent of males 20–59 years of age, and 89 per cent of females 20–54 years of age were economically active.[3] While the share for men resembles that elsewhere, that for women is greater by wide margins. In contrast, participation rates for persons over 55–60 years of age are relatively low by international standards, because in the USSR men are eligible for pensions at age 60 and women at age 55. Participation rates apparently have changed little since 1970, except for some increase for persons of pensionable age.

The quality of the labour force also improved considerably during 1971–83. In each year, several million young people graduated from high school, and 1.7–2.0 million from secondary specialized schools (tekhnikums) and higher educational institutions (vuzy). A 10-year education was made compulsory and largely implemented. As a result median years of schooling of the labour force rose from 8.4 years in 1970 to an estimated 10 years in 1980.[4] The gains were about equal for men and women, and were much more rapid for the rural labour force than for urban workers.[5] Differences among the republics, while still substantial, also narrowed considerably during the decade.

## 2. Demand for labour

As in previous decades, the demand for labour has remained high since 1970, as planners endeavoured to provide full employment and maintain high rates of economic growth. Even though growth rates slowed markedly, the labour market was tight overall because planners greatly overestimated the economy's ability to generate productivity gains. Growth rates for labour productivity decreased sharply during the period – in industry from 6 per cent in 1971–5 to 3 per cent in 1976–83, according to Soviet measures.[6] A similar fall-off was experienced in construction, and in railway transportation productivity stagnated after 1975. Towards the end of the period labour shortages appeared almost everywhere, as enterprises sought to fulfil plan targets by adding workers to make up for productivity shortfalls.

Within this general framework several factors operated to exacerbate the situation. Managers in the so-called 'productive' sectors of the economy were under much pressure to restrain employment growth, to provide labour for the rapidly expanding 'non-productive' sectors, as the government sought to increase services for an increasingly urban and affluent population. Thus, while agricultural employment declined and industrial employment rose by 20 per cent during 1971–83, the work force in the services increased by 36 per cent. High demand for labour was particularly evident in large cities: in contrast, jobs were sometimes hard to find in small towns, especially for women. Shortages were more acute for skilled workers than for the unskilled. During the decade, also, the government made a big push to develop natural resources in Siberia and to build the mammoth Baikal-Amur railroad (BAM), and chronic labour shortages appeared in these regions.

## 3. Utilization of labour

By comparison with other industrialized countries the level of labour productivity in the USSR is low and its growth rate mediocre.[7] Exploration of the many reasons for this situation is beyond the scope of this chapter. We treat here major factors that relate to the use of labour resources *per se*, recognizing, of course, that labour productivity is determined by interaction of all factors of production – land and capital, as well as labour. The impediments to a more efficient use of labour throughout the economy – prevalent in the 1970s and early

1980s as in previous decades – are conveniently grouped into those stemming largely from the behaviour of managers and those mainly related to the behaviour of workers. A third group of factors concerns the consequences of state investment policies.

## The behaviour of managers

Despite a spate of measures designed to eradicate the phenomenon,[8] Soviet enterprise managers display a strong preference for retaining more rather than fewer workers on their payrolls. The reasons are familiar. Probably most important is the fact that managerial incentives are linked primarily to meeting production targets, which are often increased in mid-plan. Since deliveries of raw materials are uncertain, a reserve of labour is needed to handle spurts of production that regularly occur at the end of each month and in the last quarter of the year. For the same reason, extra workers are desirable to prevent production losses from absenteeism and labour turnover. Moreover, managers must provide hands to help with the harvest, repair roads, help build a kindergarten, march in a parade, and the like. In addition, bonus funds have been linked to the size of the wage fund, managerial bonuses depend to some extent on the size of the funds, and managerial salary scales are based in part on the size of the enterprise as measured by employment. Finally, dismissal of a worker is cumbersome, and managers are under social and moral pressure not to fire workers (except for egregious behaviour) unless jobs can be found for them. This behavioural norm results from the state's policy of guaranteeing a job to everyone, and its strong aversion to visible unemployment.

## The behaviour of workers

Except for most graduates of colleges and secondary specialized schools obtaining their first job, workers have freedom of movement and of occupational choice. Differentiated wages are used to channel labour into industries, areas and occupations in accord with planned production and investment goals. Exercising its freedom, the Soviet labour force has proved to be quite mobile. Workers have migrated in large numbers from rural areas to the cities and from one part of the country to another. Often, however, the pattern of migration has not been that desired by planners. For example, in the late 1960s there was net out-migration from West Siberia, even though major investment projects were being launched and enterprises were scrambling for labour.

Workers have exercised their freedom to choose by changing both jobs and occupations with notable frequency. Soviet spokesmen have decried this situation with rising alarm during the 1970s.[9] Although statistics on labour turnover rates are not regularly published, some drop evidently has occurred in the 1970s.[10] None the less, the losses in work-time and other attendant costs are large,[11] and both turnover itself and the expectations of managers that it will occur are cited as causes of overmanning and low productivity. Other reasons often given are: lateness and absenteeism, both often related to alcoholism;[12] intra-shift loss of work-time (estimated to be at least 20 per cent in industry and much higher in construction);[13] running errands on company time, often with managerial permission;[14] poor scheduling of production, irregular delivery of materials, breakdown of machinery and poor coordination among shops; and a general disinclination by workers to exert themselves. The reasons for low work effort and lack of labour discipline are complex but would include guaranteed jobs for everyone and the growing imbalance between the growth of money incomes and the supply of desired goods and services, evidenced by widespread shortages, a rising marginal propensity to save, rapidly increasing prices on collective farm markets, and endemic corruption and black markets.[15]

*Factors relating to investment*

Over the years, Soviet investment policy, especially in industry, has been biased towards mechanization of basic production processes, to the neglect of auxiliary (support) functions. As a result, large numbers of persons are engaged both in auxiliary operations and in manual labour. Soviet sources report, for example, that the ratio of basic to auxiliary workers in industry is 1 to 1, compared with 2 to 1 in other industrialized countries, and that it has been stable for 20 years.[16] Many workers are engaged in manual labour even in basic processes, 27 per cent; but 71 per cent of auxiliary workers do manual labour – mainly loaders, assemblers, material handlers, sorters, packers, and the like.[17] More than 10 million persons are engaged in loading and unloading work and in intra-plant transportation, compared with only about 3 million in the United States.[18] Such large amounts of auxiliary and manual labour impact adversely on measures of labour productivity. A part of the explanation for the slow reduction in the use of manual labour lies in the proclivity of managers to hold labour in reserve to meet emergencies; in the interim, the workers must have job titles and something to do. Another reason is the deplorable state of affairs in the production of materials handling and related equipment needed to mechanize auxiliary work. Only 20 per cent of the equipment made available to enterprises goes to mechanize auxiliary operations – the rest is used to re-equip basic production facilities, whereas investment in the former is 2.8–3.5 times as effective in reducing the number of workers.[19] At present there is a great shortage of equipment to mechanize loading, lifting, hauling and warehousing activities. Production is scattered among 400 plants under 40 ministries.[20] Only 15 per cent of the total output is planned centrally, which means that many industries and plants produce their own equipment, using much manual labour and at high cost.[21]

A related factor detrimental to efficiency is the enormous amount of labour (and machines) engaged in repair work. The problem plagues all sectors and stems primarily from the poor quality and durability of Soviet-made machinery and from the generalized lack of incentives for caring for capital stock efficiently. In the early 1970s, for example, capital repair (major repairs) alone occupied one-tenth of all industrial workers and one-third of all metal-cutting tools.[22] In 1977 repair of machinery – 70 per cent of the work done by hand – reportedly engaged 18 per cent of industrial wage-workers.[23] More people are engaged in repair work than in production of machinery and equipment.[24]

## III.  GOVERNMENT POLICIES DEALING WITH THE USE OF LABOUR

Spurred by actual labour shortages and by the spectre of a potential critical situation in the 1980s, the Soviet government in recent years has taken an unprecedented number of steps to improve the functioning of the labour market and to use labour more efficiently. For convenience of analysis, the many-faceted effort will be described under the following types of measures: (1) planning, (2) organizations, (3) administrative rewards and penalties, (4) wages and managerial incentives, (5) investment designed to release labour and raise productivity. Many of these measures follow the recommendations of an All-Union Conference on the Use of Labour, published in November 1978,[25] and a number of them were incorporated in a comprehensive Party–Government decree on improving economic planning and management, adopted 12 July 1979.[26]

## 1. Planning

The principal purpose of labour force planning has been to try to ensure that demands for workers embodied in production and development plans are matched with people when and where they are needed and in the required mix of skills. The principal instrument for such planning is the labour balance, a key ingredient of the overall system of planning by balances. Over the years, poor labour force planning has been regularly blamed for localized imbalances (shortages and surpluses) that routinely arise in practice. The assorted efforts to improve regional planning by providing a greater role for local authorities have been directed towards correcting this problem by better forecasting and by taking labour supply more carefully into account in making investment. The July 1979 Decree tackles this problem anew by (1) demanding that labour balances be drawn up more 'scientifically'; (2) requiring that balances be prepared for 5-year and annual periods at all levels – from Gosplan USSR to authorities in oblasts, raions and cities (the balance of the national level must now be submitted to the Council of Ministers for scrutiny); (3) enterprises and ministries are to work with local planning bodies to draft plans for meeting manpower requirements; (4) the State Committee on Labour and Social Problems is to have an increased role in this process; (5) to help solve various labour problems, plans at all levels are to have sections on 'social development', i.e. for providing social services to match plans for the number and type of workers and for regulating and disciplining the work force.

A key part of the labour balances concerns allocation of professionally trained workers to enterprises, especially graduates from secondary specialized and higher educational institutions. Responding to mounting evidence of mismatches between qualifications of graduates and requirements of the economy, the Council of Ministers in January 1978 issued a sharply critical decree demanding that matters be set right.[27] Specifically, planning authorities and the responsible ministries were accused of failing to update programmes for training specialists to conform to changes in organization and technology of production, and also of failing to allow for changing sectoral and regional patterns of economic activity, when drawing up plans for training and for work assignments of new graduates. A follow-up decree, issued jointly with the Party Central Committee, was issued in July 1979.[28] The demands for improved planning for distribution and training of the labour force embodied in the two decrees are not new. Their stress on plans and planning procedures, however, conforms to a syndrome that has characterized reform efforts over the past 20 years; namely, the conviction that poor plans are a major cause of poor performance and that 'improved' plans will produce 'improved' performance. Up to now, this has been a vain hope.

## 2.   Organizations

Although the bulk of the labour force allocates itself among available jobs in response to wages offered, the government has played an ever larger role in the allocation of labour since the late 1950s. The process began in 1955 with the establishment of the State Committee on Labour and Wages, to monitor a major wage reform and oversee policies concerning labour matters. Since the early 1930s the government has had an elaborate system for the work assignment of graduates from tekhnikums and institutions of higher education; assignments are compulsory for a period of three years. The government also has long been involved in placing graduates from the ever-changing system of vocational-technical schools. In addition, the government has been active in the regional redistribution of workers to meet priority needs of one kind or another. This redistribution, entailing formal programmes fixed in annual labour balances, was carried out by two agencies at the national level – the All-Union Resettlement Committee and the Administration for Organised Recruitment (Orgnabor). In the post-Stalin period the resettlement activities have involved the movement of families or entire villages to meet requirements for agricultural workers in other areas. Resettlement bonuses and other benefits are offered, the largest ones for moving to Siberia and the Far East. Originally set up to assist in moving rural labour to industrial work in the cities, Orgnabor lately has been mainly concerned with recruiting urban manpower to staff major construction projects in remote areas and to provide new plants with skilled workers. Workers recruited under this programme sign fixed-term contracts and receive various kinds of benefits. The number of workers placed through Orgnabor reportedly increased by 2.4 times during 1967–76, but its share in total new hires is still only about 3 per cent.[29]

In 1976–7 the agencies dealing with labour matters were brought together in a unified state system. The USSR State Committee for Labour and Wages was renamed the USSR State Committee for Labour and Social Problems (Goskomtrud) and became a union-republic organ with the status of a ministry.[30] In 1978 a statute was approved giving the Goskomtrud system wide-ranging powers of 'control' – monitoring, checking, inspection – in respect to ministries, organizations, associations, and enterprises in matters relating to the utilization of labour.[31]

Although market forces and decentralized recruiting account for the vast bulk of new hires, the government's role may expand even further. The number of school graduates – most assigned directly to jobs – has been rising rapidly, and the labour exchanges are playing an increasingly active role.[32] A statute governing their operations was issued in 1979.[33] The government is being urged to make the use of these exchanges mandatory, for all work-seekers and for employers. The newly centralized Goskomtrud system provides the machinery for further restricting the use of market forces, should the government decide to do so.

## 3. Administrative measures

Administrative measures for coping with actual or potential labour shortages may be considered under two rubrics – those directed towards workers and those directed towards employers. We have already considered briefly the long-standing programmes to allocate graduates from colleges and tekhnikums to state-chosen jobs. There is, of course, the use of forced (prison) labour and the regular military forces to carry out economic tasks. Both groups have long been used extensively for construction and other developmental projects where civilian labour was in short supply. Finally, so-called 'antiparasite' laws, enacted in the republics, permit sentencing to corrective labour for persons who fail to hold a job in the official economy. An array of organizations, including local housing committees, are used to ferret out would-be idlers.

In the days of Stalin, legal sanctions also were used to cope with absenteeism and unwanted labour turnover. In the 1950s these sanctions were replaced with economic rewards and penalties, and workers were permitted to quit merely by giving two weeks' notice. In 1973, the government introduced new labour booklets, with tightened procedures intended to curb labour turnover,[34] and in 1977 labour booklets were made mandatory for collective farmers.[35] Tightening controls even further, the authorities in January 1980 published a sweeping Resolution, which increased to one month the period of notice required for voluntary quits, and ordered managers at all levels to get tough with violators of labour discipline.[36] Agencies concerned are 'to proceed from the premise that ... managers ... are just as responsible for the state and strengthening of labour discipline as they are for the fulfilment of plan assignments'.

In the main, the tools used to induce enterprise managers to minimize the use of labour are economic (incentive) rather than administrative in nature. With respect to administrative–managerial jobs, however, the government has persistently sought to limit their numbers by fiat. Before the 1965 economic reforms, enterprise managers had to register such positions with the State Staffing Commission, which was supposed to enforce standard staffing norms; this procedure is still required of all organizations supported by the budget. When the reforms accorded managers the right to determine their own staffing patterns, limited only by the total planned wage fund, the relative number of administrative-type jobs increased at enterprises. Also the bureaucracy – labelled 'apparat' in Soviet employment statistics – continued to grow. In response, the government imposed annual quotas on all units for reduction of administrative–management expenditures and ordered the annual planned 'savings' confiscated by the state budget.[37] This exercise yields the budget about a billion rubles annually. The freedom given managers to determine staffing patterns has now been effectively retracted. Goskomtrud and the ministries work out standard staffing patterns, which are disseminated for the 'guidance' of enterprise managers. Since 1980–1 enterprises have been subject to mandatory ceilings on employment.

## 4.  Monetary incentives

We treat this large subject under two headings: (1) the wage system in general, in terms of its use to promote efficient utilization of labour in enterprises and to direct labour to areas of actual or potential shortage; and (2) a variety of particular incentives offered to reduce labour turnover and to retain pensioners and women with children at work.

## (a) Wage regulation

Highly centralized management of the wage system enables the government to manipulate wage rates to deal with labour shortages, actual or anticipated. Wage levels by branch of the economy are set to direct labour in accord with the plan and to alter income differentials in accord with government policies.[38] Regional wage coefficients have been established to attract and retain labour in Siberia and similar regions, and to compensate for other undesirable work conditions. The coefficients, at first applicable only to workers in heavy industry in a few areas, were added to basic wage rates up to 300 rubles per month and ranged from 1.1–1.2 in the Urals, southern areas of Western Siberia, Kazakhstan and Central Asia to 2.0 in the islands of the Arctic Ocean.[39] In a general wage reform during 1971–9, the coefficients were revised and extended to new regions and sectors, including Western Siberia. These changes were designed to correct wage inequities and reduce labour turnover that resulted from the old system. Nevertheless, criticism continues to be levied at the regional differentials, the critics pointing out that they still do not apply to all workers in the services branches in the affected regions, that several different coefficients often apply in the same area, that they fail in many cases to compensate for real cost of living differences, and that they are inconsistent with the system of zonal prices for food and certain other goods.[40]

Manipulation of basic wage rates and supplements is intended to steer labour in desired directions and overcome revealed shortages in specific areas. Another arrangement, now superimposed on the basic system, is designed to induce enterprises to try to meet output assignments with fewer workers than planned, thus freeing labour for other work. This effort, referred to as the 'Shchekino experiment', began in 1967 in a large chemical plant and was gradually extended to some 1200 enterprises (in 1978)[41] mainly in the chemical, petro-chemical, paper, and maritime industries. Under this scheme the enterprise is supposed to be guaranteed a fixed wage fund and stable output targets for the year and allowed to keep all wage savings from meeting the targets with fewer workers than planned. Despite strong Party support and three sets of implementing instructions, the experiment has not been widely adopted. Evidently workers are not keen on it, because they have to take on more work; managers have resisted it, because it interferes with existing routines and because the rules of the game often are not adhered to in practice. None the less, the authorities are determined to push the scheme, and the July 1979 Decree has incorporated its principles into the general system of incentives. Specifically, beginning in 1981: (1) enterprises are to be assigned wage funds for 5-year and annual periods based on normative (standard) wage rates per ruble of output (net or gross); (2) from any savings in wages over planned sums, enterprises may pay workers wage supplements up to 50 per cent for combining jobs and taking on extra work, raise rates of pay for skilled workers, and give bonuses up to 30 per cent for managerial employees and foremen; (3) managers may pay a one-time bonus to workers who agree to revisions of work norms; (4) wage funds unspent at the end of the year are to be transferred to the general incentive funds, from which bonuses and other benefits can be paid, and are not to be confiscated.

Another measure to promote economy in enterprise use of labour is establishment of centrally set targets for growth of labour productivity, with bonuses tied to meeting them. This provision, an early modification of the 1965 reforms, was introduced in 1971–2 and has been strengthened in subsequent modifications of the rules. Specifically, fulfilling the plan for labour productivity increases incentive funds by specified percentages (normatives), set in government decrees or by ministries; the percentages are increased for over-fulfilling the plan and for meeting a voluntarily adopted, more demanding plan (counterplan). In the revision of the rules in 1976, the labour productivity target was virtually made mandatory, not only as a basis for forming bonus funds, but also as a requirement for awarding managerial bonuses. Essentially the same arrangements, with a few new wrinkles, are incorporated in the rules governing the formation and use of incentive funds in 1981–5.[42]

## (b)  Other incentives

The wage and incentive system has long contained features designed to encourage continuous service in a single enterprise, discourage labour turnover and induce women with children, and also pensioners, to remain economically active. In recent years, measures have been taken to strengthen such programmes. In 1968 benefits for workers in the Far North and equivalent regions were liberalized:[43] for the first 3 years of service, workers are paid a 10 per cent wage supplement every 6 months, with the maximum reached after 5 years. The period of vacation was also increased, and the pensionable age reduced. The Decree on Labour Discipline of 12 January 1980 adds new incentives in the form of grants to finance purchase of houses, extra vacation and additions to old age pensions.

Since the early 1960s the government several times has revised pension rules with a view to keeping persons of pensionable age in the labour force and luring retirees back to work. As a result, the proportion of old age pensioners who work rose from 12 per cent to 24 per cent during 1960–75.[44] The latest such measure, embodied in a decree of 2 October 1979 and effective as of 1 January 1980,[45] provides for supplement to pensions of 10 rubles per month for each year of work after retirement age, with a maximum of 40 rubles. The total pension plus supplement is limited to 150 rubles per month. In addition, the decree adds to the list of groups of workers entitled to receive all or part of their pensions while working. Wages plus pensions must not exceed 300 rubles per month for most eligible groups (150 rubles in the case of most office employees). In recent years the government has also been trying to encourage provision of part-time jobs and work at home for women with young children and for the handicapped.[46]

## 5. Investment

Measures considered here concern efforts to speed up mechanization of labour-intensive processes, particularly auxiliary operations. Although this theme has been stressed for years, its urgency mounted in the 1970s. The Ninth Five-Year Plan (1971–5) contained a 'broad complex' of measures, along with specific production targets, for automation and mechanization of production processes throughout the economy, with emphasis on mechanization of loading and unloading work, intra-plant transport, and warehousing operations. Reflecting dissatisfaction with progress under the Plan, a Party–Government decree issued in 1973 called for a speed-up, and demanded better organization for producing the required machinery, with explicit assignments given to particular ministries as head organizations for the effort.[47] The theme of mechanization was reiterated in the Directives for the Tenth Five-Year Plan (1976–80), with machinery ministries being assigned increased targets for production of labour-saving machinery, especially materials-handling equipment. The reform Decree of July 1979 instructed Gosplan and the ministries to draw up 'comprehensive' programmes for mechanization of labour throughout the economy, with procedures, targets and deadlines specified. One of the 'priority' programmes listed in the decree, this programme is also one of five such programmes included as separate entities in the Eleventh Five-Year Plan (1981–5).[48] Finally, the Party in July 1980 issued still another resolution on the subject, excoriating one and all for dilatory tactics and calling for a speed-up in the production of industrial robots and related mechanisms, with specific targets parcelled out once more.[49]

Despite all the decrees, production of the necessary capital equipment, as well as investment in plants to produce it, still has secondary priority for producing ministries and design bureaus. Evidently, mechanization programmes do not have priority for implementing enterprises either; even if they did, efforts to mechanize would often be frustrated by inability to obtain the requisite equipment. Production of this 'auxiliary' equipment is scattered among hundreds of enterprises and scores of ministries, and few of the facilities are specialized. Materials-handling equipment, for example, is produced in 102 plants of two major ministries but also in another 300 plants of 45 other ministries; research and design work is done by 140 organizations: only 15–18 per cent of the plants are specialized; much equipment is produced in single units or small lots at very high cost; the level of standardization is quite low, the quality of the equipment often poor, and the mix not that wanted by customers.[50] Centralization of production of materials-handling equipment under a single management agency has been proposed as a solution.

## IV.   THE LABOUR MARKET IN THE NEXT 15 YEARS

### 1.   The demographic situation

For the rest of this century the Soviet Union will face a labour market situation unprecedented in Soviet experience. As a result of a decline in birth rates since the early 1960s, the growth of the population in the able-bodied ages (16–59 for men and 16–54 for women) will drop sharply – from an average of 2.5 million in the 1970s to 1.1 million in 1981 and to about 250 000 in 1986. Thereafter, the annual increments rise slowly, but will not reach 1 million until 1997.[51] Since these age groups make up the bulk of the economically active population, annual additions to the labour force also will drop precipitously and will remain well below increments characteristic of the 1970s. Moreover, the Soviet Union will have to rely almost entirely on adult population growth for additional manpower, because labour force participation rates are now near maximum.

To provide an idea of the dimensions of the emerging manpower crunch, Table 1.1 gives estimates and projections of the population of working age and the labour force for 1950–2000. The labour force projections for the period 1980–2000 were made by me, based on population projections made by the US Bureau of the Census and assumptions about labour force participation rates and other variables indicated in Table 1.1. As shown there, the 5-year increments to the labour force range between 2.4 and 4.1 per cent in the 1980s and 1990s, compared with 5.0–8.4 per cent in the past. Unless labour can be moved out of agriculture faster than in recent years, the 5-year percentage additions to the non-agricultural labour force will be less than half those of previous 5-year periods. Under this projection, the annual increments drop from 2.3 million in 1980 to 1.1 million in 1987, rising slowly thereafter to 1.7 million in the year 2000; during the 1970s, annual increments averaged about 2.5 million.

The much slower growth of the population of working age will be accompanied by dramatic shifts in its regional structure – the result of sharply different birth rates among the republics. Table 1.2 provides data by region showing additions to the population in the able-bodied ages by 5-year periods during 1976–2000. During the 1980s and the first half of the 1990s these populations will decline in the RSFSR, the Ukraine and two of the Baltic republics, but will continue to rise elsewhere, particularly in Central Asia. In the quinquennium 1986–90, for example, the population in the able-bodied ages will rise by over 2 million in Central Asia and fall by over a million in the RSFSR. This situation is also bound to bring major shifts in the geographic composition of the labour force increments and, given the fact that the bulk of Soviet natural resources and industrial facilities are located in the RSFSR and the Ukraine, will present formidable challenges for economic decision-makers.

## 2. Management of the impending manpower shortages

The Soviet government has several options to deal with the reduced availability of manpower in the next two decades,[52] and the government's actions in 1981–4 indicate that a wide-ranging approach is being taken. First, measures taken to further raise participation rates.

*Table 1.1*   Dimension of the Soviet manpower problem

| | Increases in the population in the able-bodied ages* | | Increases in the total civilian labour force | | Increases in the non-agricultural labour force | |
|---|---|---|---|---|---|---|
| | Increment (000) | % increase | Increment (000) | % increase | Increment (000) | % increase |
| 1951–55 | 10 785 | 10.5 | 7 296 | 7.5 | 6 957 | 16.3 |
| 1956–60 | 6 026 | 5.3 | 5 195 | 5.0 | 10 970 | 22.0 |
| 1961–65 | 3 899 | 3.3 | 6 362 | 5.8 | 12 354 | 20.3 |
| 1966–70 | 7 220 | 5.9 | 9 118 | 7.8 | 11 500 | 15.7 |
| 1971–75 | 12 736 | 9.7 | 10 586 | 8.4 | 12 736 | 15.1 |
| 1976–80 | 11 026 | 7.6 | 10 336 | 7.6 | 12 990 | 10.1 |
| 1981–85 | 2 956 | 1.9 | 5 986 | 4.1 | 8 331 | 7.6 |
| 1986–90 | 2 331 | 1.5 | 3 590 | 2.4 | 5 765 | 4.9 |
| 1991–95 | 2 587 | 1.6 | 4 888 | 3.1 | 6 905 | 5.6 |
| 1996–2000 | 6 523 | 4.0 | 5 988 | 3.7 | 7 858 | 6.0 |

*Able-bodied ages, as defined by the USSR, are 16–59 for men and 16–54 for women. Increments calculated from populations as of 1 July.

*Sources:* Col. (1) Increments for 1950–70 were calculated from mid-year population data given in US Department of Commerce, Foreign Demographic Analysis Division, *Estimates and Projections of the Population of the U.S.S.R. by Age and Sex, 1950–2000*, International Population Reports, series P–91, no. 23 (1973) p. 17. Increments for 1970–2000 were calculated from unpublished estimates and projections made by the same agency, taking into account the published results of the 1979 Soviet census. The 'medium' series is used here for the projections.

Col. (2) Increments for 1951–70 calculated from data given in Stephen Rapawy, *Estimates and Projections of the Labor Force and Civilian Employment in the U.S.S.R., 1950–1990*, US Department of Commerce, Foreign Demographic Analysis Division, Foreign Economic Report no. 10 (1976) p. 19. For 1970–2000 the increments are based on estimates using the population data from the source for Col. (1) ('medium series') and the assumption that labour force participation rates remained at the level for 1970 cited in ibid., p. 15. The armed forces were assumed to remain at a level of 4 million men.

Col. (3) For 1950–75 the increments are calculated from data given in ibid., p. 19. For 1975–2000 the increments were calculated from the estimates underlying column (2) and the assumption that the agricultural labour force decreases at an average annual rate of 1.5 per cent per year, the average rate for 1971–8.

To bring in more teenagers, full-time schooling could be curtailed, an approach used in the early 1960s, which proved both unsuccessful and unpopular. None the less, the government has already moved decisively in this direction. Decrees issued in 1977–9, and the sweeping reform of the entire school system launched in 1984 aim to increase part-time schooling at the expense of full-time study, augment the vocational content of education at all levels, gear training programmes more closely to regional and occupational needs of the economy, and radically upgrade on-the-job training programmes.[53] While such measures will put more teenagers in jobs, the quality of education is likely to deteriorate as a result. The government has also taken steps recently to provide more part-time jobs for women, to make it easier for women with small children to hold jobs,[54] and to keep persons of pension age at work.[55] Despite the relatively lower education level and generally lower productivity of older workers, the government will have strong reasons for keeping them on the job rather than on pensions, because the number of persons of pension age will more than double in the 1980s. Successful implementation of such labour-force expansion policies might add several million persons to the work force. While basic trends in increments to the labour

*Table 1.2* Regional dimensions of the Soviet manpower problem: increase in the population in the able-bodied ages*

| | 1975–80 | | 1980–85 | | 1985–90 | | 1990–95 | | 1995–2000 | |
|---|---|---|---|---|---|---|---|---|---|---|
| | Number (000) | % | Number (000) | % | Number (000) | % | Number (000) | % | Number (000) | % |
| USSR | 11 788 | 100 | 3 649 | 100 | 2 341 | 100 | 2 932 | 100 | 7 240 | 100 |
| RSFSR | 4 956 | 42 | −248 | −7 | −1 081 | −46 | −645 | −22 | 1 632 | 23 |
| Ukraine | 1 393 | 12 | −39 | −1 | −13 | −1 | −262 | −9 | 184 | 3 |
| Kazakhstan | 1 148 | 10 | 772 | 21 | 670 | 29 | 674 | 23 | 891 | 12 |
| Transcaucasia | 1 162 | 10 | 800 | 22 | 519 | 22 | 502 | 17 | 875 | 12 |
| Central Asia | 2 291 | 19 | 2 106 | 58 | 2 130 | 91 | 2 569 | 88 | 3 278 | 45 |
| Baltics | 199 | 2 | 36 | 1 | −8 | — | −28 | −1 | 10 | — |
| Belorussia and Moldavia | 644 | 5 | 221 | 6 | 108 | 5 | 122 | 4 | 371 | 5 |

* 16–59 years for men; 16–54 years for women.

*Source:* Increments are calculated from population data as of 1 January given in US Bureau of the Census, Foreign Demographic Analysis Division, *Population Projections by Age and Sex for the Republics and Major Economic Regions of the U.S.S.R., 1970 to 2000*, International Population Reports, series P–91, no. 26 (1979), p. 128. The 'Medium' series was used for the projections.

force are not much altered, the availability of this extra labour could ease manpower stringencies in European Russia. For additional labour inputs, the government could also reduce the armed forces, as Khrushchev did under somewhat similar circumstances, or lengthen the scheduled work week of about 41 hours, which is low by international comparison. Both measures would have a one-time impact, however, and neither seems likely. Reduction of the armed forces would require a different international climate and Soviet global involvement from what exists now. Short of a national crisis, the government would be reluctant to increase the work week, for such a move would be highly unpopular, might prove counterproductive, would entail large overtime payments and would be viewed ideologically as a retrogressive step.

With regard to regional dimensions of the manpower situation, the government's options are to encourage or compel migration from areas of relative labour surplus (primarily Central Asia) to areas of relative labour deficit, to reallocate investment and location of new facilities to the same end, or some combination of the two policies. Although Western scholars have debated the probability of substantial out-migration from Central Asia, whose peoples have shown little inclination to do so,[56] Soviet policy-makers do not seem to be seriously considering such a 'solution' to the manpower deficit in European Russia. Rather, the discussion of how to cope with the rapidly growing populations of working age in the Southern republics is couched mainly in terms of providing more investment, locating labour-intensive activities there, and upgrading the skills of the labour force. These policies were used in the past to cope with fast-growing populations in these regions. The Southern regions have been getting about 16 per cent of total investment during the 1970s and early 1980s. Probably the government will have to maintain that share, at the least, in order for economic development to continue, if only at a snail's pace.

A different set of policies will be needed to handle the manpower situation in European Russia; indeed, the outlines of the likely policy mix are already visible. Efforts are being made to boost labour-force participation rates for teenagers and persons of pension age; some regional differentiation in the application of these measures might be attempted. Next, the government will have to curtail undesired migration of the population and encourage desired migration. These ends are being attacked through new incentives for resettlement in rural areas (e.g. to bring labour to farms in Siberia and the Far East and to the Non-Black Soil Region now being pushed as a major development project) and through a more active Orgnabor to man development projects in the Eastern regions.[57] In the interest of expediency, and to minimize investment in local infrastructure, the government is now pushing the use of 'tour of duty' brigades to meet critical needs for labour in Siberia. This method entails construction of work camps at project sites, where work crews are flown in from base cities. Tours of duty are for specified periods, followed by periods of rest in the base cities. This approach was praised as early as 1974 in a CPSU resolution concerning the timber industry, and its use has been increasing slowly since then.

Aside from the special problems of Siberia, however, the government will have to force employers throughout European Russia to make do with local manpower. Since economic plans undoubtedly will continue to provide for production growth in these regions, enterprises there will be compelled to find ways to use labour more efficiently. Nobody doubts that the ubiquitous 'hidden reserves' so often alluded to in the Soviet press do exist. Indeed, the unprecedented labour stringency in itself may bring these reserves into use. The government is leaving nothing to chance, however, and has already set in motion a broad range of measures – some carrots and some sticks. To summarize, measures include: (1) 'priority' programme to mechanize labour-intensive processes, including mandatory plan assignments for reduction of manual labour;[58] (2) imposition of ceilings on the number of employees, with wage funds geared to productivity through assignment of fixed norms for wages per ruble of output,[59] with the cost of labour increased by higher social security charges beginning in 1982; (3) enterprise and individual incentives to be tied directly to reducing employment and raising productivity; (4) a variety of measures to reward continuity of service and penalize absenteeism and job-hopping; (5) tightened work norms, and norming more jobs and staffing patterns, along with increased use of collective forms of work organization and incentives (brigade systems);[60] and (6) promoting greater use of local employment exchanges and centralization of the management of labour affairs in the State Committee for Labour and Social Problems, with broad powers to monitor use of labour throughout the economy.

Finally, to accelerate the sluggish growth of labour productivity since the mid-1970s, the Soviet leaders who succeeded Brezhnev – Andropov in late 1982 and Chernenko in early 1984 and Gorbachev in early 1985 – have been conducting a major campaign to enforce discipline and reduce corruption throughout the economy. The government has cracked down on absenteeism, tardiness and loafing on the job by ordinary workers, and many lax or incompetent managers have been fired or otherwise punished. A new Law on Labour Collectives, introduced in 1983, reinforces existing measures to use peer pressure to enforce the rules.[61] The role of the trade unions and the Komsomol in this area seems to have been strengthened. To reduce the serious economic losses caused by drunkenness, the new Gorbachev leadership in May 1985 adopted a wide-ranging set of measures to bring about a speedy reduction in consumption of alcoholic beverages.[62] Gorbachev also has endorsed an 'experiment' begun under Chernenko to boost efficiency in industry by (among other things) granting industrial enterprises greater decision-making authority over the size of their workforce, while at the same time tightening central control over wages.[63] The new arrangements are to be in effect in all of industry by 1987.

These wide-ranging measures do not entail fundamental reforms in the established ways of managing the economy. Although none of them is likely to yield large gains, collectively they should enable the government to muddle through the labour crunch and to prevent labour productivity growth rates from falling much below the levels of the past decade. Overall economic growth is bound to slow, however, because of inevitably reduced rates of growth of labour and capital, energy and raw materials constraints, and the probable inability of the government to improve factor productivity very much, given the continuance of present working arrangements in the economy. Slower growth in GNP also will entail slower growth in real per capita consumption, making it imperative for the government to restrain the growth of the money incomes. Failure to do so will undermine the efficacy of material incentives and erode the government's drive to foster disciplined work effort. Management of the closely linked quasi-markets for labour and for consumer goods over the next decade or two will present major challenges both to the administrative bureaucracy and to the political leadership.

**Notes**

1. For details see Stephen Rapawy, *Estimates and Projections of the Labor Force and Civilian Employment in the U.S.S.R., 1950 to 1990*, US Department of Commerce, Bureau of Economic Analysis, Foreign

Demographic Analysis Division, Foreign Economic Report no. 10 (September 1976) p. 19.

2.  For details, see Stephen Rapawy, 'Regional Employment Trends in the U.S.S.R., 1950 to 1975', in JEC, *Soviet Economy in a Time of Change* (Washington, DC, 1979) vol. I, pp. 603–8. Employment data for the republics do not include persons engaged in private agriculture.

3.  Data on the population by age and sex and on the economically active population are given, respectively, in USSR, Central Statistical Administration, *Itogi vsesoyuznoi perepisi naseleniia 1970 goda* (Moscow, 1972–4) vol. II, pp. 12–75 and vol. v, pp. 162–93.

4.  Central Intelligence Agency, *U.S.S.R.: Trends and Prospects in Educational Attainment, 1959–85*, ER 79–10344 (June 1979) p. 25.

5.  *Naseleniia SSSR po dannym vsesoyuznoi perepisi naseleniia 1979 goda* (Moscow, Politizdat, 1980) pp. 20–2.

6.  *Narodnoe Khoziaistvo SSSR v 1983 godu*, p. 133. Western measures of industrial production per man-hour yield rates of growth of 4.4 per cent in 1971–5 and 1.9 per cent in 1976–80. Corresponding rates for GNP per man-hour are 2.0 and 1.5 per cent.

7.  These matters are treated in Abram Bergson, *Productivity and the Social System: the USSR and the West* (Cambridge, Mass. Harvard University Press, 1978) pp. 68–116, 193–223.

8.  These measures are described in: Gertrude E. Schroeder, 'Recent developments in Soviet planning and incentives', in JEC, *Soviet Economic Prospects for the Seventies* (Washington, DC, 1973) pp. 11–38; and Gertrude E. Schroeder, 'The Soviet economy on a treadmill of "reforms"', in JEC, *Soviet Economy in a Time of Change* (Washington, DC, 1979) vol. I, pp. 312–40. Also, Gertrude E. Schroeder, 'Soviet economic "reform" decrees: mores steps on the treadmill', in JEC, *Soviet Economy in the 1980s: Problems and Prospects* (Washington, DC, 1982), Part 1, pp. 65–88.

9.  Labour turnover and absenteeism in industry are discussed and documented for the 1960s and early 1970s in Alex Pravda, 'Spontaneous workers' activities in the Soviet Union', in Arcadius Kahan and Blair A. Ruble (eds), *Industrial Labor in the U.S.S.R* (New York, Pergamon Press, 1979) pp. 334–42, 361–4; Murray Feshbach and Stephen Rapawy, 'Labor constraints in the five-year plan', in JEC, *Soviet Economic Prospects for the Seventies* (Washington, DC, 1973) pp. 538–41; David E. Powell, 'Labor turnover in the Soviet Union', *Slavic Review*, vol. 36, no. 2 (June 1977) pp. 268–85.

10. *Khoziaistvo i pravo*, no. 3 (1980) p. 27.

11. For example: over two-thirds of persons leaving construction jobs transfer to jobs in other sectors of the economy (*Sotsialisticheskii trud*, no. 12 (1979) p. 99); an average worker loses 31 days between jobs (*Planovoe khoziaistvo*, no. 10 (1979) p. 41).

12. It is reported that 37 per cent of male workers are alcoholics. *Molodoi kommunist*, no. 2 (1980) p. 65.

13. *Ekonomika i organitsatsiia promyshlennogo proizvodstva*, no. 4 (1977) p. 5.

14. Ibid. no. 5 (1980) p. 13.

15.   The situation in the 1970s is discussed in Gertrude E. Schroeder, 'Consumption', in Abram Bergson and Herbert S. Levine (eds), *The Soviet Economy Toward the Year 2000* (London, Allen & Unwin, 1983) pp. 311–49.
16.   *Voprosy ekonomiki*, no. 10 (1978) p. 148.
17.   *Sovetskaia Rossiia*, 22 July 1979 p. 2.
18.   *Trud*, 18 January 1980, p. 2.
19.   *Voprosy ekonomiki*, no. 5 (1980) p. 53.
20.   *Sovetskaia Rossiia*, 22 July 1979 p. 2.
21.   *Sovetskaia Rossiia*, 22 July 1979 p. 2.
22.   *Voprosy ekonomiki*, no. 8 (1975) p. 34.
23.   *Planovoe khoziaistvo*, no. 9 (1977) p. 20.
24.   *Trud*, 19 January 1980, p. 2.
25.   *Sotsialisticheskii trud*, no. 11 (1978) pp. 73–86.
26.   *Sobranie postanovlennii pravitel'stva SSSR*, no. 18 (1979) pp. 390–431.
27.   *Byulleten' Ministerstva Vysshego i Srednego Obrazovaniia SSSR*, no. 5 (1978) pp. 2–3.
28.   *Pravda*, 12 July 1979.
29.   L. A. Kostin (ed.), *Trudovye resursy SSSR* (Moscow, 1979) p. 240.
30.   *Sobranie postanovlennii pravitel'stva SSSR*, no. 26 (1977) pp. 543–55.
31.   *Byulleten' normativyh aktov ministerstv i vedomstv SSSR*, no. 1 (1979) pp. 3–7.
32.   In 1976, 17.2 per cent of all new hires in industry were made through labour exchanges. L. A. Kostin (ed., op. cit., p. 239. In 1977, the shares ranged (among eight republics cited) from 21.4 per cent in Latvia to 71.1 per cent in Kirgizia. A. E. Kotliar and V. V. Trubin, *Problemy regulirovaniia pereraspredeleniia rabochei sily* (Moscow, 1978) p. 156.
33.   Gosudarstvennii Komitet SSR po Trudu i Sotsial'nym Voprosam, *Byulleten'*, no. 5 (1979) pp. 6–9.
34.   *Spravochnik profsoiuznogo rabotnika*, 1976, pp. 170–3.
35.   *Sobranie postanovlennii pravitel'stva SSSR*, no. 11 (1975) pp. 209–16.
36.   *Pravda*, 12 January 1980.
37.   *Sbornik po finansovomu zakonodatel'stvu* (Moscow, 1980) pp. 519–21.
38.   For descriptions of the wage system, see: Leonard J. Kirsch, *Soviet Wages: Changes in Structure and Administration Since 1956* (Cambridge, Mass, MIT Press, 1972); Janet G. Chapman, 'Recent trends in the Soviet industrial wage structure', in Kahan and Ruble, op. cit., pp. 151–83; Janet G. Chapman, 'Soviet wages under socialism', in Alan Abouchar (ed.), *The Socialist Price Mechanism* (Durham, NC, Duke University Press, 1977) pp. 246–81; Jan Adam, *Wage Control and Inflation in the Soviet Bloc Countries* (London, Macmillan, 1979) pp. 123–34.
39.   E. F. Mizhenskaia, *Lichnye potrebnosti pri sotsialisme* (Moscow, 1973) p. 94.
40.   For example: N. S. Kistanova, *Regional'noe ispol'zovanoe trudovykh resursov* (Moscow, 1978) pp. 120–5; *Ekonomicheskie nauki*, no. 5 (1978) pp. 58–61; *Isvestiia Akademii Nauk, Seriia Ekonomicheskaia*, no. 1 (1979) pp. 60–70; *Ekonomicheskie nauki*, no. 2 (1979) p. 64; *Planovoe khoziaistvo*, no. 9 (1980) p. 29.

41.  *Voprosy ekonomiki*, no. 5 (1980) p. 58. For further discussion see, for example: Gertrude E. Schroeder, 'The Soviet economy on a treadmill of "reforms"', op. cit., pp. 329–30; *Finansy SSSR*, no. 1 (1979) pp. 59–64; *Sotsiatisticheskii trud*, no. 5 (1979) pp. 30–6; Gertrude E. Schroeder, 'Soviet economic "reform" decrees: more steps on the treadmill', *op. cit.*, pp. 69–70.

42.  *Ekonomicheskaia gazeta*, no. 15 (1980 pp. 1–8 (annex.).

43.  Gosudarstvennii Komitet Soveta Ministrov SSSR po voprosam truda i zarabotnoi platy, *Byulleten'*, no. 2 (1968) pp. 5–23.

44.  M. S. Lantsev, *Sotsial'noe obespechenie v SSSR* (Moscow, 1976) pp. 127–37. For discussion of the problems of enlisting persons of pension age in the labour force see E. v. Kasimovskii (ed.), *Trudovye resursy: formirovanie i ispol'zovanie* (Moscow, 1975) pp. 197–217; also *Khoziaistvo i pravo*, no. 3 (1978) pp. 62–6.

45.  *Pravda*, 2 October 1979. Amplification is given in *Ekonomicheskaia gazeta*, no. 47 (1979) p. 22.

46.  See *Ekonomicheskie nauki*, no. 9 (1979) pp. 44–7. Only 0.5 per cent of state employees work part-time. *Kommunist*, no. 2 (1980) p. 54.

47.  This decree is described in *Planovoe khoziaistvo*, no. 10 (1979) pp. 48–9.

48.  N. P. Baibakov, in *Vestnik Akademii Nauk*, no. 5 (1980) p. 17.

49.  *Izvestia*, 9 August 1980.

50.  *Planovoe khoziaistvo*, no. 10 (1979) pp. 50–1.

51.  These are the latest unpublished estimates of the Foreign Demographic Analysis Division, US Bureau of the Census, incorporating results of the 1979 Soviet census. The 'medium' projection is used for years after 1995.

52.  For an earlier discussion of this subject, see Murray Feshbach and Stephen Rapawy, 'Soviet population and manpower trends and policies', op. cit., pp. 113–54. For more recent discussion see Ann Goodman and Geoffrey Schleifer, 'The Soviet labor market in the 1980s', in JEC, *Soviet Economy in the 1980s: Problems and Prospects* (Washington, DC, 1982), Part 2, pp. 323–48.

53.  *Sobranie postanovlennii pravitel'stva SSSR*, no. 4 (1978) pp. 67–71; *Trud*, 30 December 1977; *Pravda*, 12 July 1979 and 11 September 1977. *Professial'no-tekhnicheskie obrazovanie*, no. 8 (1980) pp. 1–8 and no. 10 (1980) pp. 31–4; *Pravda*, 14 April 1984.

54.  *Trud*, 4 June 1980, p. 4; *Pravda*, 31 Mach 1981.

55.  *Pravda*, 2 October 1979.

56.  See, for example, Murray Feshbach, 'Prospects for out-migration from Central Asia and Kazakhstan in the next decade', in JEC, *Soviet Economy in a Time of Change* (Washington, DC, 1979) vol. I, pp. 656–709.

57.  In 1984, the CPSU and the Council of Ministers adopted a resolution upgrading the role of orgnabor and Komsomol call-ups of young people in the recruitment of workers for projects of national importance.

58.  The instructions are given in *Ekonomicheskaia gazeta*, no. 16 (April 1980) p. 6. The plan target was made mandatory by the Party-Government Decree of July 1979.

59. These provisions are a part of the July 1979 Decree. Implementing instructions are published in *Sotsialisticheskii trud*, no. 2 (1980) pp. 16–25.

60. The brigade form of organization of work is supposed to become nearly universal: a major government decree adopted in late 1983 calls for speeding up its introduction in industry. *Pravda*, December 1983. For discussions of the many problems involved see RL/RFE Research Reports 476/83 and 89/84.

61. *Pravda*, 19 June 1983.

62. *Pravda*, 17 May 1985.

63. *Pravda*, 4 August 1985.

# 2 Employment Policies in Poland

## ZBIGNIEW M. FALLENBUCHL

## I. INTRODUCTION

The maintenance of full employment has been the main explicitly stated objective of the employment policy in Poland since the end of the Second World War. The introduction of a highly centralized command system facilitated this task, as the system is well adapted to ensuring a high degree of mobilization and full employment of resources and their allocation to some priority sectors, irrespective of the profitability of such ventures.[1] The adoption of the Soviet-type 'inward-looking' development strategy, based on import substitution, the priority development of industries producing producers' goods for the domestic investment programme and attempts to achieve the highest possible rates of growth of national product, had a tendency to create an overall overcommitment of resources from the very beginning.[2] The interaction of the system and this particular strategy resulted in the emergence of the so-called 'extensive' pattern of development. The rates of growth of national product, industrial output and so on depended on increases in the quantities of inputs rather than on increases in their productivity. A certain industrial structure was created which was geared to this pattern of development.[3]

The commitment to full employment and the macroeconomic policy that tends to push the aggregate demand beyond the full employment and full capacity level of national income, the system with its strong inherent expansionist nature,[4] the strategy of development and the pattern of growth that emerged, all these factors have determined the demand side of the labour market. The strength of the demand fluctuated mainly with changes in the macroeconomic policy but it has depended also on the systemic factors and on the development strategy that was followed. Some changes in the strategy, and to a smaller extent in the system, were taking place. They had an impact on the overall strength and on the structure of demand for labour, but

27

they themselves were induced by, among other factors, the actual or the expected situation in the supply of labour.

When resources are overcommitted and the economy is operating above the full employment level of national income, when the pattern of development is extensive and the rates of growth depend on increases in the quantities of inputs, it is the supply side of employment policy that is important.

The supply of labour depends first of all on demographic factors, which are to a large extent exogenously determined, and on some other factors over which the planners could have, at least in theory, a considerable degree of control. They include the participation ratio, the working hours and the use of shifts. Some attempts have been made in Poland to control the demographic factors with an active maternity policy which was directed at first against the excessively high rates, in the opinion of the planners, of natural growth of population and later against, in their opinion, too low rates. However it appears that the impact of economic social factors, working in the same direction as the maternity policy during the early stage and against it during the later stage, was much stronger than that of the policy.

In practice the planners may not have a high degree of control even over those factors which should be the policy variables. The participation ratio depends, among other factors, on social and economic pressures that make women enter the labour force. These pressures have been very strong in Poland throughout the whole postwar period, irrespective of the planners' wishes. The participation of women is often limited by the availability of plants which could provide suitable employment for female workers in the same location in which plants with predominantly male types of work are located. Decisions in this matter may be determined by the availability of investable funds, investment priorities and factors affecting the location of industry.

The number of shifts depends on the strength of demand for the products of a given plant, which may be limited by the size of the domestic market or by the lack of complementary products. However, it also depends on the availability of fuel, raw materials and parts on the supply side, as well as on the possibility of providing transportation for the night shifts and on workers' preferences.

While the manipulation of these variables could be expected to give results in a relatively short period of time, the raising of the quality of the labour force and the adjustment of its professional structure to the structure of demand for labour, through the expansion of general education and training for special skills, usually involve a longer time lag. The regional adjustment of supply and demand is even more difficult to effect and can only be achieved, in the long run, as the result of investment policy not only in industry but also in transport, housing, urban infrastructure and other factors, which may either limit the possibility of locating industrial plants in regions with an excess supply of labour or affect geographic mobility of labour.[5]

While the system makes it possible to ignore market forces and helps in this way to achieve full employment, it is because market forces are subdued that it is difficult to ensure the efficient utilization of labour forces, to make adjustments in the structure of labour supply to changes in demand for labour, and to create the optimum mobility of labour among places of employment within a given industry in a given location and among industries and regions. The originally chosen development strategy, the extensive pattern of development, and the macroeconomic policy of continuously pushing the aggregate demand far beyond the full employment and full capacity level of national income further strengthened these difficulties. Changes in the development strategy, and systemic modifications which were taking place from time to time, did not significantly change the situation in this respect.[6]


## II. DEMOGRAPHIC FACTORS

Total population in Poland increased from 25.0 million in 1950 to 36.7 million in 1983, or by 46.8 per cent. The population at working age increased even faster: by 49.6 per cent. Its share in total population decreased from 57.8 per cent in 1950 to 54.1 per cent in 1965. Subsequently it increased and reached 59.4 per cent in 1980. However, it declined again to 58.9 per cent in 1983, although according to demographic projections it was expected to exceed 60 per cent starting in 1980 and to remain at that level until the end of the century. The natural rate of growth of population declined from about 19 per thousand during the first half of the 1950s to an average 8.5 per thousand in 1967–71. It increased again in the subsequent years and has fluctuated around 10 per thousand (see Table 2.1).

Increases in labour resources fluctuated widely from one 5-year period to another. In 1951–5 the increase was 1 130 000. This big influx was followed by a 'demographic slump': increases were 660 000

Table 2.1 Total population, population at working age, pre-working age and post-working age, 1950–83, and projections 1990–2000 (thousands)

| Year | Total Population | Working age* | Pre-working age | Post-working age | Working age % of total | Female % of: | | Natural increase per thousand |
|---|---|---|---|---|---|---|---|---|
| | | | | | | Total | Working age | |
| 1950 | 25 035 | 14 481 | 9 794 | 1 760 | 57.8 | 52.3 | 51.9 | 19.1 |
| 1955 | 27 550 | 15 608 | 9 945 | 1 997 | 56.7 | 52.0 | 51.4 | 19.5 |
| 1960 | 29 795 | 16 271 | 11 144 | 2 380 | 54.6 | 51.6 | 50.4 | 15.0 |
| 1965 | 31 551 | 17 058 | 11 571 | 2 922 | 54.1 | 51.5 | 49.8 | 10.0 |
| 1970 | 32 658 | 18 324 | 10 775 | 3 559 | 56.1 | 51.4 | 49.3 | 8.5 |
| 1975 | 34 185 | 19 962 | 10 133 | 4 090 | 58.4 | 51.3 | 49.2 | 10.2 |
| 1980 | 35 735 | 21 211 | 10 297 | 4 227 | 59.4 | 51.3 | 49.3 | 9.6 |
| 1983 | 36 745 | 21 633 | 10 737 | 4 345 | 58.9 | 51.2 | 48.7 | 10.2 |
| 1990 | 37 423 | 22 475 | 9 974 | 4 974 | 60.1 | 50.8 | 47.8 | 4.1 |
| 1995 | 38 171 | 23 035 | 9 621 | 5 515 | 60.4 | 50.7 | 43.6 | 2.2 |
| 2000 | 38 908 | 23 681 | 9 265 | 5 962 | 60.9 | 50.6 | 47.7 | 2.3 |

*Working age: male 18–64; female 18–59.

Sources: Rocznik statystyczny 1970, p. 38; 1984, p. 37; Rocznik demograficzny 1974, pp. 336, 339; 1983, p. xv.

in 1956–60 and 770 000 in 1961–5. During the subsequent five-year periods there were very big increases: 1 560 000 in 1966–70, 1 740 000 in 1971–5 and 1 400 000 in 1976–80. The 1980s are, however, characterized by a drastic decline in the addition to labour resources: 728 000 in 1981–5 and 450 000 in 1986–90. They are expected to be followed by somewhat larger increases in the subsequent decade: 560 000 in 1990–5 and 646 000 in 1995–2000.[7]

There seems to be a considerable concern about the ability of the economy to maintain sufficiently high rates of growth during the last two decades of the century because of the envisaged shortage of labour caused not only be demographic factors but also by inability to further expand the participation ratio.[8] During the whole period 1950–75, increases in employing in the national economy exceeded increases in the number of persons at working age (see Tables 2.1 and 2.2).

It was the increase in the participation ratio which was responsible for the big increases in employment even during the years of the 'demographic slump'.[9] During the 1950s and 1960s a number of persons above the retirement age were retained in employment. Particularly important was, however, a growing participation of women in the labour force. In the socialist economy (i.e. excluding private handicrafts, trade and services outside agriculture, which are all relatively insignificant, and the very important sector of individual agriculture, where it is difficult to establish which family members should be included in the labour force) the proportion of women in total employment was 30.6 per cent in 1950, 32.0 per cent in 1955, 32.8 per cent in 1960, 35.7 per cent in 1965, 39.4 per cent in 1970, 42.3 per cent in 1975, 43.5 per cent in 1980 and 43.7 per cent in 1983.[10] No further increase in the labour force in this way seems to be possible and fears have been expressed that the proportion is excessive as 'the present very high participation of women collides with the rational approach to the process of the reproduction of population.'[11]

The ratio of the number of persons employed in the national economy to the total number of persons at working age increased from 70.3 per cent in 1950 to 76.2 per cent in 1960, 79.3 per cent in 1965, 82.8 per cent in 1970 and 84.9 per cent in 1975. Afterwards the trend was reversed. The ratio declined to 81.7 per cent in 1980 and 78.6 per cent in 1983 (See Tables 2.1 and 2.2). A decline in the rates of growth of population at working age has to create problems unless labour is employed more efficiently and labour productivity increases. The Consultative Economic Council lists the labour balance together

*Table 2.2* Employment in the national economy (thousand)

| Sector | 1950 | 1960 | 1965 | 1970 | 1975 | 1976 | 1977 | 1978 | 1979 | 1980 | 1981 | 1982 | 1983 |
|---|---|---|---|---|---|---|---|---|---|---|---|---|---|
| National Economy (total) | 10 186 | 12 401 | 13 521 | 15 175 | 16 946 | 17 029 | 17 260 | 17 109 | 17 229 | 17 325 | 17 420 | 16 996 | 17 037 |
| Socialist | 4 832 | 7 194 | 8 531 | 10 325 | 12 209 | 12 302 | 12 510 | 12 632 | 12 699 | 12 718 | 12 720 | 12 184 | 12 148 |
| Private | 5 354 | 5 207 | 4 990 | 4 850 | 4 737 | 4 727 | 4 750 | 4 477 | 4 530 | 4 607 | 4 700 | 4 812 | 4 889 |
| Industry (total) | 2 107 | 3 158 | 3 728 | 4 453 | 5 150 | 5 170 | 5 233 | 5 234 | 5 237 | 5 245 | 5 237 | 4 986 | 4 974 |
| Socialist | 1 944 | 2 996 | 3 567 | 4 249 | 4 941 | 4 962 | 5 014 | 5 002 | 4 987 | 4 973 | 4 940 | 4 659 | 4 605 |
| Construction (total) | 510 | 811 | 901 | 1 075 | 1 406 | 1 385 | 1 383 | 1 394 | 1 372 | 1 337 | 1 294 | 1 224 | 1 219 |
| Socialist | 501 | 783 | 858 | 1 005 | 1 320 | 1 297 | 1 290 | 1 299 | 1 274 | 1 234 | 1 187 | 1 108 | 1 088 |
| Agriculture (total) | 5 461 | 5 367 | 5 289 | 5 210 | 5 226 | 5 235 | 5 306 | 5 049 | 5 099 | 5 143 | 5 198 | 5 174 | 5 148 |
| Socialist | 420 | 496 | 650 | 802 | 959 | 989 | 1 060 | 1 105 | 1 134 | 1 139 | 1 144 | 1 061 | 1 032 |
| Private | 5 041 | 4 871 | 4 639 | 4 408 | 4 282 | 4 267 | 4 246 | 3 944 | 3 965 | 4 004 | 4 054 | 4 113 | 4 116 |
| Forestry (total) | 92 | 150 | 173 | 183 | 155 | 162 | 161 | 160 | 158 | 155 | 153 | 154 | 158 |
| Other sectors (total) | 2 016 | 2 915 | 3 430 | 4 254 | 5 009 | 5 007 | 5 177 | 5 272 | 5 363 | 5 445 | 5 538 | 5 458 | 5 538 |

*Note:* Employment of part-time workers recalculated into the equivalent number of full-time workers.

*Sources: RS 1975*, p. 51; *1976*, pp. 55–6; *1978*, pp.42–3; *1979*, pp. 45–6; *1980*, pp. 52–3; *1984*, pp. 54–5.

with the balance of payments as the two most serious factors that will limit the freedom of manoeuvre for economic policy in Poland for a long time.[12]

## III. DEMAND FOR LABOUR

Some indication as to the strength of demand for labour can be obtained from statistics on the number of workers looking for work and the number of openings registered at labour exchanges, although these data do not present the whole situation in the labour market. It may be assumed that when the demand for labour is particularly strong not only does the number of openings increase, but also the number of workers looking for work may decline, although the latter is, of course, also influenced by the change in supply caused by an increase in the people at working age, and increases in the participation ratio and in the number of people transferring from agriculture to the non-agriculture labour force.

At the end of the reconstruction period there were still relatively large numbers of people looking for work who were registered at labour exchanges: 104 300 in 1948 and 118 800 in 1949. These numbers were the highest annual figures during the whole period 1948–83. They were higher than the numbers of openings, and the ratio of workers looking for work to the number of openings was in these two years the highest for the whole period (see Table 2.3).

The industrialization drive in the first half of the 1950s rapidly increased the number of registered openings, while the number of registered workers looking for work dropped drastically, despite the collectivization drive in agriculture which forced some individual farmers out from agriculture to non-agriculture occupations. The ratio of workers to openings declined to 0.1 in 1951–3, and three years during which investment was increasing by 12.2, 12.2 and 18.7 per cent, and net material product by 7.5, 6.2 and 10.4 per cent (see Table 2.3).

The industrialization and collectivization drive resulted in serious disturbances within the economy, shortages and maladjustments.[13] The planners were forced to reduce drastically the rate of growth of investment in 1954 and 1955. The number of openings registered at the labour exchange declined during the second half of the decade, while the number of workers looking for work increased and even exceeded the number of openings available in 1959. In that year there

*Table 2.3*  Workers looking for work, and openings (thousands)*

| Year | Looking for work | | Openings | | Looking for work openings | | Annual rates of growth | |
|------|-------|-------|-----------|-------|-------|-------|------|------------|
| | Total | Women | Total for | Women | Total | Women | DNMP | Investment |
| 1948 | 104.3 | n.a. | 37.4 | n.a. | 2.8 | — | 29.9 | 22.0 |
| 1949 | 118.8 | n.a. | 68.6 | n.a. | 2.7 | — | 17.7 | 13.0 |
| 1950 | 53.7 | n.a. | 160.2 | n.a. | 0.3 | — | 15.1 | 36.8 |
| 1951 | 5.4 | n.a. | 117.2 | n.a. | 0.1 | — | 7.5 | 12.2 |
| 1952 | 3.5 | n.a. | 197.4 | n.a. | 0.1 | — | 6.2 | 18.7 |
| 1953 | 5.9 | n.a. | 108.4 | n.a. | 0.1 | — | 10.4 | 15.2 |
| 1954 | 15.3 | n.a. | 65.0 | n.a. | 0.2 | — | 10.5 | 5.9 |
| 1955 | 30.7 | 19.9 | 46.4 | 7.2 | 0.66 | 2.76 | 8.4 | 4.0 |
| 1956 | 38.2 | 26.4 | 48.1 | 8.3 | 0.79 | 3.18 | 7.0 | 4.7 |
| 1957 | 31.9 | 21.6 | 55.8 | 11.3 | 0.57 | 1.91 | 10.7 | 7.8 |
| 1958 | 31.1 | 21.8 | 75.6 | 13.5 | 0.41 | 1.61 | 5.5 | 10.3 |
| 1959 | 42.6 | 25.9 | 31.6 | 5.2 | 1.35 | 4.98 | 5.2 | 16.6 |
| 1960 | 37.4 | 29.9 | 46.5 | 6.8 | 0.80 | 4.40 | 4.3 | 5.9 |
| 1961 | 40.6 | 33.0 | 54.6 | 7.9 | 0.74 | 4.18 | 8.2 | 7.3 |
| 1962 | 46.2 | 39.7 | 54.9 | 8.2 | 0.84 | 4.84 | 2.1 | 9.7 |
| 1963 | 60.4 | 46.8 | 25.6 | 4.1 | 2.36 | 11.41 | 6.9 | 2.7 |
| 1964 | 65.4 | 55.3 | 44.4 | 7.8 | 1.47 | 7.09 | 6.7 | 4.7 |
| 1965 | 62.0 | 54.5 | 52.9 | 12.1 | 1.17 | 4.50 | 7.0 | 9.5 |
| 1966 | 57.7 | 52.2 | 64.2 | 13.6 | 0.90 | 3.84 | 7.1 | 8.4 |
| 1967 | 52.0 | 47.4 | 58.2 | 11.9 | 0.89 | 3.98 | 5.7 | 11.3 |
| 1968 | 53.1 | 49.3 | 76.7 | 15.9 | 0.69 | 3.10 | 9.0 | 8.7 |
| 1969 | 71.1 | 64.3 | 33.6 | 8.9 | 2.12 | 7.22 | 2.9 | 8.2 |
| 1970 | 79.4 | 71.3 | 39.5 | 8.5 | 2.01 | 8.39 | 5.7 | 4.1 |
| 1971 | 81.7 | 74.9 | 84.2 | 19.4 | 0.97 | 3.86 | 8.1 | 7.5 |
| 1972 | 51.8 | 49.3 | 93.4 | 24.6 | 0.55 | 2.00 | 10.6 | 23.6 |
| 1973 | 28.1 | 26.8 | 146.9 | 41.2 | 0.19 | 0.65 | 10.8 | 25.0 |
| 1974 | 19.0 | 17.3 | 77.7 | 26.0 | 0.24 | 0.67 | 10.4 | 22.5 |
| 1975 | 15.2 | 12.7 | 94.6 | 30.1 | 0.16 | 0.42 | 9.0 | 14.2 |
| 1976 | 13.6 | 10.6 | 82.7 | 24.4 | 0.16 | 0.43 | 6.8 | 2.2 |
| 1977 | 11.7 | 9.2 | 97.7 | 28.3 | 0.12 | 0.33 | 5.0 | 4.3 |
| 1978 | 9.2 | 7.0 | 92.4 | 26.4 | 0.10 | 0.27 | 3.0 | 1.6 |
| 1979 | 6.4 | 5.2 | 128.5 | 37.0 | 0.05 | 0.14 | −2.3 | −7.9 |
| 1980 | 10.0 | 7.0 | 98.0 | 29.0 | 0.10 | 0.24 | −6.0 | −12.3 |
| 1981 | 26.0 | 12.0 | 119.0 | 39.0 | 0.22 | 0.31 | −12.0 | −22.3 |
| 1982 | 9.0 | 5.0 | 248.0 | 65.0 | 0.04 | 0.08 | −5.5 | −12.1 |
| 1983 | 5.0 | 3.0 | 234.0 | 60.0 | 0.02 | 0.05 | 6.0 | 9.4 |

*Workers looking for work and openings registered at labour exchanges. The labour exchange system does not cover all groups of workers. The statistics do not, therefore, present the whole situation in the labour market.
n.a. = not available.

*Sources:* 1950–4: M. Kabaj, 'Racjonalne zatrudnienie', in *Polityka gospodarcza Polski Ludowej* (Warsaw, 1965) p. 143. These statistics may not be completely comparable with the rest. 1955–78: *RS 1967*, p. 77; *1971*, p. 119; *1976*, p. 64; *1977*, p. 48; *1979*, p. 55; *1980*, p. 62; *1984*, pp. 67, 73, 173.

were almost five times as many women looking for work than the number of openings, although this was partly the result of a drastic reduction in the number of openings available for women.

Between 1950 and 1960 employment outside agriculture increased by 2 309 000 and employment in industry by 1 051 000. Population at working age increased by 1 790 000 during that period and employment in agriculture declined by 94 000, including a decline in private agriculture by 170 000 (see Table 2.2).

The policy of maximization of employment was followed during that period at both macro- and microeconomic levels and the previous hidden unemployment in agriculture was replaced by the hidden unemployment outside agriculture, including industry.[14] Already during the second half of the 1950s it was suggested that the objective of the policy should be changed from attempting to achieve the 'maximum employment' to ensuring the 'rational employment'.[15]

The period of a slow-down and readjustment ended in 1959. A new industrialization drive started in 1961. However, it ended in another collapse in 1963 and 1964. The rates of investment had to be reduced quite drastically in these years. The number of workers looking for work increased in 1963–5. Although the rates of growth of population at working age increased from exceptionally low rates in 1958–62, only the rate of growth in 1964 was relatively high (1.81 per cent). The ratio of workers looking for work to the number of openings increased to 2.36 in 1963, 1.47 in 1964 and 1.17 in 1965. The ratio of women looking for work to the number of openings suitable for women increased to 11.41 in 1963 (this was the highest ratio during the whole period 1955–78), 7.09 in 1964 and 4.50 in 1965 (see Table 2.3). It appears, therefore, that the demand for labour was not very strong during these three years and it is perhaps possible to talk about unemployment among female workers.

During the industrialization drive of the 1950s and early 1960s it was expected that the productivity of labour would increase as the result of, above all, increases in capital per worker and improvements in the general level of education and skills.

The average rate of growth of gross fixed capital in the national economy increased from 3.4 per cent in 1951–5 to 4.1 per cent in 1955–60 and 4.6 per cent in 1961–5. The average rate of growth of net material product per worker declined from 7.0 per cent to 5.9 per cent and 5.0 per cent during the same periods, and the ratio of the growth of net material product per worker to the rate of growth of capital declined from 2.1 to 1.4 and 1.1 respectively.[16]

The level of education was raised, particularly the share of workers with secondary vocational education (from 6.9 per cent in 1958 to 8.4 per cent in 1965) and with basic trade education (from 8.2 per cent to 11.2 per cent) (see Table 2.4).

During the Six-Year Plan, 1950–5, various administrative and legal measures were relied upon to enforce the discipline of work. They included a prohibition to leave employment without an official approval for many categories of skilled workers.[17] All these measures proved disappointing and by 1957–60 attempts were made to replace the commands and prohibitions by economic measures in order to increase productivity. The plan for 1961–5 was built on the assumption of a relatively moderate increase in employment and a big increase in productivity. Employment, however, already exceeded the planned 1965 level by 1963,[18] while the rate of growth of productivity, instead of increasing, declined in comparison with the previous period.

There was no immediate shortage of labour. The increase in the number of people at working age was 1 266 000 (737 000 male and 525 000 female) in 1965–70 and 1 638 000 (853 000 male and 785 000 female) in 1971–5 (see Table 2.1). But the demographic projections indicated a drastic decline in the increase afterwards. Moreover, the share of accumulation in national income was already dangerously large.[19]

It was recognized that it was necessary to switch from an extensive to an intensive pattern of development, i.e. to make the rates of growth of national product depend more on increases in the productivity of inputs than on increases in their quantity. In order to achieve this objective it was necessary to restructure and to modernize the economy, to effect some economic reforms and to accelerate the scientific and technological progress.[20] Gomulka was afraid of economic reforms and gave priority to the reconstruction and modernization of the economy. A new investment drive was initiated in 1965. The rate of growth of investment increased by 9.5 per cent in that year, 8.4 per cent in 1966, 11.3 per cent in 1967 and 8.7 per cent in 1968. Increases in the net material product were, however, below the planned levels.

Despite the large inflow of young people into the labour force, a shortage of labour appeared because the industrial and construction enterprises followed the old 'maximization of employment' policy.[21] The ratio of those looking for work to the number of available

**Table 2.4** Labour force according to level of education in the socialist sector (thousands)

| | 1958 | 1965 | 1968 | 1970 | 1975 | 1978 | 1979 | 1980 | 1981 | 1982 | 1983 |
|---|---|---|---|---|---|---|---|---|---|---|---|
| Total employment | 6 350.8 | 7 137.3 | 8 527.9 | 9 407.7 | 11 350.4 | 11 688.5 | 11 661.5 | 11 634.0 | 11 452.9 | 11 193.9 | 11 162.1 |
| Post-secondary | 239.9 | 310.4 | 405.5 | 502.2 | 712.3 | 860.6 | 891.2 | 937.7 | 949.0 | 972.9 | 1 008.3 |
| As % of employment | 3.8 | 4.3 | 4.8 | 5.3 | 6.3 | 7.4 | 7.6 | 8.1 | 8.3 | 8.7 | 9.0 |
| Secondary vocational | 438.7 | 598.2 | 964.9 | 1 279.4 | 1 875.6 | 2 227.5 | 2 356.2 | 2 427.4 | 2 456.9 | 2 480.9 | 2 529.3 |
| As % of employment | 6.9 | 8.4 | 11.3 | 13.6 | 16.5 | 19.1 | 20.2 | 20.9 | 21.5 | 22.2 | 22.7 |
| Secondary general | 275.6 | 313.8 | 385.4 | 529.4 | 695.6 | 742.5 | 746.3 | 740.7 | 733.2 | 720.6 | 709.9 |
| As % of employment | 4.3 | 4.4 | 4.5 | 5.6 | 6.1 | 6.4 | 6.4 | 6.4 | 6.4 | 6.4 | 6.4 |
| Vocational | 522.0 | 798.5 | 1 306.2 | 1 599.3 | 1 456.3 | 2 709.7 | 2 766.9 | 2 813.9 | 2 841.4 | 2 872.6 | 2 859.0 |
| As % of employment | 8.2 | 11.2 | 15.3 | 17.0 | 21.7 | 23.2 | 23.7 | 24.2 | 24.8 | 25.7 | 25.6 |

*Sources: Rocznik statystyczny pracy, 1945–1968* (Warsaw, 1970) p. 252; *Zatrudnieniu w gospodarce narodowej 1984* (Warsaw, 1984) pp. 8–9.

openings declined from 1.47 in 1964 to 1.17 in 1965, 0.90 in 1966, 0.89 in 1967 and 0.69 in 1968 (see Table 2.3).

The ratio of workers looking for work to the number of available openings increased from 0.69 in 1968 to 2.12 in 1969 and 2.01 in 1970. For female workers the ratio of those looking for work to the number of suitable openings available for them increased to 7.22 in 1969 and 8.39 in 1970. These were the highest levels since 1963. Again, it is possible to say that there appeared to be unemployment among female workers in these 2 years (see Table 2.3).

Further progress in industrialization was, however, made and it was reflected in changes in employment in various sectors of the economy. Employment outside agriculture increased by 1 733 000 in 1966–70, in industry by 725 000 and in construction by 174 000 (see Table 2.2).

There was also a continuous stress on improving the level of education and training for specific skills. In 1970 in the socialist sector of the economy the share of workers with post-secondary education increased to 5.3 per cent, with general secondary education to 5.6 per cent, with secondary vocational education to 13.6 per cent and those with basic trade education to 17.0 per cent.

The rate of growth of gross fixed capital increased from 4.6 per cent in 1961–5 to 6.2 per cent in 1966–70, but the rate of growth of net material product per worker declined from 5.0 per cent in 1961–5 to 3.9 per cent in 1966–70 and the ratio of the average rate of growth of net material product per worker to the rate of growth of gross fixed capital declined from 1.1 to 0.6.

Considerable improvements in the quality of labour and big increases in capital per worker did not result in an acceleration in the rates of growth of productivity but, on the contrary, were associated with a decline in the average rate in 1966–70.

It was decided that the key to the solution of this problem could be found in devising a proper system of incentives for the enterprises, which would discourage them from hiring excessively large numbers of workers and induce them to introduce various measures which would increase productivity. It was also hoped that a carefully designed system of material incentives would encourage workers to work harder, and increase the quality of work, improve discipline and discourage the excessive worker mobility among plants, which was regarded as very harmful.

A very elaborate system of incentives was introduced, together with an increase in the prices of basic consumption goods and a reduction in the prices of some consumer durables at the end of 1970. Workers' riots in December of that year forced a change in the party and government leadership, the withdrawal of the incentive system and increases in prices.

At the beginning of the 1970s a 'new development strategy' was adopted by the new leadership. It was based on the assumption that, in order to escape from a vicious circle in which the economy had found itself since at least the middle of the 1960s, it was necessary to increase simultaneously consumption – in order to give a real meaning to material incentives – and investment – in order to effect a rapid restructuring and modernization of the economy. This was only possible with the import of foreign capital. Moreover, in order to reduce the cost of scientific and technological progress and to accelerate modernization, the transfer of technology from the West was to be effected on a large scale.[22]

The introduction of the new development strategy coincided with the largest increase in the number of persons of working age that had occurred in any 5-year period since 1950. It amounted to 1 638 000. Total employment in the national economy increased by an even greater number, as the result of a further increase in the participation ratio. The increase in employment amounted to 1 711 000 (see Tables 2.1 and 2.2).

This big increase in employment was associated with extremely high rates of growth of investment, which were made possible because of the import of capital. The rates of growth of investment increased from 4.1 per cent in 1970 to 7.5 per cent in 1971, 23.6 per cent in 1972, 25.0 per cent in 1973, 22.5 per cent in 1974 and 14.2 per cent in 1975 at constant prices (see Table 2.3).

Strong pressure of demand for labour is reflected in a dramatic decline in the ratio of the workers looking for work and the number of available openings. It declined from 2.01 in 1970, to 0.97 in 1971, 0.55 in 1972 and 0.19 in 1973. It slightly increased to 0.24 in 1974 but declined again to 0.16 in 1975 (see Table 2.3).

Employment outside agriculture increased by 1 755 000 in 1970–5, including an increase by 697 000 in industry and 331 000 in construction. Employment in private agriculture declined by 126 000 but employment in the socialist sector of agriculture increased by 157 000 (see Table 2.2).

There was further improvement in the quality of labour. The share of workers with post-secondary education in the socialist economy increased to 6.3 per cent in 1975 and 8.1 per cent in 1980 and the share of those with general secondary education increased to 6.1 per cent and 6.4 per cent respectively. Again, particularly big increases took place in the number of workers with vocational education. The workers with secondary vocational education represented 16.5 per cent in 1975 and 20.9 per cent in 1980 and those with basic trade education 21.7 and 24.2 per cent (see Table 2.4).

The average growth of gross fixed capital increased from 6.2 per cent in 1966–70 to 8.0 per cent in 1971–5 and 9.1 per cent in 1976–9.

There was a very big increase in the average rate of growth of the net material product per worker from 3.9 per cent in 1966–70 to 7.0 per cent in 1971–5. This was, however, temporary and the rate of growth declined to 4.2 per cent in 1976–9. The ratio of the rate of growth of net material product per worker to the average rate of growth of gross fixed capital increased from 0.6 in 1966–70 to 0.9 in 1971–5, which was, however, a considerably lower ratio than in the first three five-year periods, when it was 23.1 in 1951–5, 1.4 in 1956–60 and 1.1 in 1961–5. Moreover, it declined to 0.5 in 1976–9 and this was its lowest level for the whole period 1951–79.

The restructuring and modernization of the economy, which was attempted on a large scale in 1971–5, did not, therefore, result in an improvement in the rates of growth of labour productivity in the long run. The process of growth did not become more intensive. On the contrary, there was a marked deterioration of the situation when the 'new development strategy' collapsed under the pressure of the balance-of-payments deficits and the mounting net hard currency indebtedness.[23]

When in 1975–8 the rates of growth of net material product and investment were rapidly declining, the ratio of those looking for work to the number of openings actually declined. Moreover, even the absolute declines in the net material product that took place in 1979–82 were not able to reduce the strength of demand for labour. In 1983 and 1984, when the positive rates of growth of net material product again started to appear but the output was still considerably below the pre-crisis level (the 1984 level was 15 per cent below the 1978 level), the ratio declined to its lowest level ever (see Table 2.3). Even a drastic reduction in the aggregate demand and the level of production is apparently unable to reduce the strength of demand for labour. This is a clear indication that there is no link between the level of employment and the level of output.

## IV. FACTORS RESPONSIBLE FOR THE UNSATISFACTORY PRODUCTIVITY PERFORMANCE

Already before the strikes of 1980–1 and the establishment of Solidarity, the leaders were often complaining that a considerable number of working hours were lost every year as the result of absenteeism. Indeed the official statistics indicate a decline in the actual working time in state industry from 87.4 per cent of the nominal working time in 1960 to 85.6 per cent in 1970, 83.6 per cent in 1975 and 83.0 per cent in 1979, the last year before the strikes and the formation of free labour unions. The decline can, however, be explained mainly by an increase in vacations and maternity leaves. Absenteeism actually declined during that whole period. Even if some of the rapidly increasing time lost due to sickness were to be regarded as 'hidden absenteeism', the proportion would still not be very large (see Table 2.5).

The actual working time in state industry declined from 83.0 per cent in 1979 to 82.2 per cent in 1980 and 80.2 per cent in 1981. It remained, however, almost unchanged at that low level under martial law in 1982 and in 1983 it did not recover even to the 1980 level. For a while there was a tendency to blame the strikes for the economic crisis which had already reached dangerous proportions in 1979. In 1980 and 1981 the increase in time lost as the result of strikes, as well as other stoppages that were caused by shortages of raw materials, components, spare parts, and other dislocations resulting from an excessive reduction in imports, was smaller than the increase in either vacation time or in time lost due to sickness, while absenteeism remained unchanged (see Table 2.5).

Similarly, contrary to various complaints expressed by the leaders, the official statistics indicate that there was a reduction in labour turnover, especially during the Solidarity period in 1980 and 1981, although some increase took place under martial law in 1982 (see Table 2.6). During the 1970s, when complaints about labour turnover became particularly strong, some economists suggested that labour productivity was hampered more by insufficient labour mobility than by the excessive turnover. This was the result of various financial and administrative obstacles and, above all, shortages of housing.[24] An increase in labour mobility, particularly geographic, was needed to improve the utilization of existing labour resources and to effect the restructuring of the economy without which it was impossible to reduce capital intensity, expand exports, reduce import intensity and

*Table 2.5* Working hours in state industry (production and development group)

| | 1960 | 1970 | 1971 | 1972 | 1973 | 1974 | 1975 | 1976 | 1977 | 1978 | 1979 | 1980 | 1981 | 1982 | 1983 |
|---|---|---|---|---|---|---|---|---|---|---|---|---|---|---|---|
| Nominal working time (million hrs) | 4775 | 6289 | 6473 | 6629 | 6725 | 6769 | 6769 | 6787 | 6862 | 6790 | 6726 | 6702 | 6246 | 5881 | 5766 |
| Overtime | 198 | 191 | 198 | 216 | 230 | 248 | 246 | 240 | 259 | 255 | 280 | 238 | 229 | 313 | 338 |
| *Percentage of nominal working time:* | | | | | | | | | | | | | | | |
| Working in normal hours | 87.4 | 85.6 | 85.3 | 84.7 | 84.4 | 84.0 | 83.6 | 83.7 | 83.3 | 83.0 | 3.0 | 82.2 | 80.2 | 80.3 | 81.1 |
| Vacations | 5.6 | 7.0 | 6.9 | 7.0 | 7.2 | 7.4 | 7.4 | 7.5 | 7.4 | 7.5 | 7.5 | 7.7 | 8.3 | 8.5 | 8.5 |
| Maternity leaves | — | 0.4 | 0.5 | 0.6 | 0.8 | 0.9 | 0.9 | 1.0 | 0.9 | 0.9 | 0.9 | 0.9 | 0.9 | 0.9 | n.a. |
| Sickness | 4.0 | 4.8 | 5.4 | 5.6 | 5.7 | 5.9 | 6.3 | 6.2 | 6.7 | 7.0 | 6.7 | 7.3 | 8.1 | 8.1 | 7.8 |
| Stoppage of work | 0.6 | 0.4 | 0.3 | 0.3 | 0.3 | 0.3 | 0.3 | 0.3 | 0.3 | 0.2 | 0.4 | 0.5* | 0.7* | 0.3 | 0.2 |
| Absenteeism | 0.5 | 0.3 | 0.3 | 0.3 | 0.3 | 0.3 | 0.3 | 0.2 | 0.2 | 0.2 | 0.3 | 0.3 | 0.3 | 0.2 | 0.2 |
| Other non-worked | 1.9 | 1.5 | 1.3 | 1.5 | 1.3 | 1.2 | 1.2 | 1.1 | 1.2 | 1.2 | 1.2 | 1.1 | 1.5 | 1.7 | 2.2** |
| Overtime | 4.1 | 3.0 | 3.1 | 3.3 | 3.4 | 3.7 | 3.6 | 3.5 | 3.8 | 3.8 | 4.2 | 3.6 | 3.7 | 5.3 | 5.9 |

*includes strikes    **including maternity leaves.

*Sources: Rocznik statystyczny przemysłu 1982* (Warsaw, 1982) pp. 128–9; *1983*, pp. 148–9; *RS 1984*, p. 221.

*Table 2.6* Labour turnover in the socialist economy*

| | Thousands of workers | | | |
|---|---|---|---|---|
| 1967 | 2188.6 | 1858.2 | 26.2 | 22.3 |
| 1970 | 2266.0 | 2079.7 | 24.2 | 21.9 |
| 1975 | 2860.2 | 2545.0 | 25.5 | 21.7 |
| 1976 | 2884.7 | 2623.4 | 25.0 | 21.7 |
| 1977 | 2696.1 | 2582.1 | 22.7 | 22.5 |
| 1978 | 2605.9 | 2566.3 | 21.5 | 21.7 |
| 1979 | 2656.6 | 2667.4 | 21.8 | 21.0 |
| 1980 | 2335.6 | 2365.0 | 19.0 | 18.3 |
| 1981 | 2041.2 | 2226.4 | 16.4 | 15.7 |
| 1982 | 2439.9 | 2685.6 | 20.1 | 20.1 |
| 1983 | 2379.8 | 2407.5 | 19.4 | 18.2 |

*Proportion of workers hired or leaving jobs to total employment in previous year.

Sources: *Rocznik statystyczny pracy 1945–1968*, op. cit., pp. 170, 182; *RS 1970*, p. 66; *Czynni zawodowo w gospodarce narodowej, 1977* (Warsaw, 1978) pp. 126–7; *Zatrudnienie w gospodarce narodowej, 1979* (Warsaw, 1979) pp. 84, 106; *RS 1984*, p. 66.

to improve the overall efficiency of production processes. This is also pointed out at present by the Consultative Economic Council as a serious problem. Neither the economic reform that was introduced in 1982, nor the compulsory use of labour exchanges in 19 out of 50 administrative districts, a clearly anti-reform measure which was imposed in 1984, have been able to increase labour mobility.[25]

No solution has also been found for another problem that prevents better utilization of labour resources. For years it has been recognized that in order to reduce the capital intensity of production and to economize scarce capital it would be desirable to increase the number of shifts. In this way the existing capital stock could be utilized more intensively. It was hoped that this policy would somewhat reduce the rates of investment and, therefore, the share of accumulation, without adversely affecting the rates of growth of national product. Despite efforts, there has been a decline in the utilization of shifts. In industry the ratio of the total number of working employed in a plant to the number of posts in one shift, the shift utilization coefficient, declined from 1.58 in 1958 to 1.40 in 1979 and has continued to decline at the beginning of the 1980s despite a drastic decline in investment (see Table 2.7).

Already before 1980 it was widely realized in Poland that the

*Table 2.7* The use of shifts in socialist industry

| | 1958 | 1960 | 1965 | 1968 | 1970 | 1975 | 1976 | 1977 | 1978 | 1979 | 1980 | 1981 | 1982 | 1983 |
|---|---|---|---|---|---|---|---|---|---|---|---|---|---|---|
| Proportion of the total number of workers to the number of posts in one shift | 1.58 | 1.57 | 1.56 | 1.57 | 1.50 | 1.48 | 1.47 | 1.45 | 1.43 | 1.40 | 1.37 | 1.37* | 1.32* | 1.30* |
| Proportion of workers at: | | | | | | | | | | | | | | |
| First shift | n.a. | n.a. | n.a. | 64.9 | 63.6 | 60.9 | 60.4 | 60.7 | 60.7 | 60.9 | 61.9 | 58.9* | 60.1* | 60.7* |
| Second shift | n.a. | n.a. | n.a. | 24.8 | 25.7 | 27.6 | 27.8 | 27.6 | 27.4 | 27.6 | 26.3 | 27.3* | 27.2* | 26.7* |
| Third shift | n.a. | n.a. | n.a. | 10.2 | 10.5 | 11.2 | 11.4 | 11.3 | 11.5 | 11.2 | 11.3 | 13.2* | 12.1* | 11.9* |

n.a. = not available    * state industry only.

*Sources: Rocznik statystyczny pracy, 1945–1968, op. cit., p. 351; Rocznik statystyczny przemysłu, 1977, p. 160; 1979, p. 208; RS 1970, p. 146; 1980, p. 155.*

inefficient use of labour resources and unsatisfactory labour productivity are the results of, above all, two factors: the lack of sufficiently strong material incentives and the operation of the system of planning and management. Starting from an extremely low level of the wartime real wages and a decline in 1952 and 1953 (to 96 and 87 per cent of the 1949 level) during the first industrialization drive,[26] the average rate of growth of real wages was 5.4 per cent in 1956–60. It dropped, however, to 1.5 per cent in 1961–5 and increased only to 2.1 per cent in 1966–70 (see Table 2.8). Stronger monetary incentives were offered as a part of the new development strategy and the rates of growth of national product increased while the average rate of growth of real wages reached 7.2 per cent in 1971–5. This improvement depended, however, on the injection of large doses of foreign capital which were not used efficiently to secure sustained growth. Serious balance-of-payments difficulties, mounting foreign indebtedness, and the way in which the planners chose to cope with the rapidly deteriorating situation reduced the rates of growth of national product and then induced absolute declines.[27] The average rate of growth of real wages declined to 2.2 per cent in the second half of the 1970s. It is, however, important to realize that in a very deep disequilibrium in the market for consumption goods, when there are enormous shortages, difficulties in obtaining various material commodities, bribes or black market prices that have to be paid to obtain them, long lines in front of stores and a decline in the quality of goods and services, the index of real wages may show an improvement under the system of officially fixed prices when there is a decline in the standard of living. This happened at the end of the 1970s and at the beginning of the 1980s. Similarly, a decline in the index of real wages in 1982 and the lack of significant improvement in 1983 and 1984 do not fully measure the decline in the standard of living.

The poor performance of workers during the working hours, lack of discipline, shoddy work, waste of materials and damage to equipment resulting from unsatisfactory maintenance can all, at least partly, be explained by the lack of material incentives. Already before 1980 many economists in Poland had expressed the view that without further improvements in these incentives, it would not be possible to effect a switch to a more intensive pattern of development.[28] The strikes of 1980 and 1981 and the establishment of free labour unions were directly related to the material situation of the workers. A catastrophic reduction in output in 1979–82, however, created very strong inflationary pressures. A conflict appeared between measures

Table 2.8 Money wages, cost of living and real wages in the socialist economy – official indices (rates of growth %)

| | Average | | | 1971–75 | 1976 | 1977 | 1978 | 1979 | 1980 | 1981 | 1982 | 1983 |
|---|---|---|---|---|---|---|---|---|---|---|---|---|
| | 1956–60 | 1961–65 | 1966–70 | | | | | | | | | |
| Money wage | 8.3 | 3.7 | 3.7 | 9.8 | 9.4 | 7.4 | 6.3 | 9.0 | 13.4 | 27.3 | 51.3 | 24.5 |
| Cost of living | 2.9 | 2.2 | 1.6 | 2.4 | 4.7 | 4.9 | 8.7 | 6.7 | 9.1 | 24.4 | 101.5 | 23.1 |
| Real wage | 5.4 | 1.5 | 2.1 | 7.2 | 4.5 | 2.4 | −2.2 | 2.2 | 3.9 | 2.3 | −24.9 | 1.1 |

Sources: RS 1979, pp. xxxiv–xxxv; 1984, p. 114.

which were required to reduce the aggregate demand to the reduced level of aggregate supply and those which could increase the aggregate supply. The former required drastic restriction in real personal incomes, including wages, the latter suggested increases in wages to stimulate efforts.

Equally important as material incentives are systemic factors. The interaction of the overcentralized and inflexible command system with the development strategy that was adopted created an industrial structure which was geared to the extensive pattern of development. No significant improvements in the standard of living were, therefore, possible. Moreover, no effective employment policy could have been introduced so long as the system remained unreformed. Five different wage systems were tried before the 1982 reform: (1) 1945–9; (2) 1950–6; (3) 1957–64; (4) 1964–71; and (5) 1972–81. Complicated manipulations with piece work, bonuses, the creation of various special funds within the enterprise, the size of which depends on performance and the use can be beneficial in various forms to the workers or the enterprise, were introduced and changed to stimulate individual and group efficiency of work and to achieve some other objectives such as improvements in the quality of products, reduction of cost, elimination of waste, technological improvements and so on.[29] At the beginning of the 1980s a very large number of economists in Poland reached the conclusion that no modifications along these lines could really improve the situation and that a major systemic reform was absolutely necessary.[30]

## V.   ECONOMIC REFORM AND EMPLOYMENT POLICY

A decline in national product in 1979 and a quickly deteriorating situation in 1980 increased demands for economic reforms. Under the pressure of the strikers' demands and public opinion, supported by the resolutions of the meeting of the Polish Economic Association, a proposal for a comprehensive economic reform was adopted by the Ninth Special Party Congress in July 1981 to be introduced at the beginning of 1982.[31] It was based on three principles: (1) the autonomy of the enterprises; (2) their self-government; and (3) self-financing. The role of the planning commission and the branch ministries (i.e. the ministries responsible for various sectors of the economy) was to be reduced and changed from decisions concerning day-to-day operations of the enterprises to those affecting macroeconomic and main structural problems. The middle administrative level in the form of the so-called associations of the enterprises were to be abolished. The enterprises were to be 'steered' by economic 'parameters', such as prices, interest rates, taxes, exchange rates and various 'norms' which would indicate the desirable input-output or time required, and the role of economic instruments was to increase gradually while that of administrative commands was to decline.

Financial results of the enterprises were to become the only success indicator for their management, although not one but two indicators were accepted for this purpose: profit and net production. It was expected that inefficient production would be discontinued, except in some special cases, and that financially weak enterprises would not be able to expand, or even to exist in the long run. The reform was to lead to the rationalization of prices and wages and to result in a more rational allocation of resources, including labour, and, therefore, to their more efficient utilization. This was a mixed system of parametric socialist market economy and administrative steering. Although not sufficiently far-reaching or fully internally consistent, and particularly weak in foreign trade which, because of the increased dependence of the economy on import and enormous indebtedness became the most important field, it was a major step forward in the direction of a fully-fledged socialist market economy.[32]

It implied that workers could be dismissed from the enterprises which would be forced to reduce their labour costs, that for the dismissed worker it might not be easy to find alternative jobs without changing location or qualifications, accepting work at a later shift or at a lower wage, that the lack of labour discipline and neglect of duties would not be tolerated by the enterprises any more, that the enterprises would be allowed to attract the right type of labour by offering competitive wages and that the workers who prepared to work harder and better should be able to improve their remuneration. This would unavoidably lead to greater inequality of income but, as is usually pointed out, remuneration according to the amount and quality of labour is the basic systemic principle of the socialist economy.[33]

The anticipation of the reform, together with the declining output and frequent stoppages of work, caused by the shortage of raw materials, components, spare parts and machines, resulting from the abrupt cuts in imports from the West, created widespread expectations of unemployment. For this reason early retirements, permanent disability leaves and special child-care leaves for mothers with small children were already encouraged in 1978 and 1979.[34] The number of people who availed themselves of these possibilities declined during the period of great hopes and optimism among the workers in 1980. It increased, however, again in 1981 and, especially, under martial law in 1982. In 1983 the number was smaller than in the previous year but still considerably above the 1981 level (see Table 2.9).

This policy has been recognized as a serious mistake. Overimposed on the demographic decline, it created a shortage of labour while the reform, as we have seen before, failed to reduce the excessive demand for labour (see Table 2.3).

The reform was introduced under the conditions of martial law with the economy paralysed by administrative chaos, interrupted telephone connections and restricted mobility of persons. Various specific instructions were issued with a delay of two or three months and the enterprises were left in a vacuum.

Despite official declarations stressing the authorities' full commitment to the reform as adopted by the Ninth Party Congress, some significant modifications were made, at first in order 'to adjust the reform to the requirements of martial law'.[35] Originally the reform seemed to be accepted as an absolutely necessary condition for recovery from the crisis and for effecting the switch to a more intensive pattern of development which was the only way to achieve selfsustained growth in the long run. Since the time of its introduction, however, the attitude of the authorities has changed and the official line is now that the reform cannot be introduced under the conditions of a deep internal and external disequilibrium, that its full implementation has to be delayed and that a period of transition is needed which is likely to last several years, during which many features of the command system must be retained.[36]

Although the enterprises have been given a considerable degree of autonomy *de jure*, in practice their activities are considerably limited by officially fixed prices, by the administrative allocation of raw materials and foreign exchanges, by the retention of the middle level administrative units in the form of new voluntary associations (which are not quite voluntary, because joining them is often necessary in order to obtain some raw materials of special financial considerations) or even compulsory associations in some sectors of the economy. Moreover, some sectors, such as coal mining, power generation and distribution, the sugar industry, meat processing, transportation, communications, etc., have been entirely excluded from the reform.[37]

*Table 2.9* Retirements and disability leaves, earlier retirements and child-care leaves (thousands)

| | 1970 | 1975 | 1976 | 1977 | 1978 | 1979 | 1980 | 1981 | 1982 | 1983 |
|---|---|---|---|---|---|---|---|---|---|---|
| Retirements and disability leaves | 132.9 | 167.2 | 193.3 | 216.8 | 249.4 | 333.9 | 248.1 | 369.7 | 556.2 | 235.3 |
| Early retirements | | | | | | | | | | |
| male employees | — | — | — | — | 26.2 | 10.26 | 20.2 | 168.8 | 327.1 | 27.2 |
| female employees | — | — | — | — | 10.6 | 41.6 | 6.7 | 103.8 | 203.9 | 18.4 |
| Child-care leaves | 50.4 | 219.2 | 285.4 | 352.4 | 15.6 | 60.9 | 13.5 | 65.0 | 123.2 | 8.8 |
| | | | | | 403.2 | 442.6 | 487.2 | 624.6 | 795.3 | 877.7 |
| Early retirements and child-care leaves | 50.4 | 219.2 | 285.4 | 352.4 | 429.4 | 545.2 | 507.4 | 793.4 | 1122.4 | 904.9 |
| As % or population at working age | 0.3 | 1.1 | 1.4 | 1.7 | 2.1 | 2.6 | 2.4 | 3.7 | 5.2 | 4.2 |

*Source: Zatrudnienie w gospodarce narodowej 1984* (Warsaw, 1984) pp. 14–17.

In the employment field, rationalization of wages was accepted as one of the main tasks of the transitional period. The main stress was to be put on the creation of the dependence of wages on the financial results of the enterprise activity. The central 'steering' was to be limited to: (1) the determination of the minimum wage; (2) methods of compensation for rise in the cost of living; (3) preparation of lists of maximum and minimum wages for various types of jobs; and (4) preparation of the general rules of wage determination.[38]

Progress in this field has, however, been slow and subject to reversals. In 1982 an attempt was, indeed, made to increase the enterprises' autonomy in this field by limiting the central control of wages and retaining the control by (1) the lists of maximum and minimum wages for various types of jobs and by (2) introducing a tax on wages. However, in practice about two thirds of all wages increases in that year were the result of centrally determined wage adjustments and individual exemptions or modifications of the wage tax rates, effected in a purely administrative way on the basis of the bureacrats' judgement, subject to negotiations between the enterprises and the branch ministries often with intervention by new associations on behalf of their enterprises. The situation was similar in 1983 and 1984.[39]

In January 1984 a new law was enacted by the Sejm (parliament) which permits the enterprises to choose, if they so wish, their own system of wages providing that the range between the maximum and minimum wage is not smaller than a certain centrally determined range, and that the enterprises meet some strict conditions. A very detailed administrative control has, however, been retained.[40]

It has been pointed out that 'there are more initial conditions, limitations and exemptions than any real autonomy of action.'[41] Until the end of the year 'only an insignificant number of the enterprises expressed interest in taking advantage of this possibility.'[42]

In the opinion of at least some Polish economists, so far 'changes in the wage policy have been small and insignificant' and they are 'completely insufficient from the point of view of the principles of the reform: the autonomy, self-government and self-financing of the enterprises.'[43]

At the same time the experience of the early 1980s has demonstrated once again that the administrative methods are unable to solve the problem of irrational and excessive employment in various sectors of the economy.[44] There is still a lot of unnecessary labour hoarded by the enterprises because the low wage bill, the cost formula of the price determination and the rule of the 'justified costs' make it possible for the enterprises to obtain permission to raise prices to the level that cover the cost of all unnecessary labour which may one day be necessary. In this respect the introduction of the obligatory use of labour exchanges has aggravated the situation. The enterprises have an additional reason to keep unnecessary workers because with the rationing of labour it may be difficult to obtain them if they are needed in the future.[45]

In this situation it appears that the so-called 'employment barrier of growth is simply a myth',[46] resulting from what Professor A. Rajkiewicz has described as 'unemployment among the employed'.[47]

It is clear that very limited progress has been achieved in the field of employment since the introduction of the reform. However, as has been stressed by another distinguished Polish economist recently, 'if there will be no progress in the systemic field and no rationalization of economic policy, there are no reasons for optimism' about the future of the economy.[48]

## Notes

1.  The author discussed this point in Z. M. Fallenbuchl, 'How does the Soviet economy function without free market?', *The Queen's Quarterly*, LXX (4) (1964), reprinted in M. Bornstein and D. R. Fusfield (eds), *The Soviet Economy: A Book of Readings* (Homewood, Irwin, rev. edn 1966) pp. 34–66; (3rd edn, 1970) pp. 24–36; (4th edn, 1974) pp. 3–16; an abbreviated text is included in R. T. Gill, *Economics: A Text with Included Readings* (Pacific Palisades, Goodyear, 1973) pp. 80–4.

2.  Z. M. Fallenbuchl, 'The communist pattern of industrialization', *Soviet Studies*, XXI(4) (1970) pp. 451–78.

3.  Z. M. Fallenbuchl, 'Industrial structure and the intensive pattern of development in Poland', *Jahrbuch der Wirtschaft Osteuropas*, 4 (1973) pp. 233–54.

4.  J. Beksiak, *Społeczeństwo gospodarujące* (Warsaw, 1972) pp. 113–26.

5.  This aspect of employment policy has been discussed by the author in Z. M. Fallenbuchl, 'Internal migration and economic development under socialism: the case of Poland', in A. A. Brown and E. Neuberger (eds), *Internal Migration: A Comparative Perspective* (New York, Academic Press, 1977) pp. 305–27.

6.  For a more detailed discussion see Z. M. Fallenbuchl, 'The Polish Economy in the 1970s', in JEC, *East European Economies Post-Helsinki* (Washington, DC, US Government Printing Office, 1977) pp. 816–64.

7.  J. Holzer, *Nowe Drogi*, no. 2 (1979).

8. Z. Schulz, *Gospodarka planowa*, no. 5 (1976) pp. 266–71; M. Kabaj, *Życie gospodarcze*, no. 20 (1979), pp. 1, 4; M. Kabaj, *Życie gospodarcze*, no. 41 (1979) pp. 1, 4.
9. A. Karpiński and J. Pajestka in *Polityka gospodarcza Polski Ludowej* (Warsaw, 1965), pp. 41–3.
10. *Rocznik statystyczny pracy 1945–68* (Warsaw, 1970), pp. xxiv, xxv; *Zatrudnienie w gospodarce narodowej* (Warsaw, 1979), p. 2; (1984) p. 3.
11. Schulz, op. cit., p. 268.
12. *Życie gospódarcze*, no. 47 (1984) p. 8.
13. M. Olęcdzki, *Polityka zatrudnienia* (Warsaw, 1974), p. 307; the author has discussed this point in Z. M. Fallenbuchl, 'Collectivization and Economic Development', *The Canadian Journal of Economic and Political Science*, XXXIII (1) (1967) pp. 1–15.
14. A. Rajkiewicz, *Zatrudnienie w Polsce Ludowej w latach 1950–1970* (Warsaw, 1965), p. 230; H. Jędruszczak, *Zatrudnienie a przemiany spolecene w Polsce w latach 1944–1960* (Wroclaw, 1972), pp. 168–9.
15. J. Górski, and M. Kabaj, *Polityka gospodarcza P.R.L.* (Warsaw, 1974) pp. 194–5; Jedruszczak, op. cit., p. 169.
16. *Rocznik dochodu narodowego 1971* (Warsaw, 1971) pp. 17, 18, 184.
17. Olędzki, op. cit., p. 306.
18. Ibid, p. 309; Rajkiewicz, op. cit., p. 230.
19. The author has presented an analysis of the optimum rate of accumulation and some examples of overshooting it in Eastern Europe during the 1950s in Z. M. Fallenbuchl, 'Investment Policy for Economic Development: Some Lessons from the Communist Experience', *The Canadian Journal of Economic and Political Science*, XXIX (1), (1963) pp. 26–39.
20. Z. M. Fallenbuchl, 'The Strategy of Development and Gierek's Economic Maneuvre', in A. Bromke and Y. W. Strong (eds), *Gierek's Poland* (New York, Praeger, 1973) pp. 52–70.
21. Olędzki, op. cit., p. 310.
22. For the discussion of this policy and its implementation see Z. M. Fallenbuchl, *East–West Technology Transfer-Study of Poland, 1971–1980* (Paris, OECD, 1983).
23. The author has discussed the collapse of the new development strategy in Z. M. Fallenbuchl, 'The Polish Economy of the Beginning of the 1980s', JEC, *East European Economic Assessment* (Washington, DC, US Government Printing Office) pp. 33–71.
24. A. Melich, *Życie gospodarcze*, no. 24 (1977) pp. 1–2; J. Gordon, *Życie gospodarcze*, no. 32 (1979) p. 8.
25. *Życie gospodarcze*, no. 47 (1984) p. 8.
26. J. Meller, *Place a planowanie gospodarcze w Polsce 1950–1975* (Warsaw, 1977) p. 55.
27. The author discussed the crisis in Z. M. Fallenbuchl, 'Poland: Command Planning in Crisis', *Challenge*, 24(3) (1981) pp. 5–12 and Z. M. Fallenbuchl, 'Poland's Economic Crisis', *Problems of Communism*, XXXI(2) (1982) pp. 1–21.
28. S. Felbur, *Gospodarka planowa*, no. 4 (1977) pp. 187–93.
29. W. Krencik, *Gospodarka planowa*, no. 2 (1981) pp. 68–75.

30. B. Przywara, *Gospodarka planowa*, no. 12 (1982) pp. 485–490.
31. *Kierunki reformy gospodarczej* (Warsaw, 1981).
32. For the discussion of the official and other reform proposals see Z. M. Fallenbuchl, 'The Origins of the Present Economic Crisis in Poland and Issue of Economic Reform', in A. Jain (ed), *Solidarity: The Origins and Implications of Polish Trade Unions* (Baton Rouge, Oracle Press, 1983) pp. 149–66.
33. I. Dryll, *Życie gospodarcze*, 9 June 1985.
34. Z. Dach, *Gospodarka planowa*, no. 11 (1984) pp. 503–4.
35. For more details see Z. M. Fallenbuchl, 'The Polish Economy Under Martial Law', *Soviet Studies*, XXXVI(4) (1984) pp. 513–27.
36. 'Report of the Consultative Economic Council on the System of Functioning of the Economy', *Życie gospodarcze*, no. 45 (1984) p. 1; W. Baka, *Życie gospodarcze*, no. 6 (1985) p. 1.
37. C. Józefiak, *Życie gospodarcze*, no. 5 (1985) p. 5.
38. C. Józefiak, *Życie gospodarcze*, no. 4 (1985) p. 7.
39. Józefiak, op. cit., no. 5 (1985), p. 5; Report of the Consultative Economic Council, *Życie gospodarcze*, no. 14, 1984.
40. I. Dryll, *Życie gospodarcze*, no. 6 (1984) p. 3; I. Dryll, *Życie gospodarcze*, no. 8 (1984) p. 4.
41. Józefiak, op. cit., no. 5 (1985) p. 5.
42. J. Elbanowski, *Życie gospodarcze*, no. 50 (1984) p. 11.
43. Józefiak, op. cit., no. 5 (1985) p. 5.
44. Dach, op. cit., p. 507.
45. Ibid.; T. Kramer, *Sztandar mlodych*, 7 May 1985.
46. Z. Gontarski, *Życie gospodarcze*, no. 5 (1985) p. 10.
47. Ibid.
48. J. Mujżel during a panel discussion reported in *Kierunki*, 9 June 1985.

# 3 Manpower Problems in the GDR

## JIRI KOSTA

## I. INTRODUCTION

The East German labour market is marked by an increasing shortage of manpower resources. 'The complaint about lack of labour is being heard in nearly all plants and organizations, beginning with the pub at the corner up to the big industrial combine';[1] statements of this kind are found not only in professional writings but also in the GDR mass media every day. The following data illustrate this situation.

The participation rate (the ratio of the gainfully active population to the total population) has grown from 46.4 per cent (1960) to 48.2 per cent (1970) and to 53.1 per cent (1983), the participation rate of women from 37.7 per cent at the beginning to 49.4 per cent at the end of this period.[2] Because military and security forces are not included in the GDR statistics, these rates should be raised by about 3 points in order to make them comparable with international data.[3] The high participation rates become more evident when they are compared with those of other countries. Thus the 1980 participation rate (Western definition) amounted to 55.2 per cent in the GDR and to 41.9 per cent in the FRG,[4] the corresponding ratios for women of working age (15–60 years) in 1980 were 84.4 per cent (GDR) and 50.6 per cent (FRG). The women's participation rate in 1970 (which has to be accepted with some reservation) was 30 per cent in Austria and in the FRG, 32 per cent in Switzerland, 39 per cent in Hungary and 42 per cent in the CSSR, while it was 43 per cent in the GDR.[5]

Are there any prospects that the gap in the demand for manpower in the GDR economy will be bridged or, at least, diminished in the 1980s? In order to answer this question, the present situation has to be investigated. In the following section, therefore, labour supply and labour demand are discussed. Then the policy measures which have been taken by the East German government in order to cope with the apparent problems are analysed. The conclusion contains an evaluation of the efforts to overcome labour shortages and, in this context, a tentative consideration about the prospects for this issue.

## II. THE EAST GERMAN LABOUR MARKET – DEVELOPMENT AND PRESENT SITUATION

There are many causes of labour shortages in the GDR economy: demographic, economic, historical, cultural and motivational. The question why the present situation is characterized by a supply gap can be answered more precisely after the development of labour supply and labour demand have been investigated separately.

The supply of labour depends first of all on demographic factors. The development of the population, particularly its age and sex composition, determines the manpower potential. The corresponding figures are given in Tables 3.1 and 3.2

*Table 3.1*  Development of population in the GDR

| Year | Population (annual averages) | Females per 100 males | Live births (per 1000 inhabitants) | Deaths (per 1000 inhabitants) | Natural population growth |
|------|------|------|------|------|------|
| 1960 | 17 241 | 122 | 17.0 | 13.6 | + 3.4 |
| 1965 | 17 020 | 119 | 16.5 | 13.5 | + 3.0 |
| 1970 | 17 058 | 117 | 13.9 | 14.1 | − 0.2 |
| 1975 | 16 850 | 116 | 10.8 | 14.3 | − 3.5 |
| 1977 | 16 765 | 115 | 13.3 | 13.5 | − 0.2 |
| 1978 | 16 756 | 114 | 13.9 | 13.9 | 0 |
| 1979 | 16 745 | 114 | 14.0 | 13.9 | + 0.1 |
| 1980 | 16 737 | 113 | 14.6 | 14.2 | + 0.4 |
| 1981 | 16 736 | 113 | 14.2 | 13.9 | + 0.3 |
| 1982 | 16 697 | 113 | 14.4 | 13.7 | + 0.7 |
| 1983 | 16 699 | 112 | 14.0 | 13.3 | + 0.7 |

*Source: SJD 1984*, pp. 61, 62.

The size of the East German population declined during the whole period; the excess of the death rate over the birth rate was alarming in the first half of the 1970s. Both rates have been approximately in balance only since 1977, so that the number of inhabitants was almost constant in the second half of the 1970s. It was the loss of men in both world wars which has had an unfavourable impact on labour re-

*Table 3.2* Manpower resources

| End of year | Working age population*<br>(per 100 inhabitants) | Children†<br>(per 100 inhabitants) | Retirement age<br>population‡ |
|---|---|---|---|
| 1950 | 64.1 | 22.1 | 13.8 |
| 1960 | 61.3 | 21.0 | 17.6 |
| 1965 | 58.2 | 23.2 | 18.6 |
| 1970 | 57.9 | 22.6 | 19.5 |
| 1975 | 59.7 | 20.6 | 19.6 |
| 1979 | 62.8 | 19.1 | 18.1 |
| 1983 | 64.4 | 18.7 | 16.9 |

*Males 15–65 years old; females 15–60; and five-twelfths of all population between the age of 14 and 15.
†Up to 15 years + seven-twelfths of all 14–15-year-old children.
‡Males 65 years and more; females 60 years and more.

*Source: SJD 1984*, pp. 346, 347.

sources. The consequence has been the high share of the female population, which has decreased only gradually (Table 3.1).

The proportion of the working age population (Eastern definition) decreased during the 1950s. Here the widespread flight to West Germany up to 1961 (construction of the Wall) was of decisive relevance.[6] In the past decade the situation has improved. On the one hand the birth losses caused by the Great Depression of the early 1930s continue to have an effect in 1980. On the other hand, the numerically weak age-groups born during the First World War will reach retirement age during the 1980s, and the present 15–30-year-old age group, which is much stronger numerically, will move up. At the same time, however, the strong birth losses from the Second World War will reduce the labour potential in the near future. All these factors taken together, mean that after 1985, the labour force will remain constant for a couple of years.

In the past the system of education in East Germany expanded similarly to other developed countries. The corresponding increase in students reduces, of course, the work force potential. A glance at statistical figures shows that the number of young people over 15 who go on to vocational school and university education has grown continually during the last two decades.

The proportion of vocational school students per 10 000 inhabitants grew from 73 in 1960 to 101 in 1979 and university students from 58 in 1960 to 77 in 1979. The decline of the latter during the 1970s, and the latest discussions in the GDR, indicate that the expansion of the university sector is being restricted since a certain surplus of qualified individuals has developed.

People of retirement age are not included (statistically) in the working age population; however, they are being utilized as much as possible. In 1975, for instance, the participation level of working retirees amounted to 650 000 persons and at present to 350 000.[7]

*Table 3.3*   Student–inhabitant ratio

| Year | Vocational school students (per 10 000 inhabitants) | University students (per 10 000 inhabitants) |
|------|------|------|
| 1960 | 73.1 | 58.1 |
| 1965 | 66.7 | 65.5 |
| 1970 | 97.9 | 83.9 |
| 1975 | 93.0 | 81.4 |
| 1979 | 101.3 | 77.1 |
| 1983 | 100.5 | 77.9 |

*Source: SJD 1984*, p. 56.

The labour potential depends, after all, on the average working hours spent by the gainfully active population. The world-wide trend to shorter working time has not passed East Germany by: in 1967 the work-week was shortened from 45 to $43\frac{3}{4}$ hours. For three-shift workers the work-week was set at 42 hours and reduced to 40 hours in 1977 (in the same year to $43\frac{3}{4}$ hours for two-shift workmen). Other constraints placed on employment resources consist of benefits for mothers. For all working mothers the work-week was shortened from $43\frac{3}{4}$ hours to 40 hours in May 1977 (the same work-week had already been set for female shift workers in 1972). Since 1976 mothers have received a year's paid holiday (Babyjahr) after giving birth to the second or subsequent children, with a general prolongation of holidays amounting to 3 days at least, since 1979, and other benefits.[8] It is not possible to determine how far the shortening of working hours has been compensated by overtime work (originally not intended but unavoidable in order to fulfil the plan targets).

All the data mentioned above concerning the demographic development; then the expansion of education; finally, the shortening of working time contribute to a decrease in labour supply. Consequently it is necessary to consider where there are reserves in the GDR which could be mobilized. Given the high utilization of domestic labour, recourse to foreign workers seems to be reasonable. The relevant information tells us that in 1983 there were about 50 000 foreigners employed in the GDR, particularly Poles, Hungarians, Vietnamese, and Mongolians; with the exception of Poles, most of them were trainees.[9] This number has not increased to any substantial degree because for political reasons the Honecker regime wants to limit the contact of its own population with people from abroad.

Having investigated the supply situation, we will move to the problems of labour demand. East German enterprises and other organizations express their labour needs in the framework of plan targets, assigned to them by supervisory authorities. The number of gainfully active persons ($L$) depends on the volume of goods (services) produced ($Y$) and on labour productivity ($p$). In terms of economic growth, the demand for labour is given by the ratio of production growth to the growth of labour productivity, i.e.

$$L_2/L_1 = \frac{Y_2/Y_1}{p_2/p_1}$$

where 1 is the first and 2 the second period. This relationship can be shown for the past in Table 3.4.[10]

*Table 3.4.* Growth of national income, employment and labour productivity (annual growth rates as percentage)

| Indicator | 1950–5 | 1955–60 | 1960–5 | 1966–70 | 1971–5 | 1975–80 | 1980–5 |
|---|---|---|---|---|---|---|---|
| National income produced | 13.1 | 7.1 | 3.4 | 5.2 | 5.4 | 4.1 | 3.9 |
| Workers in the material sphere | 0.8 | −0.2 | −0.3 | 0.0 | 0.1 | 0.4 | 0.6 |
| Labour productivity in the material sphere | 12.2 | 7.3 | 3.7 | 5.2 | 5.3 | 3.7 | 3.3 |

*Source: SJD 1984*, pp. 17, 98.

Since the GDR statistics include in national income only output of the material sectors, i.e. the production of goods and 'material' services (including transport, trade, but excluding administration, culture, etc.) the data for the period 1950–78 as shown in Table 3.4 are based exclusively on figures concerning the 'material sphere' of the East German economy.[11]

In the second half of the 1950s (figures for the early 1950s refer to the postwar reconstruction period and are therefore not comparable), labour demand did not expand because of high productivity growth (a possible statistical bias can be neglected). An insignificant decrease in employment was the consequence of slightly lower output growth compared with productivity growth in 1961–5. Then in the late 1960s, and also in the first half of the 1970s, the number of working people stagnated since both growth rates (output and productivity) were the same. A small increase in the labour force appeared from 1976 to 1980 and in the early 1980s which was due to a slightly higher output growth rate compared with the increase in labour productivity. These results for the whole economy may have been less favourable than indicated because, firstly, productivity in the 'non-material' sphere grew more slowly than in the 'material' sphere and, secondly, the productivity indicator could be 'inflated' because of overestimates of output (no matter whether output is calculated on the basis of gross output or commodity production).

Some data concerning the development of the employment structure by economic sectors and industries will complete the analysis of labour demand (see Table 3.5).

*Table 3.5*  Employment structure by economic sectors

| Year | Industry and handicraft | Construction | Agriculture and forestry | Transport and communication | Trade | Other sectors |
|---|---|---|---|---|---|---|
| 1950 | 37.5 | 6.5 | 27.9 | 6.3 | 9.4 | 12.5 |
| 1960 | 41.4 | 6.1 | 17.0 | 7.2 | 11.6 | 16.7 |
| 1970 | 42.0 | 6.9 | 12.8 | 7.5 | 11.0 | 19.8 |
| 1979 | 41.3 | 7.1 | 10.7 | 7.5 | 10.3 | 23.1 |
| 1983 | 41.0 | 6.9 | 10.7 | 7.4 | 10.1 | 23.9 |

*Source: SJD 1980*, p. 85, and *1984*, p. 109.

From the early 1950s up to the late 1970s, the share of the labour force in the secondary sector (industry and construction) increased by 4.4 per cent, the share of employees in the service sector (transport, trade, others) grew by 12.7 per cent (public administration, health and education services grew particularly fast). The employment ratio for the first sector (agriculture) decreased by more than 17 per cent.

Compared with other CMEA countries the basic tendency will be similar although the trend will be modified by the stage of industrial development.[12] Thus from 1960 to 1983 the share of the labour force in the secondary sector grew from 48.3 to 50.6 per cent in the GDR (the figures for 1960 differ slightly from those in Table 3.5 due to the different sources), similarly from 45.6 to 47.4 per cent in Czechoslovakia, from 32.4 to 38.5 per cent in the USSR, from 34.0 to 39.2 per cent in Hungary and from 32.4 to 37.2 per cent in Poland. The corresponding decline for the primary sector was: GDR, 17.2 per cent (1960), 10.4 per cent (1983); Czechoslovakia, 25.9 per cent, 13.6 per cent; USSR, 38.8 per cent, 19.8 per cent; in Hungary, 38.9 per cent, 23.4 per cent; Poland 44.1 per cent, 30.3 per cent. Completing the residuals to 100 per cent the share of the tertiary (service) sector in 1983 will be 39.0 per cent for the GDR being the highest developed and 30.1 per cent for Poland, the lowest developed, of the countries compared.

In order to compare the GDR with the FRG, a comparable Western economy,[13] the following figures are relevant. In 1980 in the FRG the employment shares by sectors were 5.9 per cent (primary), 44.8 per cent (secondary) and 49.3 per cent (tertiary) whereas in the GDR the corresponding data were 10.1, 48.8 and 41.9 per cent. The differences are caused not only by the level of development, but also by different development strategies and differing functioning of the economic systems. This will become even clearer by examining employment by industries (branches) as indicated in Table 3.6.

Table 3.6   Employment by branches of industry (percentages)

| Year | Industry | Fuel and energy | Metallurgy | Machinery | Chemicals | Textiles | Food |
|------|----------|-----------------|------------|-----------|-----------|----------|------|
| 1960 | 100.0 | 7.3 | 4.1 | 24.4 | 11.3 | 12.2 | 8.2 |
| 1970 | 100.0 | 6.2 | 4.3 | 28.7 | 11.5 | 8.8 | 7.7 |
| 1977 | 100.0 | 6.4 | 4.2 | 29.0 | 10.7 | 7.6 | 8.4 |
| 1981 | 100.0 | 6.8 | 4.3 | 29.5 | 10.7 | 7.1 | 8.7 |

*Source: RGW in Zahlen* (Wiener Institut fur internationale Wirtschaftsvergleiche), 1978, p. 152, and 1983, p. 154.

The structural change in the East German economy which had taken place in the past was characterized by the growing share of machinery. This was a consequence of the plan priorities resulting from the specialization arrangements within the CMEA according to Soviet initiatives.[14] This new orientation can be seen even more distinctly if we follow the employment structure by industry from prewar time to the early 1960s. This is shown in Table 3.7.

*Table 3.7* Employment by branches of industry in West and East Germany (percentages)

|  | FRG | | | GDR | | |
|---|---|---|---|---|---|---|
|  | *1936* | *1950* | *1962* | *1936* | *1950* | *1962* |
| Industry (total) | 100.0 | 100.0 | 100.0 | 100.0 | 100.0 | 100.0 |
| Basic materials | 27.9 | 30.8 | 25.3 | 19.8 | 24.2 | 26.7 |
| Metal-working industry | 33.4 | 32.7 | 42.7 | 31.3 | 33.3 | 38.7 |
| Consumer goods | 30.0 | 29.6 | 25.9 | 40.3 | 35.0 | 27.1 |
| Food, beverages, etc. | 8.7 | 6.9 | 6.2 | 8.6 | 7.5 | 7.5 |

*Source:* G. Leptin, *Veränderungen in der Branchen- und Regional Struktur der deutschen Industrie zwischen 1936 und 1962* (Berlin, 1965) pp. 47 ff., quoted according to *Materialien zum Bericht der Lage der Nation* (Bonn, 1974) p. 337.

Comparable data indicate that the share of workers employed in investment goods industries, particularly in basic materials production (coal, steel), on the present territory of the GDR in 1936 lagged remarkably behind the corresponding West German figures. The forced growth of heavy industry after 1945, continuing a trend which had already begun in the late Hitler era, resulted in GDR's catching up to the lead of West Germany: in 1962 the employment share in basic materials was even higher in the GDR, and in the metal-working branches the gap in favour of the FRG was at least diminished. It should be stressed that the extreme expansion of labour-intensive heavy industry implied extraordinary demand for labour inputs.

The last aspect, which might explain the excessive demand for manpower in the GDR, is the high share of personnel in sectors such as the state and planning administration, the military and security forces and the political institutions (Communist Party, trade unions, youth organization, etc.). Moreover these systemic peculiarities, which cannot be quantified because of a lack of data, are burdening the labour balance to a large extent.

The investigation of supply and demand has shown how the imbalance in the labour market – the supply gap or the demand excess – has arisen. The unfavourable situation can only be overcome if the productivity lag behind the Western industrial countries such as the FRG can be made up (compare Table 3.4).

A further weakness of the East German labour market lies in the insufficient adaptation of professional categories to the structure of labour demand.[15] This problem will be discussed in detail below under 'Results and Prospectives'.

## III. EMPLOYMENT POLICY: GOALS AND MEASURES

This policy – in terms of East European 'manpower planning and control' – is an integral part of the all-embracing planning system in the GDR.[16] The manpower objectives and targets are subordinated to the objectives of production output. In other words, the demand for manpower depends on the economic growth strategy.

Growth and structure of output in the GDR always determine the number of workers and their professional composition. Labour planning is linked with demographic projections, with the education plans and other institutional data (regional, transport, etc.). Given the background of these relationships and interdependences, policy measures in the GDR are orientated to two aims (as was shown above): (a) to an increase of labour productivity in order to overcome the scarcity of manpower, and (b) to a better adaptation of labour resources to the regional, sectoral and professional demand as it is expressed in the plan.

The mandatory targets (number of workers, etc.) which are set by the superior planning bodies are handed down to the enterprises. Because there is a relatively free choice of jobs for each worker it is then the task of the enterprise management to take care of the fulfilment of the labour input plans. The recruitment of workers can be handled – if free choice of jobs is to be guaranteed – mainly by indirect means, i.e. by material incentives. These methods are supported by some administrative measures and by ideological ('ideal') motivation as well.

## 1. Administrative methods of labour control

Binding labour plan targets are quantitative directives which the enterprise receives from the superior planning authority (combinate, regional body, ministry). For the last 5-year plan (1981–5), in the plan section 'Labour productivity, Manpower, Earned Incomes' and 'Professional Training', different mandatory targets for enterprises have been set, among them indicators showing the development of labour productivity, size and composition of manpower (in accordance with regional manpower balances), wage fund, average wage, cadres and qualifications.[17]

Whether the labour force is used efficiently or not must be proved first of all, by indicators, 'labour productivity based on' 'value added' (Eigenleistung), and 'release[18] of manpower to other sectors – number of persons'.[19] In the decrees for drawing up the one year plans for 1981, 1982, etc., highly detailed instructions to the ministries, combines and enterprises were given on how the 'release of manpower' target, i.e. labour savings, was to be fulfilled.[20]

The labour administration plays an important role, especially the State Secretariat for Labour and Wages and the subordinated District (Bezirk) and county (Kreis) Offices for Labour and Wages founded in 1973.[21] It is their task to oversee the employment policy implementation, to control and analyse whether manpower is rationally used, and to participate in setting up the labour plans and balances worked out by the central planning bodies. According to a government decree published in 1979 the regional authorities can 'impose on the enterprise targets additional to the labour plan targets'.[22]

A further administrative measure applied is a directive of the government to limit the cost of management and administration in 1980 in the state-owned economy ('volkseigene Wirtschaft') to the level achieved in the year before.[23] It is hoped that this will prevent the operation of 'Parkinson's Law'.

The autonomy of individual choice is restricted by some bureaucratic practices. In the course of allocating graduates of vocational and other schools to jobs individual priorities can prevail only to a small extent in spite of a job consultation service.[24] The number of school enrolments is limited, too, and admission depends not only on school results, but also on the 'political engagement' and the social origin of the young worker.

In addition job changes within the enterprise are frequently effected by command; to the extent that workers' involvement is allowed; it is done under the watchful eye of the Party or trade unions.

## 2. Incentives

Like administrative measures incentives are used primarily for the two purposes mentioned above: firstly to stimulate enterprises and their staff to labour savings, and secondly to induce labour to take jobs which correspond to plan priorities (industrial, regional and occupational).

The main incentives to increase labour productivity are wages[25] and bonuses.[26] The share of wages in the workers' earning amounted to 92 per cent in 1973, the remaining 8 per cent represented the bonuses (it seems that this relationship has not changed very much up to now). According to GDR textbooks there are some differences with regard to the functions of both wages and bonuses.[27] In addition to stimulating labour efficiency the wage ought also to promote improvements in skill and support the distribution of the labour force according to the plan targets. Wages depend, first of all, on the performance of the individual worker. Bonuses, depending on the collective performance of the plant, have to stimulate the fulfilment of the enterprise plan targets and, besides, initiate the drawing-up by the enterprise management of higher plan objectives compared with the original plan targets assigned from the centre. From these principles the following institutional regulations have been set up in the GDR.

The main instruments of wage determination and regulation are job evaluation, wage rates, piece-work rules and the wage fund indicator.[28]

Wage (skill) grades are allocated to all jobs to be performed on the basis of criteria spelled out by the so-called branch wage catalogues which are in fact job-evaluation handbooks. There are nowadays six to eight wage grades for blue-collar workers, three for foremen, eight for technical and administrative personnel, and five for experts, including those with university education. According to East German sources of 1980 the wage rate (which is the money value attached to the wage grade) for the eighth grade is 1.61 times higher than for the third grade (the first and second grades are not used).[29]

The wage rates differ not only with regard to the skill requirements but also according to the various branches. Thus both policy aims – labour productivity growth and manpower allocation in accordance with the plan – are taken into consideration. The wage itself not only includes the part given by the wage rate. As in other CMEA countries the rate portion in the total wage decreases between two wage rate reforms in favour of an additional payment which the East German planners call 'surplus wage' ('Mehrlohn', sometimes 'Mehrleistungslohn'). In the GDR the share of the wage rate declined in the middle of the 1970s to 50 per cent,[30] and lost, therefore, its stimulation effect.[31] That is why after 1976 a wage reform was started in order to raise the share of the wage rate to 70–90 per cent of the basic wage until 1980 (there are no published data about the results which have been achieved so far, but it seems that up to 1980 'new basic wages' were introduced[32]).

Wages ought to orientate the enterprise not only to an efficient utilization of labour but at the same time, as we have shown, to an allocation of manpower according to the regional, sectoral, professional, and training plan objectives. The distribution of the labour force in accordance with the plan is promoted by the wage rates and the 'surplus wage' mentioned above. Figure 3.1 shows the wage rate differentials by 8 wage grades in 10 GDR industries in the early 1970s. (It is not likely that the main relationship would have changed substantially up to now.)

The heights of the columns shown in Figure 3.1 indicate the different branch priorities with regard to labour scarcity, at the top the mining industry down to 'light' machines and instruments (which might be surprising) and, at the bottom, the food industry. Within branches the wage rates are further differentiated corresponding to the 'macroeconomic relevance of a given production line and with regard to regional aspects . . .'.[33]

As we have learned, a worker's income does not only include the wage rate, but an additional 'surplus wage' and the bonus as well. This is why the income differentials for work need not, necessarily, be identical with the wage rate differences shown in Figure 3.1. In Table 3.8 the differentials of incomes for work performed by blue- and white-collar workers according to selected industries are shown. Their incentive effect is more relevant for the distribution of manpower than the differences resulting from the wage rates.

The data shown in Table 3.8 indicate the high priority of metallurgy, energy and fuel production and, in the early 1970s, construction. These

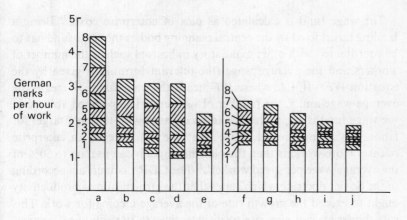

(a) Ore-mining (underground).
(b) Brown coal-mining (open-cast).
(c) Metallurgy.
(d) Heavy machinery.
(e) Machines, instruments, optics.
(f) Chemicals.
(g) Railway transport.
(h) Construction.
(i) Textile, clothing, leather.
(j) Food industry.

*Figure 3.1* Wage rate differentials by industries

are the branches where labour shortages were alarming. The incentives given by the higher incomes in the priority branches had to be supported by better social conditions such as housing for the employees, holiday facilities, etc.

*Table 3.8* Income differentials in selected industries (monthly incomes for work)

| Year | GDR economy | Industry (total) | Energy, fuel | Metallurgy | Machinery | Textile industry | Construction | Agriculture | Trade |
|------|------|------|------|------|------|------|------|------|------|
| 1970 | 100 | 101 | 109 | 115 | 106 | 81 | 109 | 93 | 88 |
| 1983 | 100 | 101 | 112 | 109 | 104 | 89 | 104 | 96 | 88 |

*Source: SJD 1984*, pp. 27, 55.

The wage fund is calculated as part of enterprise costs.[34] Being a binding target fixed by the central planning bodies the wage fund has to be coordinated with other mandatory indicators such as the number of workers and the average wage (the relevant formula is given by the equation $WF = \bar{W} + L$, where $WF$ means the wage fund, $\bar{W}$ means the average wage and $L$ the number of workers). The planned volume of the wage fund is set, moreover, in accordance with the plan target for labour saving mentioned above (see note 20). In case an enterprise releases more workers than the plan envisages it can use 'up to 50% of the average wage per saved worker'.[35] The GDR planners act according to the Soviet doctrine which states that the growth rate of productivity ought to exceed the growth rate of the average income for work. This rule, however, can give rise to disincentives to performance, particularly if overstressed.

Bonuses are paid out of special funds, the size of which depends on the economic results of the enterprise. It is the 'bonus fund' ('Prämienfonds') and the 'performance fund' ('Leistungsfonds') which are of particular importance with regard to the productivity goal. Both funds are fed from net profit.[36]

The bonus fund is a relic of the economic reform of the 1960s ('Neues Ökonomisches System der Planung und Leitung'); at that time it was financed from the profit achieved. Since 1972 it has been imposed as a central target. Its size depends on the fulfilment of the indicators commodity production and net profit, and eventually on additional targets (export, labour productivity, etc.). The resources for the fund are created (a) in the stage of target bargaining if the enterprise voluntarily accepts higher figures, and (b) in the course of carrying out the plan if it is overfulfilled (in that case degressively). The bonus fund is used first of all for the year-end reward (Jahresendprämie) which in 1975 amounted to 764 Marks on the average. It seems that this bonus paid out at the end of the year acts as a means of financial improvement rather than as an incentive for better performance. Smaller bonuses may be paid from the fund for individual effort, particularly within the framework of socialist competition.

The performance fund, as another instrument of stimulation, has existed since 1972. It is sponsored if the planned growth of labour productivity is overfulfilled and/or if the enterprise accepts higher plan targets than foreseen. Another criterion for extending this fund is energy, material saving and quality improvements. The average volume of the performance fund amounts roughly to a quarter of the value of the bonus fund and is to be used for the 'improvement of working and living conditions of working people' and for 'socialist rationalization'. Since 1984 the central planners have been trying to boost growth of productivity by increasing labour cost. Industrial and construction enterprises are obliged to pay 70 per cent of the wage fund as a 'contribution to social funds' to the state.[37]

Another means of supporting the social environment of the workers is the fund for cultural and social purposes (Kultur und Sozialfonds): it serves, along with some other financial resources of the enterprises' budget, for housing and other amenities which are distributed by the management in cooperation with the trade unions according to the workers' performance.[38]

The East German planners also use disincentives: overfulfilment of the employment plan adversely affects bonuses. In such a case the enterprise has to pay part of the profit up to 5000 Marks per 'excess' worker to the state budget (1980).[39]

Another traditional way of strengthening the incentive effect is the use of piece rates wherever performance is measurable. Both rates, those for piece-work and those for time-work, are applied in different forms; the time rates usually in combination with a premium payment for special performance indicators such as quality, material (or other) savings, etc.

Though the incentives discussed so far should have a speedy effect on regulating the supply of labour, the GDR authorities have also introduced a series of provisions in order to improve the manpower situation in the long run. Since the early 1970s the political leadership has strived to stop the decline of the population by means of social policy. Besides the 6 weeks' leave for pregnant women (introduced in 1965) the maternity leave has been prolonged from 8 weeks (introduced in 1963) to 12 weeks in 1972, then once again, to 20 weeks in 1976, with, in addition, a 1-year's leave after the second child ('Babyjahr').[40] These and some other measures (increase in family allowance for each child, housing and consumer credit for young married couples) lead to the improvement in population growth shown in Section II. These policy provisions will bring about, no doubt, an increase in the labour force in the long run (in the 1990s), but will, however, affect public finances. According to the calculations of H. Vortmann family allowances will amount to 3.3 per cent of net incomes.[41]

### 3.  Non-material motivations

According to the East German mass media – and even in many of the more specialized publications – non-material incentives are of great relevance. The different forms of socialist competition, pledges, innovator-movements, plan discussions, etc., and the flood of orders, medals and honorary titles, which the GDR citizen is everywhere confronted with, will not be reproduced in detail. The motivation created by these measures may have been correctly evaluated by a West German author when he said that the effect of moral incentives is reduced by 'too many of them', further by an excess of ideological phrases and, finally, by including political conformism in the criterion of competition.[42] It is hard for an outsider to judge the success of public campaigns such as the one started by the petrochemical combinate Schwedt, which appeals to all plants to save labour.[43]

## IV.  RESULTS AND PROSPECTIVES

An evaluation of the results achieved by the employment policy measures has to be based on the planned objectives. These have consisted, as has been shown, in overcoming labour shortages by productivity increases and improving the allocation of manpower. The latter means primarily the matching of the skill structure of the work force with the skill requirements of jobs in the economic development plan.

Let us cast a glance, first of all, at the productivity rates (although the calculation of labour productivity has to be accepted with some reservation). It is true that the increase in productivity in the late 1960s and early 1970s shown in Table 3.4 is remarkable. This favourable trend may have resulted from a 'reform effect' – as a consequence of the reform period after 1963 – and may also have been caused by technological transfer from the West.[44] The data in Table 3.4 show a decline of productivity growth after 1975 which would be even more distinct if the labour-intensive service sector were included, because of an extraordinary expansion of education and health. According to the calculations of the DIW-Berlin 'the lag in labour productivity *vis-à-vis* the FRG which was rated by Walter Ulbricht as 25 per cent on the average in 1963, has meanwhile increased. The inadequate efficiency of the factor inputs is the most important problem of the GDR-economy'.[45] In another report of the same institute it is said: 'The labour productivity in the GDR [reaches] only about 68% of the West German level'. According to a statement made by Honnecker in November 1983, there was 'a productivity gap of up to 30 per cent compared with France and West Germany'.[46]

Although our productivity figures are only fragmentary, the negative trend which they indicate is confirmed by critical East German publications. It has been said in the media that labour saving between 1976 and 1978 amounted to 7700 jobs but capital-widening investments created at the same time 30 000 new jobs (ratio 1:3.9). The corresponding ratios were, it is said, 1:3.5 in 1979, and improved to 1:2.1 in 1980.[47]

Some labour economists suggest that displaced manpower should be employed for social reasons within the plant rather than outside.[48] This is the goal of the combinate Schwedt (mentioned above) which was supposed to displace 2400 workers, i.e. 20 per cent of its personnel, from 1978 to 1982, and this goal was even to be raised later. Following the 'Schwedt initiative' a campaign under the slogan 'Fewer produce more' was started, but did not seem to be very successful until 1981.[49] Yet later on some remarkable achievements in labour savings were claimed to have been realized in the Frankfurt/ Oder district: allegedly 10 848 workers have been released since 1981 for other tasks, following the Schwedt initiative.[50] The problem of overstaffing 'could be solved', another source says, 'thanks to a consistent socialist policy of rationalization. Now the problems of reallocation of work time and of the labour force come to the fore ...'.[51] The latter may be true, but the aim of increasing labour productivity in general has not yet been met (note 46), though some partial success was probably achieved. A breakthrough in this direction, however, will not succeed in our view as long as command planning is maintained. The transition from quantity targets to efficiency criteria in monetary terms, which, by the way, has been pushed back in the course of the 1970s, will be only a small step forward if these criteria are still imposed on the enterprise as binding indicators. If they are, any order from the centre will cause the well-known reaction of the economic unit: the firm uses its information advantage to bargain with the authorities for low outputs and high inputs including labour. The 'ratchet effect'[52] works even then if the incentives are used for a voluntary acceptance of higher targets by the enterprise in the course of setting up the central plan. Concerning our problem the logic of central-administrative planning necessarily leads to labour hoarding.

Some further factors connected with the political and economic system are the increasing wasteful use of manpower. Let us metnion some of these features such as:[53]

(a) the fear of risk-taking by the management which is a serious obstacle to innovation,[54]
(b) a lower level of mechanization in general, and in the field of auxiliary work in particular, such as transport, storage, maintenance, etc.;[55]
(c) the high number of white-collar workers as a consequence of bureaucratic planning and control;[56]
(d) the uneven production process which forces the directors responsible to hoard labour in order to make up the losses towards the end of each plan period.

The result of all these shortcomings finds its expression in the low level of productivity compared with the advanced economies in the West.[57] A decisively positive change would require, in our view, a radical reform of the system, which is not in sight. It does not seem to us that the reorganization of enterprises in the GDR from the late 1970s consisting of the extension of 'combines' as the main 'mezzo-institution' between the central authorities (central planning commission, ministries) and the enterprises can be considered as such a systemic reform.[58]

If the key objective – the increase of labour productivity – has not been achieved, what about the second goal consisting of a proper allocation of manpower according to the needs of the economy? It will be appropriate to differentiate between the macro economic and the micro economic levels. From a macro economic point of view both instruments, the administrative measures and the incentives, have caused, by and large, a flow of labour resources to the priority sectors and branches.[59] Less successful has been the micro economic coordination, primarily the coordination of the workers' skill with the requirements of the job. For a long time the idea prevailed that technical change would bring about a general rise in the qualification level. A strong expansion of the educational and training system in the last 10–15 years and, as a consequence, a considerable increase in the highly qualified blue- and white-collar workers therefore flooded the economy. The latest discussion in the GDR indicates that there is an 'over-production' of skilled workers who cannot make use of their qualifications.[60] This seems to refer, to a certain extent, to the technical staff on the middle management level, too. It is difficult to guess whether the opposite feature, namely the occupation of upper-echelon jobs by insufficiently qualified persons, is a fact as it is in other CMEA countries[61] since there is no published information on this problem in East Germany.

Another feature which is being discussed in public more than any other is labour turnover.[62] This phenomenon shows that the expectations of the worker as to his working conditions are often not satisfied. It can be caused by the discrepancies in qualification mentioned above, but also by other dissatisfactions such as low income, work strain, bad social facilities, stress caused by a bad working climate in the department, etc.[63] The discussions about (undesirable) turnover excluded the other side of the coin, namely the (desirable) mobility of labour. It seems that often the East German economists are more and more aware of the fact that a permanent adaptation of modern economy to unavoidably changing conditions requires a certain degree of manpower mobility.[64]

A further difficulty is the contradiction between efficiency requirements and needs of work humanization.[65] Two examples may illustrate this: the problem of shiftwork and the crucial problem of women's participation in the work force. The party and union functionaries do their utmost to persuade the workers that shifts are necessary because of the common interest in extending output. Negative aspects of shift jobs such as health damage, stress in family life, etc., are being countered by 'moral suasion'. It is obvious that the dissatisfaction caused by shift work does not contribute to productivity improvements.

The participation of women in economic activities is a consequence of labour shortages, and has little to do with the 'emancipation of women' as the propaganda claims. If women take jobs voluntarily in the field of production or services it is because they want to increase the income of the family, and not for emancipatory goals since they know that their taking a job creates a double burden caused by housework (including procurement of supplies), education (since facilities for children do not suffice), etc. Equality of women in employment and private life is out of the question. Can anyone think, in this situation, of a real motivation for employed women to increase labour productivity?

Taking into consideration the analysis of the past, our reflections on the present situation and some calculations made by experts on future development, the following conclusions concerning long-term prospects can be drawn:

(a) The number of GDR inhabitants of working age (Eastern definition) will increase by roughly 300 000 persons up to 1985, and keep this level until 1990. According to estimates of (West and East German) experts in the 1980s the number of employed pensioners will decrease and the number of children will grow. Only after 1990 will an improvement in the labour force potential take place.[66]

(b) Secondly, the 'explosion of education' of the last two decades is coming to an end since there is much less need for higher education in the economy. Moreover, it is the need to cut educational costs and to recruit more young people for jobs which favours a limitation of school and training capacities.

(c) Thirdly, in spite of all efforts made by the party leadership there is little hope for a better penetration of technical progress into the production process which is a precondition for productivity growth. Only if this took place could the labour shortage – which, with regard to the low productivity level, is a fictive one – be overcome. But there is hardly a chance of succeeding in this direction since a radical economic reform is not in sight.

(d) Fourthly, the existing instruments, incentives and motivations are scarcely able to harmonize the skill and qualification structure of workers with the changing requirements of the workplace.

**Notes**

1. F. Rudolf, *Berliner Zeitung*, 11 October 1979, p. 3.
2. *SJD 1984*, pp. 16, 61 and 112.
3. H. Vortmann, in H. H. Höhmann (ed.), *Arbeitsmarkt und Wirtschafts-planung. Beiträge zur Beschäftigungsstruktur und Arbeitskraftepolitik in Osteuropa* (Köln–Frankfurt a.-M., 1977) p. 105.
4. *Zahlenspiegel BRD-DDR. Ein Vergleich, Bundesministerium fur inner-deutsche Beziehungen*, 2, edition 1983 (hereafter cited as *Zahlenspiegel*), p. 40.
5. For the GDR: Vortmann, op. cit., p. 107; for other countries: F. Levcik, *Research Reprot No. 26* (Wiener Institut für internationale Wirtschaftsvergleiche, April 1976) p. 19.
6. Vortmann, op cit., p. 102.
7. *Handbuch DDR-Wirtschaft*, Deutsches Institut für Wirtschaftsfors-

chung (DIW) (Berlin, 4th edition, Reinbek, 1984) (hereafter cited as *Handbuch*), p. 57.

8. *Wochenbericht*, no. 31 (1978), DIW, pp. 299–300; *Handbuch*, p. 51.
9. *Handbuch* pp. 45–6, 292.
10. We do not intend to discuss here other aspects of the data shown in Table 3.4 such as growth trends and performance problems in the GDR economy in general. To do so one would be obliged, first of all, to take into consideration one of the main difficulties in the 1970s, i.e. the unfavourable development of the terms of trade.
11. As to the methodology of comparing national account calculations in East and West Germany see *Handbuch*, pp. 98–114.
12. *Statisticheskii ezhegodnik SEV* (Moscow, 1979) pp. 441–3 and 1984, pp. 363–6.
13. *Zahlenspiegel*, p. 83.
14. The most developed economies within the CMEA – the East German and the Czechoslovak economies – have been obliged to make enormous deliveries of investment goods to the Soviet Union and the other member countries which have restricted their export capacities to their important partners in the West (more about this problem see J. Kosta, *Abriss der sozialökonomischen Entwicklung der Tschechoslowakei 1975–1977* (Frankfurt, 1978) in particular pp. 72–87).
15. E. Sachse, *Sozialistische Arbeitswissenschaft*, no. 4 (1978) p. 277.
16. As to the manpower planning in Soviet-type systems see J. Kosta, in C. Watrin (ed.), *Struktur- und stabilitätspolitische Probleme in alternativen Wirtschaftssystemen* (Berlin, 1974) pp. 108–12.
17. *Gesetzesblatt der DDR*, 1980, Sonderdrunk no. 1020 n; ibid., 1981, part I, no. 14; ibid., 1983, no. 1122; ibid., 1984, sect. VII.
18. 'Release' ('Freisetzung') does not necessarily mean dismissal, but labour savings in general, achieved mainly by technological advance (see also the contribution of Anna-Jutta Pietsch in this volume).
19. W. Klein, *Deutschland-Archiv*, no. 1 (1978) p. 39.
20. *Gesetzesblatt der DDR, 1980*, part I, nr. 20, section 17.1.
21. G. Kunter and W. Müller, *Sozialistische Arbeitswissenschaft*, no. 1 (1974) pp. 1–9; R. Döhler, *Sozialistische Arbeitswissenschaft*, no. 5 (1974) pp. 356–60.
22. *Gesetzesblatt der DDR, 1979*, part I, nr. 15, pp. 1, 2.
23. *Gesetzesblatt der DDR, 1979*, part I, nr. 28, ziffer XI, 1.
24. W. Jaide, *Deutschland Archiv*, nio. 2 (1977) pp. 176–9.
25. The term 'wages' is being used in this contribution for money remuneration for work including salaries, but excluding bonuses.
26. For both wages and bonuses see: H. Bley *et al., Ökonomik der Arbeit* (Berlin (GDR), 1974) pp. 494–500.
27. Ibid.
28. Ibid., pp. 500–54.
29. *Ökonomisches Lexikon*, Q-L, III edn (East Berlin, 1980) p. 298.
30. J. Strassburger, *Deutschland Archiv*, no. 9 (1976) pp. 950–8.
31. *Deutschland Archiv*, no. 11 (1977) pp. 1226–8.
32. According to information of the DIW Berlin (Mr Vortmann).
33. Bley, op. cit., pp. 524–5.

34.   For the wage fund and the bonus fund see Bley, op. cit., pp. 500–10; see also *Ökonomisches Lexikon* H–P (Berlin, 1978), 'Lohnfonds', pp. 434–5, 'Prämienfonds', pp. 730–1; *Handbuch*, p. 106.

35.   *Gesetzesblatt der DDR, 1980*, part I, section 17.3, p. 206.

36.   For more details concerning the 'bonus fund' and the 'performance fund' see A. Bley, *Leitfaden zur Finanzierung der volkseigenen Industrie* (Berlin (GDR), 1978) pp. 139–41; W. Klein, op. cit., pp. 40–5; *Handbuch*, pp. 78–81; J. Körner, *Deutschland Archiv*, no. 10 (1977) pp. 1080–92; H. W. Stenzel and H. Uebermuth, *Finanzen und Preise* (Berlin (GDR), 1978) pp. 84–90.

37.   *Gesetzesblatt der DDR, 1983*, part I, no. 11; *Handbuch*, pp. 237, 238.

38.   The social funds granted by the state budget (for education, medical care, pensions, subsidies for housing, local transport, etc.) function to a certain extent like another incentive 'in direct dependence from quantity and quality of performed labour': A. Keck, *Sozialistische Finanzen*, no. 6 (1976) pp. 6–9.

39.   *Gesetzesblatt der DDR, 1979*, part I, nr. 28, III, 1.

40.   This has been mentioned partially earlier (compare note 8).

41.   All information given in this paragraph was provided by Mr Vortmann, DIW Berlin.

42.   F. Gratz, *Deutschland Archiv*, no. 10 (1977) p. 1079.

43.   See, e.g., F. Rudolf, *Berliner Zeitung*, 18 April 1980, p. 3.

44.   The remarkable growth of labour productivity in the early 1970s could have been caused by the increasing transfer of technology from the West due to detente policy at that time (for this explanation I am grateful to Professor Carson who discussed my paper at the Calgary conference in November 1980). The technology transfer can be shown by the following data: the share of Western technology ('investment goods') imported from the OECD countries (excluding the FRG) in total GDR imports amounted to 20.1 per cent from 1961 to 1965, to 32.2 per cent from 1966 to 1970, and to 31.4 per cent from 1971 to 1975 (*Wochenberichte*, DIW Berlin). The share of investment goods imported from the FRG into the GDR in total GDR imports increased from 17.3 per cent in 1961–5 to 22.8 per cent in 1966–70 and to 23.8 per cent in 1971–5 (*Handbuch*, pp. 357, 366).

45.   *Handbuch*, p. 34.

46.   Jaide, op. cit., p. 177; *Neues Deutschland*, 27 November 1983.

47.   K. H. Arnold, *Berliner Zeitung*, 17 April 1980, p. 3; Arnold, *Berliner Zeitung*, 18 April 1980, p. 3; J. Blady, *Tribune*, 16 January 1980, p. 3; R. Gericke, F. Haberland, *Erfahrungen und Aufgaben sozialistischer Rationalisierung*, Abhandlungen der AdW (Berlin (GDR), 1983) p. 21.

48.   S. Grund, *Sozialistische Arbeitswissenschaft*, no. 3 (1972) p. 239.

49.   L. Humel, *Zum Stand und den weiteren Aufgaben bei der Gewinnung von Arbeitskraften durch sozialistische Rationalisierung*, Abhandlungen der AdW (Berlin (GDR), 1983) p. 66.

50.   *Neuer Weg*, no. 6 (1984) p. 223.

51.   H. Grabley, *Sozialistische Arbeitswissenschaft*, no. 6 (1983).

52.   The 'ratchet effect' means the behaviour of a firm in a centrally planned economy of the Soviet type which consists in keeping permanent input

reserves according to achievements in the past planning period (compare, e.g., V. Vincentz, 'Über die Ausgestaltung von Prämiensystemen', paper delivered at a conference of the Ausschuss zum Vergleich von Wirtschaftssystemen, Tutzing, 18 and 19 September 1980).

53. Those and others are explained convincingly in a study investigating the same problem in Czechoslovakia: J. Adam and J. Cekota, *Revue d'études comparatives Est-Ouest*, no. 4, 1980.

54. The reasons for the slow rate of technology progress in a centrally planned economy are shown in H. G. J. Kosta, H. Kramer and J. Sláma, *Der technologische Fortschritt in Österreich und in der Tschechoslowakei* (Wien/New York, 1971) in particular p. 82.

55. Grund, op. cit., p. 240.

56. Ibid.

57. In spite of this the performance of the GDR economy is no doubt better than that of other CMEA countries such as Poland and Czechoslovakia. This may be caused; among other factors, by more direct access to the advanced Western economies by means of GDR–FRG trade ('Innerdeutscher Handel') and, in our view, by a better way of dealing with administrative and monetary instruments than the planners of the partner countries have.

58. M. Melzer and A. Scherzinger, *Vierteljahreshefte zur Wirtschaftsforschung* (DIW Berlin) no. 4 (1978) pp. 379–92.

59. Yet there are complaints expressed in an article by a well-known GDR expert about a 'remarkable underfulfilment of the manpower plans in the material sectors with overfulfilment in the non-material sectors at the same time' and shortages in several industrial centres as well (Sachse, op. cit., p. 277).

60. Ibid., pp. 276–9; a particular phenomenon is the unexpected tendency of technological change to lead to workers' dequalification (see, e.g. R. Deppe and D. Hoss, *Sozialistische Rationalisierung* (Frankfurt a.-M., 1980).

61. Adam and Cekota, op. cit., p. 8.

62. K. Lubcke, *Arbeit und Arbeitsrecht*, no. 4 (1980) pp. 152–3; A. Tomm, *Sozialistische Arbeitswissenschaft*, no. 6 (1976) pp. 421–7.

63. Compare K. Belwe, *Deutschland Archiv*, no. 6 (1980) pp. 601–11; A. Scherzinger, *Vierteljahreshefte zur Wirtschaftsforschung*, no. 3 (1979) pp. 237–40.

64. An exception, to a certain extent, is an article by a labour economist who points out that labour mobility is by and large a necessary feature of the intensive type of growth and one should find 'criteria for optimal tendencies of labour mobility' (A. Tomm, *Sozialistische Arbeitswissenschaft*, no. 6 (1979) pp. 421–6).

65. Scherzinger, op. cit., pp. 241–8.

66. The estimates of the population developments in the future are based on two sources: (a) *Wirtschaftswissenschaft*, no. 7 (1979) pp. 769–89; (b) calculations of the DIW Berlin (Mr Vortmann).

# 4 Employment Policies in Czechoslovakia

## FRANZ-LOTHAR ALTMANN

## INTRODUCTION

The aim of this chapter is to describe the main features and causes of the present labour shortages in Czechoslovakia as well as to explain the governmental responses to this challenge. In an investigation undertaken in the first half of the 1970s it was discovered that in Czechoslovak industry at that time approximately 300 000 machine operator positions were not filled.[1] This number has increased substantially in recent years according to a report given by the Chairman of the Federal Assembly of the CSSR, A. Indra.[2] He stated that the number of vacant posts in the machine building industries alone reached 600 000 in 1980. For the whole economy job vacancies numbered 738 000 in 1983.[3]

The labour market situation must be regarded as a result of both demographic development (which determines the supply of labour) and economic policies (which entail changes in volume and structure of the demand for labour). Thus, the first section of this study depicts the demographic trends and related developments which influence the supply of labour, and in section two factors aggravating these shortages are discussed in more detail. Finally section three deals with policy measures which aim at a quantitative improvement of the supply of labour as well as at the more effective utilization of labour.

## I. SUPPLY OF LABOUR

In a balance sheet of the labour force for an economy the following three groups of persons form the supply side of the balance sheet:

(a) population of working age: in the CSSR 15–59 for men and 15–54 for women;
(b) people over retirement age, but still working;

78

(c)  foreign workers employed in the domestic economy less domestic workers employed abroad.

Of course, not all persons of working age are willing or able to take jobs for various reasons such as education and/or career training, military service, maternity leave or physical handicaps. Certainly, however, the growth of the working age population is the most important factor which has to be considered when discussing possible prospects for the supply of labour. Pensioners working longer than normally foreseen can only serve as a temporary relief for a tense labour market, whereas migratory (foreign) workers in some countries (e.g. West Germany) can achieve an indispensable role in the economy.

## 1.  Demographic development

Much has been written about Czechoslovakia's demographic development[4] in the past. Therefore only the main trends will be repeated here as far as they are of any importance for the present and future situation in the labour market.

Since on average the rate of mortality (deaths per thousand inhabitants) has remained the same over the years in Czechoslovakia, the dynamics of population growth are influenced mainly by the birth rate (births per thousand inhabitants). In the first postwar decade natality in Czechoslovakia was quite high, reaching more than 22 per thousand (in Slovakia between 1952 and 1957 as high as 26–8 per thousand), a figure which has never been achieved since. Obviously some compensation effect with regard to the low fertility during the war took place, because not only young women, but older women as well, showed higher fertility. In the following 15 years (1955–69) a steady decrease in natality occurred, due first of all to the introduction of a relatively liberal abortion law in 1958.[5] In 1968 the absolute nadir was reached when a birth rate of only 14.9 per thousand ranked Czechoslovakia in one of the very last places in the world. In that year only Belgium/Luxemburg (14.2 per thousand), Sweden (14.3 per thousand) and East Germany (14.7 per thousand) lagged behind, but the CSSR's position was solely due to the Slovakian birth rate (of 18 per thousand which still was the lowest in her history). The Czech Lands alone would have occupied the last place in world ratings, with a mere 13.9 per thousand! The implementation in 1971–3 of a set of sociopolitical pronatal measures, together with an improvement in the age structure of women, effectuated a baby boom in 1974 (19.9 per thousand). At least two-thirds of the increase in births is attributed to the stimulus provided by the pronatalist policy.[6] However, in the last few years a slow decrease in the birth rate is again observable, as shown in Table 4.1.

Table 4.1   Birth rates in postwar Czechoslovakia (annual rates of live births per thousand inhabitants)

| 1945–54 | 1955–59 | 1960–64 | 1965–69 | 1970–74 | 1975–79 | 1980 | 1983 |
|---------|---------|---------|---------|---------|---------|------|------|
| 22 | 18.5 | 16.3 | 15.5 | 17.7 | 18.8 | 16.3 | 14.8 |

Sources: Seidl, op. cit. (see note 4), pp. 79–80; SRC, 1984, p. 96.

## 2.  Demographic projection, 1980–2000

In 1977 the Federal Statistical Office, and in 1978 the Statistical Offices of Slovakia and the Czech Lands, calculated long-term projections for the expected growth of the labour supply until the year 2000. The results are given in Table 4.2. In the long-term perspective the

Table 4.2   Growth of the population of working age in 1980–2000 (men: 15–59; women: 15–54)

| Year | Absolute (000s) | | | Rate of increase (1975 = 100) | | |
|------|------|-----|-----|------|-----|-----|
| | CSSR | CSR | SSR | CSSR | CSR | SSR |
| 1978* | 8655 | 5812 | 2843 | 101.9 | 101.0 | 103.8 |
| 1980 | 8729 | 5842 | 2887 | 102.7 | 101.6 | 104.9 |
| 1985 | 8806 | 5851 | 2955 | 103.6 | 101.8 | 107.4 |
| 1990 | 9183 | 6087 | 3096 | 108.8 | 105.9 | 112.5 |
| 1995 | 9659 | 6339 | 3320 | 113.6 | 110.3 | 120.7 |
| 2000 | 9937 | 6425 | 3512 | 116.9 | 111.8 | 127.7 |

*Actual.

Source: V. Srb, Hospodářské noviny, no. 30 (1979) p. 4.

growth of the work force potential looks rather favourable, because the number of people of working age will increase between 1975 and 2000 by 16.9 per cent, whereas the growth rate of the total population will only reach 13.5 per cent. This is in particular true for the Czech Lands where the respective figures are 11.8 per cent against 8.0 per cent. In Slovakia an almost balanced development is expected when the working age population will grow by 27.7 per cent and the general population increase will be around 26.6 per cent.

However, for single 5-year periods, distinct deviations from this positive trend can be forecast. Between 1976 and 1980 the relationship was the reverse, the working age population increased by 2.7 per cent (CSR: 1.6 per cent; SSR: 4.9 per cent) wheras total population growth was 3.5 per cent (CSR: 2.5 per cent; SSR: 5.7 per cent). An even less favourable development is expected for the years 1981–5 when the population of working age will reach a growth rate of just 0.9 per cent (CSR: 0.2 per cent; SSR: 2.4 per cent) and the total population will increase by 2.4 per cent (CSR: 1.1 per cent; SSR: 5.0 per cent).[7] Only after 1985 will the increases in the population of working age outdo those of the total population. Finally, in the last 5-year period, an almost balanced development is predicted (cf. Figure 4.1).

From Table 4.2 we can see that, particularly in the first 5-year period after 1980, only very little relief for the labour market will come from the natural growth of population: an absolute increase in the working age population of approximately 77 000 for the whole period 1981–5 denotes a mere annual increase of 0.18 per cent! Only after this nadir is reached is a 10-year period of enlarged supply of labour expected. However, if one remembers that in 1983 about 738 000 vacant jobs were registered then it becomes evident that even the 454 000 additional persons of working age, the number unrealistically predicted until 1990, cannot suffice to meet the needs of the economy. Furthermore, one must consider that in the last few years only 83 per cent of this age group in fact were economically active. The figure of 454 000 must be reduced, therefore, to a considerable extent when talking about the number of those persons who will actually be available for employment. This will be discussed in the following paragraph.

## 3. Other factors influencing the supply of labour

No substantial change is expected in the number of handicapped and disabled persons of working age. Having registered 243 000 in 1975,

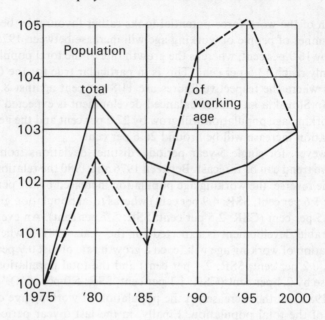

*Source:* V. Srb, op. cit.

*Figure 4.1* Growth of total population and of population of working age

this figure increased slightly to 267 000 until 1984.[8] A great impact on the available labour resources will result from the expected increase in the number of persons who either attend high school or university or serve apprenticeships. In the years 1975–90, 21 per cent of the increment of the population of working age (in the Czech Lands even 28 per cent) will – due to these educational commitments – not be at the planners' disposal. Thus in 1990, 10.5 per cent of the total population of working age will be engaged in educational or job training (1975: 9.6 per cent).

In the past the rise in the economic activity of the working age population was one of the decisive sources of an increase in the rate of employment. Since the early 1960s no further shift of labour from agriculture to the other growing and labour-demanding sectors of the economy has been possible. Therefore only an increase in women's participation rates could help Czechoslovakia to supply its economy with the required additional labour. The first line in Table 4.3 shows how large this rise in women's (gross) participation was, especially in the 1970s. However, the dramatic decline in the birth rate in the late

*Table 4.3*  Women's participation rate and maternity leave

|  | 1960 | 1965 | 1970 | 1972 | 1974 | 1976 | 1980 | 1984 |
|---|---|---|---|---|---|---|---|---|
| Women's participation rate (%) | | | | | | | | |
| Gross* | n.a. | 44.8 | 46.7 | 47.4 | 47.8 | 48.1 | 48.2 | 48.3 |
| Nett† | n.a. | n.a. | 45.6 | 45.6 | 45.5 | 45.3 | 45.5 | 46.0 |
| Women on maternity leave (1000s) | n.a. | n.a. | 152 | 238 | 330 | 382 | 380 | 33.9 |

*Share of women in total employment including women on maternity leave.
†Share of women in total employment without women on maternity leave.
n.a. = not available

*Sources: SRC, 1966, 1975, 1981, 1985.*

1960s (see Section I.1) forced the government to start the long-term pronatalist programme. Children's allowances were raised on 1 January 1973, and again on 1 January 1985; the family now receives Kčs 200 monthly for the first child, Kčs 650 for two children, Kčs 1210 for three, Kčs 1720 for four and Kčs 350 for every additional child. Also a non-recurring payment of Kčs 2000 is given for extra expenditures for each newborn child. Much more important – and hence affecting women's labour participation – was the set of measures concerning prolonged maternity leave which came into force in 1971. For a period of 26 weeks maternity leave a young mother receives 90 per cent of her net salary. If she is single, this time is prolonged to 35 weeks. Furthermore, having two or more children already, she can stay home until the youngest child reaches the age of 2 years without losing claim to her job, and receive Kčs 600 per month. If she has to take care of two children younger than 2, the allowance amounts to Kčs 900, if there are three children, the payment totals Kčs 1300. This maternity contribution is also offered to women who have not been employed before.[9]

As one can see from Table 4.3, line 3, this offer was soon accepted, in particular after 1973, when an additional stimulus was introduced for young couples: a credit of up to Kčs 30 000 can be obtained to purchase an apartment or furniture. This credit is good for 10 years and offers the possibility of writing off Kčs 2000 when the first child is born. Each additional child reduces the debt by Kčs 4000.

Considering the economic activity of the population in Czechoslovakia one finds that there are still quite considerable differences between Slovakia and the Czech Lands: the number of people actually working[10] in 1984 reached 86.7 per cent of the total working age population in Bohemia/Moravia and only 80.3 per cent in Slovakia. It would, however, be wrong to conclude from this fact that there are still labour reserves which could be activated for the Czech Lands. There are two explanations for this difference: firstly, relatively more young people in Slovakia than in the Czech Lands enter employment only after having finished their education; and secondly, Slovakia possesses a higher number of women having three or more children, thus making more extensive use of maternity leave.

Thus, a further increase in the raise in the participation rate of the population of working age is obviously not possible. There are only two more groups of people to consider when looking on the supply side of the labour market in Czechoslovakia: old-age pensioners and foreign (migratory) workers. The question of employment of people over working age will be discussed later. Nevertheless it should be stressed here that in mid-1984 employees of post-productive age (men aged 60 and more; women 55 and more) numbered approximately 900 000, this representing almost 12 per cent of the total labour force.[11]

Finally some remarks on the foreign workers' issue. In the late 1950s some 4800 Bulgarian workers were employed in construction and agriculture, of whom only 550 remained in 1975. The largest contingent of foreign workers still comes from Poland and is employed mainly in consumer goods industries like textiles. Although the contract had provided for 26 000 Polish workers, only 18 830 actually were enrolled during the period 1963–73.[12] Nowadays there are approximately 47 000 foreign workers in Czechoslovakia, of whom almost 30 000 are Vietnamese, 13 000 Polish and 4600 Cuban, whereas only some 1000 Czechoslovak workers cross the border for work.

## II.  REASONS FOR THE SHORTAGE OF LABOUR

Searching for the reasons for the existing shortage of labour in the Czechoslovak economy one comes across quite a few explanations which probably may be summarized under the term 'deficiencies in the utilization of labour'. It is openly discussed in Czechoslovakia that considerable reserves of labour exist within enterprises and administration due to ineffective allocation of qualified manpower and underutilization of working time.

## 1. Growing number of white-collar workers

To back up the statement that the number of white-collar workers is increasing at a faster rate than the overall number of workers, two reports will be cited:

(a) The government commission for rationalization of work and wage systems checked, for the years 1970–7, the development of employment groups in the general management (generální ředitelství) of 36 industrial and construction enterprises. The results of this sample, given in Table 4.4, indicate clearly that in industry

*Table 4.4* Average annual increases of employment groups in industry and construction (percentages)

| | Employed persons total | | Technical–economic workers | | Employed persons in general management | |
|---|---|---|---|---|---|---|
| | Industry | Construction | Industry | Construction | Industry | Construction |
| 1970–5 | 0.7 | 2.1 | 1.5 | 2.6 | 5.8 | 6.1 |
| 1975–7 | 0.7 | 1.2 | 1.7 | 2.0 | 3.6 | 6.2 |

*Source:* M. Kotek, *Hospodářské noviny*, 13 (1979).

as well as in construction both groups of white-collar workers (technical-economic workers and pure administrative employees) grew faster than the total number of employed persons.

(b) An inspection at the end of 1979 by the People's Control Committee of the Czech Lands established that administrative apparatus at the level of industrial general managements had grown by 2344 persons since 1978 alone, while at the same time the overall number of workers and employees in industry controlled by the Czech Lands state administration had declined.[13]

The reasons for this development are manifold. On the one hand more written reports are required by superordinate levels of management and/or administration; on the other hand bureaucracy is steadily finding new fields of administrative activity even in Czechoslovakia and demanding new personnel since defunct activities do not seem to release any manpower at all.[14]

## 2. Growing number of workers and low degree of mechanization in auxiliary work

In 1974 workers in auxiliary jobs numbered approximately 600 000 in industry (i.e. 29.9 per cent of all industrial workers),[15] mainly in maintenance and repair services for machinery and buildings, and in transport and stock-keeping. What are criticized most in this respect are the very low level of the over-age technical equipment and the very low degree of mechanization: 77 per cent of all stock-keeping is not mechanized and exists quite often for up to 100 years in the same shape. The degree of mechanization of the handling of materials reached just 20–2 per cent in Czechoslovakia in the mid-1970s while the corresponding figure for West Germany and the USA was close to 80 per cent.[16] Furthermore stock-keeping is very little concentrated in Czechoslovakia. It was reported that about 110 000 warehouses of an average size of 385 m$^2$ are in existence, whereas the world standard reaches 1000 m$^2$. A research institute[17] therefore calculated that approximately 100 000 persons, and two-thirds of all warehouses, could be saved by better organization of work and by mechanization.

## 3. Underutilization of working time

The Federal Minister for Labour and Social Affairs disclosed in a recent article that time losses in industry amount to 15 per cent and in construction to as much as 30 per cent of the given working time.[18] These losses in working time, which do not include absenteeism and malingering, already amounted in the mid-1970s to more than 100 million hours annually on the national level, thus having the same effect as if there were 55 000 workers less. In 1980 the losses quoted above in industry and construction alone corresponded to 66 000 workers! Shortcomings in the organization of the production process as well as poor working time discipline are the main causes of such enormous waste of working time.

## 4. Labour planning and enterprise behaviour

The process of balancing supply of, and demand for, labour can only be successful if enterprises report their real requirements to associations, general management and branch ministries, and if calculations and estimates of the available manpower and labour productivity growth correspond to actual developments. However, national planning committees tend to have optimistic expectations, in all fields of economic planning. Thus labour supply figures become the desired numbers rather than the estimated, due to the fact that very often unrealistic assumptions are made with regard to the willingness of people to undertake employment or to stay longer in work (pensioners) than necessary.[19] Unfounded optimism must also be attributed to the planners' forecasts of labour productivity growth. Therefore fulfilment of output targets requires more labour than assumed, and this in turn generates strains in the labour market.

On the other hand, enterprises do not disclose all their reserves – for several reasons. The first and most simple may be seen in the fact that they already consider themselves to be in a competitive situation in a labour-short economy. Having hidden reserves makes the enterprise more able to react when sudden changes in the centre's demand or in normal plan fulfilment arise. Another cause for employing more workers than really needed is the fact that the salary of managers is directly connected with the number of his subordinates. Furthermore, the larger an enterprise, the greater its prestige and, consequently, the more likely it is to obtain acceptable plan targets.

Finally the practice of investment planning and performance is accused of creating excess demand for labour. Due to the well-known manpower shortage the central authorities have to exert pressure on enterprises applying for approval of investment projects to save not only financial means but also labour. Therefore, enterprises rather underestimate their requirements for labour for new investments in order to obtain the centre's place for the start of the project. Once the venture is in an advanced stage, and it turns out that 'in contrast to all calculations' the originally estimated funds and manpower do not at all meet the real needs, then it is much easier to receive additional financial and labour supplies to complete the otherwise non-completable construction.[20]

It is clear that under these circumstances (over-optimistic expectations of the supply of labour by the planning authorities and excessive demand for labour by the enterprises) deficits in manpower are almost unavoidable.

## III. GOVERNMENT PROVISIONS FOR EXPANSION, REDISTRIBUTION AND IMPROVED UTILIZATION OF LABOUR SUPPLY

Retardation of economic growth, which occurred particularly in the second half of the 1970s, is not only caused by manpower shortages. However, for the single firm a lack of labour may serve as an excuse for not being able to fulfil the output targets. Much more important in this respect is the fact that labour shortages to a great extent curtail structural changes in the economy which are regarded by Czechoslovak planners as the only way to improve the efficiency of the national economy.

Government provisions aiming to alleviate the problems caused by labour shortages can be divided into two groups: administrative, direct provisions and non-administrative, indirect measures.

### 1. Administrative provisions

#### (a)  Education and job requirements

Relying exclusively on direct instruments in employment policy would impede free choice of occupation and jobs, and would 'militarize' the whole labour market. In principle the socialist countries claim that young people can decide freely on their education and their place of work. This, however, does not fit very well into a planned economy, in particular when labour shortages become a serious problem. Schools of the different educational types, therefore, are assigned binding indices by the planning offices with regard to the number of school-entrants and graduates. The latter must correspond to the requirements of the respective branches of the economy. Recently, increasing complaints about discrepancies between the qualifications required by the firms and the educational and professional training of the school-leavers have been reported. Therefore, contacts between school and economy have been intensified through organization of practical training in the firms for pupils and students.[21]

In this context some figures should be mentioned concerning the effective utilization of skilled labour. In September 1979 two-thirds (68.2 per cent) of all skilled workers were employed in the branches where they had originally received their qualifications. It is striking that this percentage is smaller in the Czech Lands (65.7 per cent) than in Slovakia (74.9 per cent). Figures for 1983 are no better; they reveal that in machinery only 72.5 per cent of technicians and economists possessed exactly the qualifications required by the job they occupied! The respective figures for other branches were: chemistry 72.2 per cent, construction 67.3 per cent, electrotechnics 73.6 per cent, and agriculture 62.0 per cent.[22]

## (b)  Absolute limits of labour increases

In 1970 manpower limits were introduced for enterprises in order to stop steady increases in the firms' demands for labour. Control over the implementation of the new measures was entrusted to the national committees of the counties (kraj)[23] which generally are the supervisory organs of the enterprises with respect to the allocation of labour.[24] This does primarily apply to the assignment of fresh new manpower to the enterprises' associations, called 'productive economic units' (Výrobní hospodářská jednotka = VHJ), where the national committees of the counties (Krajský národní výbor = KNV) are obliged to check the disaggregated labour plans of the associations concerning the utilization of labour. Until 1977 enterprises were not allowed to exceed the assigned percentage increases in manpower. Beginning with 1978 these increases are no longer expressed in percentage terms but are given in absolute figures to the association, thus eliminating the differences which frequently appeared between planned and realized increases in manpower.

In the new set of measures for the improvements of the system of planning of the national economy after 1980, this determination of absolute (instead of relative) figures for the increases in labour has been established as one of the main instruments of labour planning. Each ministry (resort) received an absolute number for employment in its organizations and is not allowed to exceed it. If it turns out that in one organization the planned increase in labour will not or cannot be utilized *in toto*, a shift of this labour surplus to another organization can only be made after the approval of the KNVs or the planning commission of Slovakia or the Czech Lands.[25] Even then the absolute amount of employment as determined in the state plan for the respective ministry must not be exceeded.

There is an exception to every rule. The absolute binding limit for the increase in labour may be exceeded, if manual and auxiliary workers are available locally. Those persons may be employed over and above the plan in selected shops or sales organizations for foodstuffs and groceries in their own locality. In Prague, Bratislava and in the North-Bohemian basin they can also be employed in selected sales organizations for industrial goods and in canteens. Similar possibilities exist for local people who would not otherwise be utilized in greater quantities than foreseen in the plan, to be employed in selected service and repair branches. Usually the following two groups of persons may be regarded as so-called free, locally bound labour resources:

(i) housewives, who have not been employed before and who cannot regularly go to work (due to age or because they have to take care of children);

(ii) workers who cannot regularly go to work for health reasons, i.e. mainly people with changing working ability and/or more serious injuries to health.

However, there has been already an amendment to the new regulations, valid for the years 1983–5, according to which the number of employed persons in all organizations is no longer a compulsory limit but has to be handled as an 'informative' indicator.[26]

Labour requirements for new capacities have become an extremely important issue. Associations (VHJ) and KNVs are now obliged to give separate evidence in their general labour plans of their labour requirements for new capacities. In particular they have to prove from what resources and to what extent this required labour force will be recruited.[27] In addition, they must submit a programme of qualification training as well as guarantees for the existence or preparation of housing facilities and special services.

*(c)   Central registration of persons employed*

In order to facilitate employment policy measures of different kinds – direct and indirect, individual and general – a central registration of all employed persons was started in 1968. All enterprises are obliged to draw up this so-called 'Uniform register of employed persons' (JEP = Jednotná Evidence Pracujících) but obviously in the first half of the 1970s there was little progress in the development of this centrally coordinated registration system.[28]

In 1976 the CSSR Government passed an amendment to the JEP system, according to which in 1981–5 an automatized register of the working population was to be compiled by listing individual (selected) data for every employed person. In a preparatory and experimental stage more than 200 000 workers from 60 organizations (mainly enterprises from industry) were listed in this automatized manpower register with 34 indicators (of which 12 concerned wages) during the years 1974–9.

In addition, in six counties, a stepwise introduction of an automatized subregister on manpower movements took place, consisting of a collection of 27 indicators for every employed person. Quarterly reports can now be provided on the movements of manpower between branches and regions, and more information can be received on changes in the structure of professions, qualifications, age and the like. By 1985 the majority of the enterprises should have created the basis for the automatized processing of personnel and wage data, offering also at that time the possibility of forwarding data to the state information system on magnetic tapes. In the long run it is intended to form a hierarchic system of automatized registration of the labour force.

## (d) Limits for employment in administration

In spite of all restrictions and one-time actions, like the 10 per cent reduction in 1970, the disproportionate growth of the number of administrative and managerial workers continued in the 1970s. The regulation of the number of administrative and managerial workers, as introduced in 1976 on the basis of the government resolution No. 293/1975, was extended to all technical-economic employees in the construction sector in 1977 and in industry in 1978. This regulation imposes binding limits for the above categories in the form of percentages of the total labour force or in absolute figures. Since 1979 the number of technical–economic employees has been regulated in selected branches of the economy in a more detailed way by defining specific professional groups.[29] In general, percentage shares for administrative, managerial, and technical–economic employees in the total number of employees of an organization are used. A special programme of overall economizing (program hospodárnosti), released in September 1981 (gvt decree no. 346/1981), demands a reduction in employment in the administrative apparatus of 70 000 persons during the period 1982–5.

*(e)   Other administrative measures*

In the 1960s a gradual reduction of working time was carried out in
Czechoslovakia ending with the introduction of the five-day week in
1968. However, §84 of the labour code contains the possibility of
designating Saturdays as compulsory working days for individual
years in order to fulfil the requirements of the government decree of
1975 which stipulated that in the period of the sixth 5-year plan
(1976–80) the number of working days per year had to be 260.[30] This
rule is still valid for the 1980s.

Of course, tightening of labour discipline is also discussed, but
obviously no real improvement can yet be ascertained. Although the
revised labour code of 1975 makes the dismissal of workers easier
(§53), such cases seem to be quite rare.

In Slovakia the government promulgated a resolution in 1977 (No.
349/1977) embracing a whole set of regulations for the reduction of
time losses and the tightening of labour discipline. Its realization
brought about some partial improvements, but commentators still are
not at all content with these minor changes.[31]

## 2.   Non-administrative provisions

*(a)   Incentives to individuals*

In the 1950s fundamental changes in the structure of the Czechoslovak economy occurred. In that period a greater part of the population
was willing to move from one region to another when job opportunities promised better prospects for their individual future. Also,
reserves in the agricultural population eased the recruitment of fresh
manpower for new production, in particular for the extensive development of industry and construction. This flexibility of the work
force has disappeared since only young women are still willing to
some extent to change their employment when jobs are offered
elsewhere.

However, structural changes are still needed; only the profile of
these changes has been altered. The individual sectors and branches of
the Czechoslovak economy now present very different patterns of
efficiency. Structural changes in the sense of priority shifts, mainly
between industrial branches, are thus regarded as extremely import-

ant when perspectives are discussed concerning the increase in overall productivity and export competitiveness.

For carrying out these intra-sectoral structural changes so-called development and slow-down programmes were introduced, numbering 31 in industry. Through these programmes 15 per cent of all industrial workers (25 per cent of all employees in engineering) are affected. During 1976–80 the number of persons additionally employed in the development programmes should be 40 000, i.e. 42 per cent of the total increase in industrial employment.

However, redistribution of the work force between less and more efficient enterprises turned out to be extremely difficult. According to experts it would be possible and useful to close production lines employing approximately 20 per cent of all industrial workers. In the first stage, 1976–80, only 32 000 jobs (1 per cent of the total number) were scheduled to be eliminated. In the first 2 years (1976–7) only 60 per cent of this still modest goal was reached, i.e. 6600 jobs were actually eliminated.[32]

Hindrances to a quicker and more effective execution of these structural change programmes are found not only in shortcomings of national economic planning, but also in the lack of sufficient material incentives for both enterprises and workers. In particular, on the side of the workers 'social barriers' which are connected with such questions as wage differentials, housing facilities, supply of municipal and/or enterprise services (kindergarten, schools, etc.) and the like, diminish their interest in moving to priority branches. Therefore, better incentives for workers who voluntarily decide to change employment become necessary, at least as long as free choice of employment is maintained.

Of course, the main issue in this respect must be financial security for people who have changed or want to change their jobs. In 1967, for the first time unemployment benefits were introduced for workers who, despite the help of their previous employer and the local administration (KNV), cannot find jobs corresponding to their abilities and qualifications. According to this still-valid regulation such a worker is entitled to 60 per cent of his net monthly income to a maximum of Kčs 1800 in the first 6 months. If he still has not found an adequate job he may receive 30 per cent up to a maximum Kčs 900 for another 6 months. This claim is forfeited if he rejects an adequate job offer without giving proper reasons or refuses to participate in a short-term agricultural brigade organized by national committees.[33]

Workers who do find new jobs within a short time in another

organization will receive a 3 months' compensatory payment covering
the difference between their average gross income in their previous job
and the new one. If the new job requires considerably different
qualifications which the employee has to acquire within a certain
period of time, he is entitled to a compensatory payment for the time
necessary for this training, but not longer than 6 months. Only in
cases where a journeyman's examination is foreseen can this compensatory payment be extended to 12 months.[34] It is perhaps noteworthy
that the previous limit of Kčs 3000 monthly for such a compensatory
payment was repealed in 1979 due to the steady increases in average
wages.

Apart from this compensatory wage levelling payment workers
who join priority enterprises that are included in the programme of
'most important structural changes',[35] can claim recruitment allowances. These allowances are differentiated on the one hand according
to branches and groups of organizations, on the other hand according
to the length of the new employment contract, and will be paid in part
when the employee starts his new job. The rest is granted after half a
year or after the first or second year. If the worker signs a contract for
1 year he may receive between Kčs 400 and 1600; if he decides for 3
years this recruitment allowance is between Kčs 1200 and 6500.

Given the branch ministry's approval, an enterprise belonging to
the programme of 'most important structural changes' can even offer
so-called increased recruitment allowances up to a maximum of six
average monthly (gross) wages achieved in the previous organization
provided that the worker is willing to sign a contract for at least 5
years.

*(b)   Wage regulation policies*

In a discussion of problems relating to a labour-short economy two
objectives can be formulated for wage regulation:

(1) to restrict the ability of enterprises to increase the wage-bill and
    the work force above certain (wanted) limits, and
(2) to motivate by wage differentiation workers or apprentices/
    students to enroll in specific priority branches.

Since J. Adam has elaborated on the development of Czechoslovak
wage regulation policies in detail,[36] this chapter will only present the

main features of the present wage system as far as they affect the two objectives mentioned above.

The system of wage regulation, introduced in 1970 after the end of the 1966 reform, basically meant a return to the old pre-reform system of wage-bill determination. The central authorities assign enterprises, via branch ministries, mandatory limits for the wage-bill, usually expressed as a fixed share in marketed output (formerly gross value of output).[37] The new tax on the wage-bill, introduced in 1970 in lieu of the former stabilization tax, only punished increases in average wages which were taxed in a progressive way – it did not affect increases in employment, nor did it encourage labour saving.[38] In 1978, this tax was abolished and replaced by a tax on (average) wage increases above the planned rate of increase. According to the new provisions for 1981–5 the wage-bill is set as a normative related to planned output and number of employees. If an association or enterprise plans a higher rate of labour productivity by a slower growth of employment than envisaged in the 5-year plan the resulting increase in the average wage is not subject to the new tax.[39] A similar mechanism was introduced for the so-called budgetary organizations (which are directly financed by the state or county budgets and do not work on a profit basis).

Also in the last third of the 1970s the Czechoslovak planners started, for the period 1978–80, an experiment in 150 enterprises with the purpose of finding ways to promote quality and efficiency. For these enterprises a modification in the system of wage regulation was introduced by dividing the overall wage fund of each year into two components:

(1) A fund for basic wages, which makes up approximately 80 per cent of the total wage sum. This basic wage-bill is determined as before, i.e. the central authorities assign mandatory limits to enterprises, but now expressed as a fixed share in net output (instead of marketed output).
(2) A fund for bonuses, which makes up the rest of the total wage sum (approximately 20 per cent). This fund is set as an absolute sum, but is conditioned by the fulfilment of some indicators.

In fact, as the minister responsible for the experiment and the introduction of the new system after 1980, L. Lér, stressed, it turned out that during 1978–9 the experimental enterprises employed 4000 persons less than foreseen in the long-term plan. Obviously the enterprises were interested in the distribution of bonuses among fewer employees.[40]

Generally, however, material incentives did not play an important role, either in stimulating enterprises to save labour or in trying to better utilize work time. Bonus indicators were often determined in a very formal and global way. They were easy to fulfil and difficult to supervise. Therefore they were very often fulfilled and the bonuses paid, but the enterprise as a whole has not fulfilled its plan targets.[41] For the new system of planning and management, therefore, a completely revised set of bonus rules was demanded with new and more precise indicators.[42]

In the set of provisions for the years after 1980 a separate section is dedicated to the effectiveness of wages.[43] It calls for a consistent enforcement of the principle of remuneration according to performance. 'Even in socialism wage differentiation is unavoidable',[44] is echoed by two Czechoslovak economists. This so-called complex programme for the improvement of the effectiveness of wages is realized in two stages[45] the first stage ran from 1981 to 1983. During this time the central branch organizations and the production units (VHJ) had to scrutinize the labour intensity of different norms, adjust them to the concrete conditions of production and work, and at the same time extend the basis of production norms, so that the number of 'unnormed' working employees would be diminished by at least 15 per cent.

In this first stage also new and more effective wage forms were to be developed with the aim of increasing the initiative of the workers. In selected working collectives the so-called brigade-form of work and remuneration was tested. In this context much more emphasis was to be laid on significant wage differentiation depending on job requirements and actual performance.

Not everything developed during this first stage as planners expected. In particular, narrow wage differentials remained practically unchanged.

It should not be too difficult to introduce increased differentiation in the wage system, since in Czechoslovakia wage differentials among different occupational groups are probably the smallest in the industrialized part of the world. To underline this statement findings from a microcensus of 1970 are given in Table 4.5. Of course, within these highly aggregated groups of qualifications wage differentiations

*Table 4.5* Wage differentiation according to differences in education and/or occupational training in 1970

|  | 8 years of elementary school | Journey-man | 2 years at technical school | 4 years at technical school | University |
|---|---|---|---|---|---|
| CSSR | 100 | 109 | 115 | 121 | 151 |
| Hungary | 100 | 150 | — | 170 | 220 |
| GDR | 100 | 150 | — | 220 | 270 |
| Netherlands | 100 | 115 | — | 148 | 296 |
| USA | 100 | — | — | 140 | 235 |

*Source:* L. Kalinová, *Máme nedostatek pracovních sil?* (Prague, Svoboda, 1975) p. 162.

according to job characteristics are applied, but still the tendency in the CSSR has been to smooth out differences in renumeration rather than to increase them.

Apart from the individual incentives offered to workers who are willing to sign contracts with firms belonging to one of the development programmes, one would expect that, due to shortcomings in the supply of labour, selected branches and sectors as a whole would be able to pay substantially higher average wages. As one can see from Table 4.6 in the last eight years only minor changes in the sectoral wage distribution were initiated.

A slightly more distinct attempt to widen wage differentials can be observed in industry. The intended preferential treatment of fuels and energy is quite clearly expressed in the figures presented in Table 4.7. Whether these differences will be more effective than hitherto as incentives for job-hoppers cannot yet be known. However in recent years, and to an increasing extent, people in Czechoslovakia no longer regard higher wages as the most important motivation for changing jobs. They rather wish to improve the individual conditions of work, to enhance the prestige of the occupation, and to see more promising perspectives for the significance of the work they do. Last but not least, people who consider changing jobs also include in their reflections factors like housing, school facilities and other local service benefits.

The second stage runs from 1985 to 1987. In this stage a further 'objectifying' of norms is scheduled: each year at least 20 per cent have to be analyzed and at the same time again the number of 'unnormed'

*Table 4.6*  Differences in average monthly wages between the main sectors of the CSSR economy

|  | Total economy | Industry | Construction | Agriculture | Forestry | Transport | Commun-ications |
|---|---|---|---|---|---|---|---|
| 1975 | 100 | 101.5 | 111.0 | 96.4 | 100.8 | 115.6 | 88.3 |
| 1980 | 100 | 103.1 | 109.3 | 97.2 | 101.9 | 119.2 | 88.6 |
| 1983 | 100 | 104.7 | 109.9 | 100.0 | 102.4 | 119.4 | 89.8 |

|  | Trade and restaurants | Science and R & D | Education | Culture | Health and social security | Local services | State admin-istration |
|---|---|---|---|---|---|---|---|
| 1975 | 83.4 | 112.9 | 96.1 | 89.1 | 90.4 | 77.0 | 106.6 |
| 1980 | 82.2 | 113.1 | 95.4 | 70.0 | 87.1 | 76.6 | 105.5 |
| 1983 | 80.6 | 113.9 | 93.4 | 65.5 | 93.3[a] | 76.6 | 100.5 |

[a] Public health services only.

*Source: SRC 1981*, p. 203; *1984*, p. 193.

employees has to be reduced by 10 per cent. The main emphasis is placed on further savings in the consumption of raw materials and fuels, but manpower shortages are also to be overcome. More important amendments are planned in the system of wage rates where, again, more differentiation is demanded as the main characteristic. It

*Table 4.7*  Differences in average monthly wages between industrial branches

|  | Total industry | Fuels | Energy | Metallurgy | Engineering |
|---|---|---|---|---|---|
| 1975 | 100 | 134.4 | 109.7 | 117.9 | 101.3 |
| 1980 | 100 | 137.1 | 111.7 | 117.2 | 100.1 |
| 1983 | 100 | 144.1 | 112.4 | 118.2 | 104.1 |

|  | Construction materials industry | Chemical industry | Textiles | Consumer goods industry | Foods and beverage industry |
|---|---|---|---|---|---|
| 1975 | 105.0 | 100.6 | 80.9 | 88.1 | 95.1 |
| 1980 | 102.4 | 100.6 | 81.8 | 87.7 | 91.4 |
| 1983 | 101.7 | 101.8 | 81.8 | 86.3 | 92.4 |

*Source: SRC, 1981*, p. 358; *SRC, 1984*, p. 366.

is interesting that in the discussion the example of Western industria-lized countries is quoted where allegedly 15 to 35 per cent of productivity increases can be attributed to differences in wage rates among branches. However the additional financial means for higher wages must be created by the enterprises themselves, either through increased profits or by diminishing the number of employees. In January 1985 two enterprises started this second stage of the wage system, others were to follow in the course of the same year.[46]

## (c) Incentives for pensioners

Many employed persons reaching the retirement age (men 60; women 55) are still able to work and can perform useful work due to their many years' experience. Therefore the Czechoslovak government tries to make use of this additional labour reserve. The rules, valid until 1983 (according to government decree nos. 135/1975 Sb. and 11/1980 Sb.), were presented in the first edition of this volume on pages 91 and 92. Although in 1981 already 877 000 pensioners were employed, representing 11.4 per cent of the total labour force at that time it was argued that those persons were not always appropriately and effec-tively employed. Therefore, beginning with 1 January 1984, all former rules for the employment of pensioners were abolished. Government decree no. 142/1983 Sb. replaced the former variety of rules by two new rules which make it possible for old-age pensioners and widows over 57 to receive their pension in full while being further employed:[47]

(1) If those pensioners are employed as blue-collar workers, operat-ing and service personnel (except in leading positions), or in some other (specially listed) occupations, e.g. middle or lower jobs in health care and social services (section 2).
(2) In other occupations than those listed in section 2, if the employ-ment is contracted for not longer than one year, and if the gross earnings from this occupation do not exceed Kčs 22 000 per calendar year (section 3). The average monthly salary in 1985 was Kčs 2908.

Beside these two new forms of a pensioner's employment with parallel payment of wage and pension, it is still possible for an employee having reached retirement age to continue working without receiving his/her pension. In this case, each additional working year increases the future pension by 7 per cent. At present (beginning 1985) 723 000 pensioners are still employed in the state sector of the economy, while another 167 000 can be found in the collectivized sector of agriculture. This represents altogether about 12 per cent of overall employment and 29 per cent of old-age and widow pensioners in present-day Czechoslovakia.[48]

## IV. CONCLUDING REMARKS

Although the figures reported on labour shortages in Czechoslovakia seem to indicate that this has indeed become a serious problem for the economy (because in addition to present employment approximately 11–12 per cent more positions could be filled) a closer look at some of the causes of this situation leads to the conclusion that a great part of this labour shortage is due only to such phenomena as: weak labour discipline, underutilization of working time, over-employment in some sectors and/or branches of the economy (administration, white-collar workers), also low degree of mechanization in some labour-intensive branches, and last but not least, the behaviour of enterprises (hoarding of labour, over-stated requirements of labour). Just the few estimates about the possible and quite easy savings of labour by the Czechoslovak government or attached research institutes (which have been reported in this paper in Sections III.2 and III.3) indicate that this extremely high over-employment in fact can only be regarded as very relative. In particular, if one considers that Czechoslovakia has not yet been seized to the same extent as Western industrialized countries by the micro-chips ('job-killers') revolution of most recent years, then a wide field of rationalization possibilities must also be included in the discussion of future labour shortage problems. One should mention here also that machinery and equipment to a great extent are already over-aged in Czechoslovakia, thus using valuable manpower in an inefficient way. By the way, this is already known in other countries (e.g. in Yugoslavia) as the 'Czechoslovak disease'.

However, at the moment Czechoslovakia has to cope with the problems of labour shortages as they appear. Faced with quite unfavourable demographic trends the government can only hope that the provisions introduced in the last years, and those foreseen for the future, will bring a slight relief. But it seems that fundamental changes in the labour market cannot be expected as long as it still remains almost impossible to close inefficient production lines or threaten lazy workers with dismissal. Also, material incentives in the form of higher wages differentiated according to work performance, or granted as recruitment allowances in priority branches, must lose part of their effect when the economy on the other hand is not able to improve the supply of consumer goods, services, housing facilities and the like. Since all other reserves (housewives, pensioners) are practically exhausted, provisions aiming at a greater participation of these persons will also not bring a substantial change in the Czechoslovak labour market in the near future.

## Notes

1. *Československá ekonomika v sedmdesátých letech* (Prague, Academia, 1975) pp. 54–77.
2. *Rudé právo*, 17 October 1980.
3. I. Klacanský, *Nové slovo*, 1 December 1983.
4. Cf. *inter alia*: A. Elias, *Manpower Trends in Czechoslovakia: 1950 to 1990*, US Dept. of Commerce, International Population Statistics Reports, Series P-90, no. 24 (Washington, DC, 1972); V. Seidl, *Plánované hospodářství*, no. 5 (1980) pp. 78–87; J. Adam and J. Cekota, *Revue d'etudes comparatives Est-Ouest,* no. 4 (1980); L. Pisca, *Sociologia,* no. 1 (1980) pp. 21–5; S. Černý *et al., Pracovní síly v československém hospodářství* (Prague, Práce, 1970); J. Kosta, 'Beschäftigungsstruktur und Arbeitskräftepolitik in der Tschechoslowakei', Berichte des Bundesinstituts für ostwissenschaftliche und internationale Studien, no. 23 (1976); P. Sokolowsky, *Der Arbeitsmarkt in der Tschechoslowakei* (Vienna, 1980).
5. *Sbírka zákonů*, no. 68 (1980) came into force on 1 January 1958.
6. Seidl, op. cit., p. 80.
7. The actual development in 1981–4 was worse than the prognosis; the total population grew by 1.0 per cent and the working age population by only 0.07 per cent. *SRC 1985*, p. 23.
8. *SRC 1984*, p. 187.
9. *Sbírka zákonů*, nos. 8 (1982) and 112 (1984).
10. This means that women on maternity leave, students, apprentices, and disabled persons are not included here.
11. J. Kux, *Hospodářské noviny*, no. 50 (1984) p. 4.
12. M. Kmetková, *Ekonomický časopis*, no. 1 (1979) pp. 76–8; *Zemědělské noviny*, 11 July 1983; *Rudé právo*, 26 January 1985.
13. *Czechoslovak Situation Report*, no. 3 (1979) RFE, December 1979.
14. *Rudé právo*, 11 December 1979.
15. E. Mikes and J. Steinich, *Plánované hospodářství*, no. 11 (1975) p. 24.
16. Ibid.
17. Institut manipulačních, dopravních, obalových a skladovacích systémů.

18.  M. Štancel, *Tribuna*, no. 49 (1980) p. 14.
19.  Cf. T. Vais, 'Manpower Policy in Eastern Europe', mimeographed, p. 18.
20.  Ibid., p. 19.
21.  Kosta, op. cit., p. 44.
22.  *Statistické přehledy*, no. 10 (1980); I. Žilová, *Plánované hospodářství*, no. 1 (1985) p. 33.
23.  Cf. Adam and Cekota, op. cit. County National Committees (Krajské národní výbory) are the middle link in Czechoslovakia's administrative organization. In addition to the two capitals Prague and Bratislava, which possess the status of counties, there exist seven Czech and three Slovak counties.
24.  'Zákonik práce' §26 (2), *Sbírka zákonů*, no. 55 (1975).
25.  K. Formánek, *Plánované hospodářství*, no. 5 (1978) p. 55.
26.  K. Ujházy, *Plánované hospodářství*, no. 8 (1982).
27.  Ibid., p. 56.
28.  K. Štětka, *Hospodářské noviny*, no. 26 (1980) p. 5.
29.  Kotek, op. cit.
30.  Adam and Cekota, op. cit., p. 14.
31.  Cf. V. Tevecová, *Pravda*, 12 November 1980.
32.  M. Pick, Introduction to V. Šusta, Supplement to *Hospodářske noviny*, no. 4 (1979) p. 3.
33.  Adam and Cekota, op. cit., p. 19; Šusta, op. cit., p. 9.
34.  U. Šusta, op. cit., p. 7.
35.  For a more detailed description of these 'most important structural changes' cf. Šusta, op. cit., p. 10.
36.  J. Adam, *Wage, Price and Taxation Policy in Czechoslovakia, 1948–1970* (Berlin, Duncker & Humblot, 1974); J. Adam, *Wage Control and Inflation in the Soviet Bloc Countries* (London, Macmillan, 1979).
37.  It is doubtful whether, in practice, the difference between marketed output and gross value of output entails fundamental changes, because in most cases marketed output includes not only the value of sold products but also the value of unfinished products and changes in inventories. (See J. Adam, *Wage Control . . .*, p. 172.)
38.  Adam and Cekota, op. cit.
39.  Cf. J. Velek, *Plánované hospodářství*, no. 9 (1980) p. 12.
40.  L. Lér, *Hospòdářské noviny*, no. 32 (1980) pp. 1 and 4.
41.  Cf. J. Müller, *Hospodářské noviny*, no. 13 (1980) p. 1.
42.  L. Štrougal, *Rudé právo*, 17 March 1980.
43.  Supplement to Hospodářské noviny, no. 12 (1980) paragraph D.
44.  M. Majtan and A. Suchá, *Hospodářské noviny*, no. 12 (1980) p. 3; J. Vesel, *Plánované hospodářství*, no. 7 (1979) p. 70.
45.  *Zemědělské noviny*, 30 August 1984.
46.  J. Zima, *Rudé právo*, 18 December, 1984; *Rudé právo*, 21 February 1985.
47.  *Sbírka zákonů*, no. 142 (1983); 'Zaměstnávání pracujících důchodců', Supplements to *Hospodářské noviny*, nos. 2 and 3 (1984).
48.  *Zemědělské noviny*, 14 December 1984.

# 5 Employment Policy in Hungary

## JÁNOS TIMÁR

## I. MANPOWER RESOURCES – MANPOWER SUPPLY

The size of the manpower supply is determined by the potential manpower resources and their changes. Manpower resources depend primarily on the numbers of the working-age population.[1] The resources are increased by the number of economically active people beyond working age and reduced by the number of retired of working-age persons and students of working age as well as by women on special maternity leave. Thus manpower resources depend upon demographic flows, welfare and the development of education as well as on policies that influence these factors.

Hungary's demographic conditions were shaped by two world wars and several waves of migration which resulted in a significant loss of people, a low level of fertility and a comparatively high mortality rate. These factors explain why the working-age population had grown in the last thirty-five years from only 5.6 million to 6.1 million (by 9 per cent) and why this growth has taken place amid significant fluctuations.

The number of economically active people beyond working age declined significantly (by 7 per cent of potential manpower resources) in past decades because of a gradual extension of *old age pension eligibility* and the reduction in the retirement age for people active in agriculture.[2] As a result economic activity of women over the age of 54 and men over 59 appears to be extremely low by international standards.[3]

Potential manpower resources were also reduced (by 4.4 per cent) by *disability* and by early retirement allowed in some special cases. The former was caused in part by unfavourable working conditions and by shortcomings in health and occupational rehabilitation, and in part by a vested interest in disability pensions, since the second economy provides a favourable opportunity for supplementary incomes.

103

In 1984 there were 224 000 women on maternity leave, taking advantage of the *child care aid* introduced in 1967.[4] In keeping with its original project this system had a favourable influence on balancing female employment and child care, but the 'cost' was a decline in the potential manpower resources (by 3.8 per cent).

The development of *education and specialized training* necessarily increased the number of full-time students of working age (4.1 per cent of potential manpower resources). Significant fluctuations in numbers are also caused by fluctuations in birth rates and age structure.

Table 5.1 shows changes in potential manpower resources.

On the whole, in the past thirty-five years, the potential manpower resources have reduced from 6 million to 5.3 million people (by 11.4 per cent). Two-thirds of this decline has been in the female workforce and one-third in the male.

## II.   UTILIZATION OF LABOUR – DEMAND FOR LABOUR

Between 1949 and 1984 the number of persons economically active in the national economy rose from just under 4.1 million to nearly 5 million. This was an extensive and rapid change compared to the pre-1945 period, and the favourable development of the world economy in most of the period was conducive to this change. The number of economically active persons showed a similar or even greater increase in other countries, particularly where the employment of migrant and guest workers enabled richer nations to take advantage of the unused manpower resources of the less advanced countries.

Noteworthy in Hungary's development is, in the first two to three decades of its postwar dynamic development, the gradual exhaustion of all free manpower resources within the country. Above and beyond the well-known demographic factors, the expansion and improvement of the general pension system resulted in a significant growth in the number of economically active persons who retired, while the number of young people entering the workforce has gradually declined. Thus, from the early 1970s on, the natural reserves were less and less adequate to cover the natural decline in active manpower. As a result of the closed nature of the national labour market, the role of housewives gradually expanded until they became the sole source of manpower increases. This can be seen in Figure 5.1 and Table 5.2.

The above factors explain how the use of potential male manpower

*Table 5.1* Manpower resources 1949–84 (in thousands)

|  | 1949 | 1960 | 1971 | 1976 | 1981 | 1984 |
|---|---|---|---|---|---|---|
| Population of working age[1] | 5608 | 5754 | 6100 | 6237 | 6143 | 6093 |
| Economically active population below and beyond working age | 572 | 655 | 372 | 283 | 195 | 142 |
| Pensioners of working age | 82 | 56 | 133 | 252 | 341 | 346 |
| Students of working age | 150 | 269 | 463 | 396 | 374 | 395 |
| Working age population on maternity leave | — | — | 168 | 265 | 254 | 224 |
| Manpower resources, total | 5948 | 6084 | 5708 | 5607 | 5369 | 5270 |
| Mining and manufacturing | 793 | 1329 | 1767 | 1782 | 1648 | 1545 |
| Construction | 91 | 289 | 383 | 420 | 393 | 363 |
| Agriculture and related | 2196 | 1832 | 1254 | 1085 | 1058 | 1072 |
| Transport and communication | 181 | 309 | 370 | 403 | 400 | 397 |
| Commerce, hotels and related | 215 | 298 | 420 | 469 | 489 | 504 |
| Water works and supply | 4 | 11 | 62 | 71 | 77 | 77 |
| Services | 605 | 693 | 752 | 864 | 905 | 935 |
| Economically active population, total | 4085 | 4760 | 5010 | 5093 | 5015 | 4940 |
| Economically inactive population of working age | 1863 | 1324 | 686 | 504 | 350 | 328 |
| Rate of utilization of manpower resources (%) | 68.7 | 78.2 | 87.8 | 90.8 | 93.4 | 93.7 |

[1] Male 15–59 years, female 15–54 years.

*Source: SE* of various years.

resources which had already exceeded 90 per cent in 1949 reached a peak of 97 per cent in the mid-1970s. However, in 1949, nearly two-thirds of the women of working age (1.8 million) were still in the households; by 1984 their number was only 260 000. In 1949 only 66 per cent of the total potential manpower resources was used, while the figure for 1984 was 94 per cent. These changes are shown in Figure 5.2.

Even the small manpower resources that still exist in the house-holds are no longer a real 'reserve'. The majority of the roughly

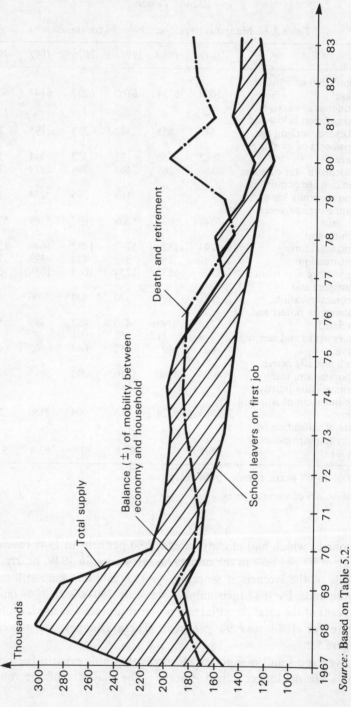

*Source*: Based on Table 5.2.

*Figure 5.1* Labour supply and demand

*Table 5.2*  Changes in the economically active population 1967–83 (in thousands)

| Year | Exit | | | Entrance | | | Changes in the economically active population |
|------|------|------|------|------|------|------|------|
| | Mortality of working age population | Retirement | Total | School leavers on first job | Balance of mobility between household and economy | Total | |
| 1967 | 19.6 | 147.7 | 167.3 | 147.0 | 77.4 | 224.4 | 57.1 |
| 1968 | 20.0 | 160.9 | 180.9 | 179.0 | 121.7 | 300.7 | 119.8 |
| 1969 | 19.3 | 170.7 | 190.0 | 186.5 | 96.6 | 283.1 | 93.1 |
| 1970 | 19.1 | 156.5 | 175.6 | 170.2 | 35.5 | 205.7 | 30.1 |
| 1971 | 19.5 | 151.7 | 171.2 | 176.1 | 23.4 | 199.5 | 28.3 |
| 1972 | 19.2 | 153.5 | 172.7 | 162.1 | 33.2 | 195.3 | 22.6 |
| 1973 | 20.1 | 162.2 | 182.3 | 153.4 | 41.3 | 194.7 | 12.4 |
| 1974 | 21.0 | 165.3 | 186.3 | 150.4 | 47.8 | 198.2 | 11.9 |
| 1975 | 21.9 | 163.4 | 185.3 | 149.3 | 43.7 | 193.0 | 7.7 |
| 1976 | 22.5 | 162.9 | 185.4 | 141.1 | 32.3 | 173.4 | − 12.0 |
| 1977 | 22.2 | 144.1 | 166.3 | 135.9 | 18.0 | 153.9 | − 12.4 |
| 1978 | 23.4 | 126.1 | 149.5 | 132.7 | 29.0 | 161.7 | 12.2 |
| 1979 | 23.0 | 132.6 | 155.6 | 128.1 | 20.1 | 148.2 | − 7.4 |
| 1980 | 24.5 | 165.2 | 189.7 | 116.2 | 14.4 | 130.6 | − 59.1 |
| 1981 | 23.1 | 140.4 | 163.5 | 124.7 | 26.2 | 150.9 | − 12.6 |
| 1982 | 23.0 | 152.8 | 175.8 | 124.2 | 19.8 | 144.0 | − 31.8 |
| 1983 | 23.5 | 156.6 | 180.1 | 128.0 | 17.0 | 145.0 | − 35.1 |

*Source: SE* of various years.

260 000 housewives of working age are over 40, unskilled, with most of them living in small agricultural villages; in other words they are a stratum which cannot really be mobilized. According to the latest data collected from questionnaires by the Hungarian Central Statistical Office, barely 10 per cent of them said that they would seek employment within the next 2 years. Most of them, to explain their unreadiness to enter employment, cited the lack of job opportunities, work in family farming and activities related to raising children.[5]

Table 5.1 and Figure 5.3 show that the employment figures and the sectoral pattern did not change smoothly. Three-quarters of the entire growth in manpower took place in just a little over one decade, up to 1960. In the first half of the 1970s the growth was still positive and then started to decline, culminating, in the first half of the 1980s, in a drop in employment.

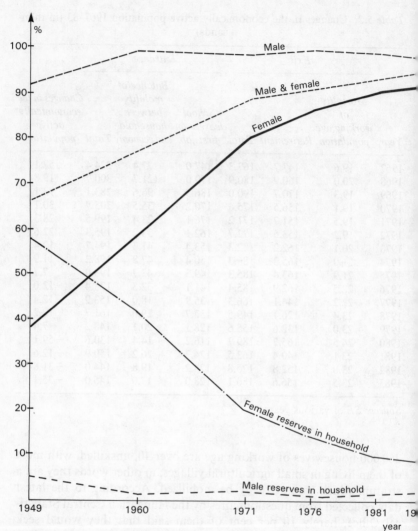

*Source:* Based on Table 5.1.

*Figure 5.2* Potential and employed manpower resources by sexes

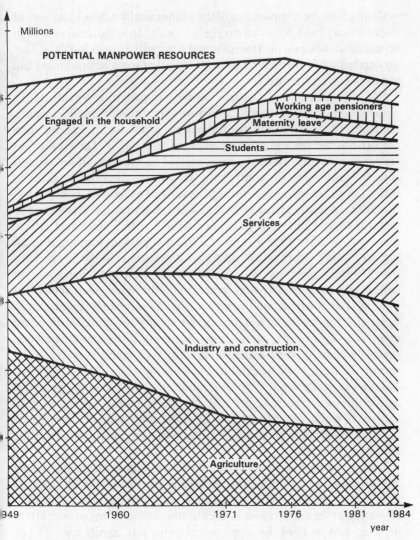

Millions

**POTENTIAL MANPOWER RESOURCES**

Engaged in the household

Working age pensioners

Maternity leave

Students

Services

Industry and construction

Agriculture

1949    1960    1971    1976    1981    1984

year

*Figure 5.3*  Potential manpower resources and their distribution

Changes in the composition of the economically active by sectors of the economy have followed on the whole the international course of economic development. International comparison also indicates that service branches are undermanned (as in other socialist countries) and industry is overmanned.[6]

For a long time now a debate has been in progress to evaluate the number and ratio of people active in agriculture.[7] This is, in part, related to the fact that the sectoral pattern is diverse, depending upon the various figures and calculations used to judge it. The fact is that Hungarian sectoral statistics are compiled on the basis of an 'organizational' approach (in contrast to an 'activity' approach, used by IOT); the entire manpower (as well as the full output) of an organization is listed in the sector according to its main profile. According to sectoral (organizational) statistics of the Central Statistical Office, there was in early 1984 a total of 1 072 000 persons employed in all sectors of agriculture taken together. Of these nearly 330 000 persons (in 1976 the figure was only 180 000) worked on state farms and on collective farms in activities other than the basic one, mostly in industrial or construction operations. At the same time, employment figures for this sector do not include the volume, or the corresponding manpower figures, for work done in private plots and small businesses, which in 1980 exceeded in terms of manpower the work volume of total basic agricultural activity by about 11–12 per cent. Taking the foregoing into consideration, the ratio of employment in agriculture is currently 22 per cent, calculated by the 'organizational' approach, while, according to the 'activity' approach, it is 15 per cent, though, when taken according to total work time input, it should be 28–30 per cent.

During the past thirty-five years the rate of employment in industry initially showed a sudden rise: in 1949 it was below the 20 per cent level and by the mid-1970s it peaked at nearly 36 per cent. Since then employment in industry as a sector has declined by over 200 000 persons, and in 1984 the employment ratio was hardly over 31 per cent. According to international comparisons this ratio cannot be considered either particularly high or 'distorted'.

An important role in the continuous change in sectoral pattern is played by labour turnover. In recent years statistics have registered 600 000 to 650 000 job changes a year. (This means therefore that the rate of turnover is over 14–15 per cent.) In connection with this there have been in recent years a number of objections voiced in Hungarian economic literature, saying that the rate of turnover is 'too high' while others say that 'manpower mobility is insufficient'. There are two types of realistic considerations behind these apparently contradictory views. The point of departure of the first is that every entrance into employment, and termination of employment, are of significant cost to the employer; therefore, goes the argument, labour turnover should be reduced because this would reduce production costs and increase the productivity of labour. The other, equally justified concept, however, states that the dynamic development of the economy requires the results in more rapid changes in sectoral employment patterns and in the job structure.

The number of job changes, however, do not give us much information on turnover since there is no yardstick with which to compare it in order to be able to qualify it as 'high' or 'low'. What is, however, significant is to what extent job changes reflect the requirement for economic efficiency and to what extent competition on the labour market is becoming sharper because of a manpower shortage. The fact is that in the vast majority of cases in Hungary, job changes are initiated by employees and not by employers, and it is quite probable that the requirement for enterprise efficiency affects turnover only a little.

A few of the latest figures show that, in the second half of the 1970s, the changes in economic policy and the latest steps in the economic reform have shifted the job changes in a positive direction. From the experience of certain enterprises it is possible to conclude that, if the ratio of dismissals openly initiated by the enterprises increases, it will reduce the number of job changes initiated by the workers themselves and thus will also reduce average labour turnover.

In keeping with generally accepted practice, we have confined ourselves up to now to the examination of equilibrium in the labour market by comparing the manpower resources with their use, and the demand for labour with its supply, all measured in numbers of persons. However, the latest studies show convincingly that in analysing either the manpower market or employment policy, work time is essential, and it is also vital to observe the use of other time for activities outside of official work time.

The development of modern industry has definitely separated the 'economy' and the household from each other, and with this the duration of activities spent in the workplace from 'household' work which directly serves the reproduction of human existence. While industrialization in Hungary has reduced small-scale commodity production to a minimum, a special new type of economic activity has recently evolved, wedged in between the 'economy' and the 'house-hold'. It is called the 'second economy'.[8] Finally, more than a small amount of time is required for transport. The total time inputs of these activities which differ in nature are separate from one another; nevertheless they are closely related and are termed 'the time base for *social reproduction*'. Based on existing work-time budgets we estimate that in Hungary today about 36–7 per cent of the total time base is used by the 'first' economy (socialist sector); 17–18 per cent is used up in the second economy. The amount of time spent in transport is estimated to be 11 per cent, most of which goes for travel to and from work. Finally, 'household work' in the strict sense of the term accounts for 24–6 per cent of this time base.[9]

In Hungary up to 1968 the official work week was 48 hours. During 1968–74 it was reduced to 44 with a five day week each second week. In 1984 the working week in industry, construction and state admini-stration was reduced to 40 hours. The reductions in working time reduced the work time base of the economy, but this was for some time offset by an increase in the number of economically active persons. However, in the period of work time reductions beginning with 1980, the number of the economically active also declined. The result of this dual effect is that now the total work-time base of the economy is also showing a decline.

Within the time base of work in the second economy small-scale agricultural production has a dominant share. This production is carried on partly on the household plots of the collective farm members and other agricultural workers, and partly in the small-scale farms of people living in the villages but with jobs in non-agricultural sectors. In 1967 the household plots used up 58 per cent of the total amount of time required for small-scale agricultural production, and the independent small farms used up 42 per cent. To 1982 the proportions were reversed: 58 per cent of the total time base used was taken by the small-scale farms and 42 per cent by the household plots. An even more important change occurred: while, at the end of the 1960s, 70 per cent of the total time base was devoted to production by the households for their own consumption and only 30 per cent went for commodity production, in the early 1980s 60 per cent of the total time base went for commodity production.[10]

The economic activity of women in the socialist countries is high, and women generally, with the exception of the GDR, work full-time. At the same time socioeconomic development has not led to any important change in the amount of housework for the same strata of the population, either in Hungary or in other countries,[11] and the total time base for the household, including transport, significantly exceeds the work time base for the first economy.

According to Hungarian time budget studies, in 1963 the economically active male spent an average of 2 hours a day working beyond official working hours in the household and the second economy, while economically active women spent almost 5 hours. Up to 1977, when practically all women of working age worked full-time, the distribution of these activities between the economically active male and female hardly changed; the work done by the men increased to 2.5 hours, while that of the women only declined to 4.5 hours.

The existing conflicts between the first and second economies and between the economy and households can only be reduced with a reduction in the number of economically active people with 'dual status'[12] and a more rational distribution of the burden of the 'double shift'. This requires manifold and complicated social and economic organizational activity in, among other things, the area of employment policy, if we want to improve economic efficiency so that there is also an improvement in the 'quality of life'.

## III. EMPLOYMENT POLICY: OBJECTIVES, METHODS AND RESULTS

In Hungary the 'building of socialism', begun in the late 1940s, was based upon the traditional socialism model which included an economy based on a directive planning system. The goal of employment policy at that time was the achievement of 'real full employment', free from any type of unemployment through 'a planned and proportionate development'. At the same time it was claimed that the obligation to work and the right to work of the able-bodied population in socialism were 'really the right of *every member of society of working age* to receive secure jobs *remunerated* with wages in keeping with the quantity and quality of the work done.'[13]

This goal of full employment, which encompassed the liquidation of private small-scale production and the transformation of the owners into wage earners, was in complete harmony with the fundamental political and economic policy objective: the introduction of a forced pace of industrialization into countries that had been left behind historically and were on the European periphery, so that they would close the gap between the advanced capitalist countries (that stood in the vanguard of industrialization) and themselves. Due to capital scarcity and the level of qualifications and experience of the labour force, the acceleration of economic growth required as rapid as possible an increase in the number of persons employed, primarily in socialist industry and construction.

This employment policy was also in harmony with a social policy aimed at completely eliminating the unemployment inherited from the past and aggravated by war destruction, at reducing inequality of income and at raising the level of social equality for women.

In principle the national economic planners calculated the manpower requirements of the national economy as a function of production and productivity. However, neither in Hungary nor elsewhere was it possible to elaborate a method of planning productivity so exact that it could substantially reduce the uncertainties in the global estimation of productivity. Therefore 'planning of labour demand was rather planning the employment of an expected labour supply, and only the distribution of this supply among the sectors can be related directly to the planned development of these sectors.'[14] The implementation of the objectives of employment policy in the planning process depended upon the causes of expected disequilibrium in demand for and supply of manpower. In some cases the planners of production were under pressure to create more job opportunities, and in other cases the manpower planners were urged to initiate higher growth in the labour supply.

Based upon the theoretical axioms and planning practice mentioned earlier, in the early 1950s the transfer of manpower from the private to the socialist sector was carried out on the one hand by price, tax and financial policies which were used on liquidate private small-scale production and, on the other hand, by the rapid development of the socialist sector itself, which had a strong suction effect. The transfer was facilitated by retraining programmes.

Employment policy had the special task of 'planned distribution of qualified manpower'. A multitude of decrees and executive decrees specified the formal education and trade qualifications required for the various workplaces in the state-owned enterprises. Young professionals were subject to 'compulsory professional practice', that is, legal regulations specified that young people concluding secondary and higher specialized educational institutions were obliged to work for a definite period of time (e.g., two years in the case of higher education) in a job stipulated by the minister.

Free choice of jobs was restricted in keeping with the principles and measures discussed above. Workers dismissed for disciplinary reasons, or workers quitting, were subject to various sanctions; paid holidays and sick pay were reduced significantly, and for a time they could only seek re-employment through an employment agency run by the council of the region.

The regional councils took over the job of employment agencies from the trade unions in the late 1940s. At this time their main role was to satisfy the manpower needs of state enterprises. Accordingly, they organized or granted permits for a 'recruitment' of labour in line with 'national economic interests', which meant finding and contracting free manpower reserves within the administrative areas under their jurisdiction. They also placed job-seekers, including 'migratory birds', (workers who change jobs three or more times within one year).

Despite restrictions on freedom of choice of jobs, the 'right to work' was implemented. By the early 1950s the huge amount of open unemployment inherited from the past had been eliminated, and by the mid-1960s the hidden and latent unemployment within agriculture had for all practical purposes been eliminated. The rapid development of education and trade training, the mass inclusion of women in trade training courses, and the expansion of job opportunities unquestionably contributed to the realization of the original, progressive goals – the reduction in inequalities in income and in the unequal social position of women.

This is not to say that these achievements were due to employment policy. They resulted rather from the fact that the basic goals of the employment policy fitted in well with an economic policy aimed at rapid economic growth and with the working of the system of management of the economy. The change in ownership relations, elimination of incomes from capital and private small-scale production, or their restriction to a narrow field, necessarily reinforced the willingness of the able-bodied population to seek employment. At the same time in this growth-oriented economy, enterprises' demands for resources, including labour, we not restricted by the requirements of economic efficiency. This meant that economic growth was paralleled by an increase in employment, until the rise in employment reached the natural constraints of a closed national labour market.[15]

At the same time employment policy was not really able to implement the 'planned distribution and restructuring' of manpower. While job changes by young specialists finishing school each year were sharply restricted, it was less practicable to influence the job changes of people who had already finished their 'compulsory professional practice' and had been working for some time. The system of compulsory placement did not live up to the hopes placed in it, for the enterprises became less and less eager to hire new workers.

There is no doubt that the Hungarian system must be credited with creating security and comparative well-being for 'people willing and able to work'. This came about despite shortcomings in the management and performance of the economy which were addressed in party and government documents calling emphatically for an improvement in economic efficiency.[16] The idea of economic reform gained ground and in 1965 became the official party platform. In 1968 an economic reform under the name of the 'New Economic Mechanism' (NEM) was introduced. As is generally known, the main objective of NEM was to change the Hungarian system from an administrative planning based upon directives to a 'planned socialist market economy'.

Based upon the long-term manpower forecast elaborated in the early 1960s a new employment policy concept was laid down as early as the beginning of the 1960s which stressed that 'an increasing employment of the able-bodied population does not mean that the objective should be full employment in any absolute sense. The extent of employment is determined not only by the level of economic development but also by the demographic characteristics of the population, primarily by its distribution according to age and sex.' According to this concept 'manpower allocation cannot be realized through a system of administrative measures, particularly not through compulsion, ... but ... we must create conditions under which the reproduction and allocation of manpower according to the needs of society are realized ... as a result of conscious actions by individuals acting according to their own decisions.'[17]

Under the new conditions that had evolved by the mid-1960s the objective of 'full employment' had increasingly lost its original significance, since the system of management of the economy continued to make dynamic growth possible. This growth was fostered by the world economic upswing and resulted in a continued demand for manpower, while, as has been noted, the rapid exhaustion of manpower reserves had begun. The shortage of manpower, which initially characterized only Budapest and the rapidly developing new industrial centres, gradually spread throughout the country, and by the end of the 1960s it had become general. As a consequence keen competition developed between enterprises, local labour markets for the new labour force and for the redistribution of labour already in employment. At the same time structural contradictions in the relationship between demand for and supply of labour developed. While among certain groups of qualified manpower signs of oversaturation began to appear, there was a shortage of workers willing to perform unskilled or strenuous work.

The new stage in development required a reformulation of the fundamental targets of employment policy and a setting of new methods for its implementation. This was facilitated by the upswing in Marxian theory. It was accepted by a steadily growing circle in Hungary that labour in an economy of socialist commodity production continues to be a 'commodity' and that there is 'a labour market', although, in keeping with the socialist socio-economic system, it differs in nature and operation from the capitalist 'labour market'.[18] 'Full employment' continued to be the guiding principle of employment policy, but it had been stated clearly that under the given conditions of the socialist economy there is 'a special state of the labour market where the demand for labour is attained and then increasingly exceeds the labour supply, and a labour shortage prevails on the labour market.'[19] Correspondingly the spotlight was on the requirement for equilibrium in the labour market and on an 'economical', 'thrifty' and 'efficient' use of manpower.

Already in 1965 the leading body of economic policy of the Hungarian Socialist Workers' Party stated that the implementation of full employment should be principally a social, government goal in which a significant role was to be played by the regional government administration, while the main job of the enterprises was to ensure efficient use of manpower.[20]

In keeping with the new concept, the methods used earlier were re-evaluated and amended. After the introduction of the economic reform of 1968 a new 'Labour Code' was issued; it eliminated all pre-existing sanctions against the movement of manpower and it strengthened the right of workers to change jobs according to their wishes. The 'planned distribution' or 'organized regrouping' of manpower became the task of enterprises; it was based principally upon the assumption that the more efficient enterprises which were therefore able to pay higher wages would siphon off manpower from slowly developing enterprises with low wages. Since proper cost sensitivity, interest in profit and market competition were lacking, it was decided to use wage regulation as a tool of labour economy and reallocation of manpower. For the sake of economic efficiency increasing stress was put on 'differentiated wages based upon individual performance'.

The initial provisions of the economic reform of 1968 were: the elimination of plan directives in the control over enterprises, the building up of the institutional framework for enterprise autonomy, the gradual liberalization of prices and other significant measures – all these indicated that Hungary was shifting from a 'conventional socialism model' to a new type of model that was to be more efficient socially and economically. However, the elan of the reform was eroded in the beginning of the 1970s. The positive influence of market operation was felt only in a limited sphere and to a limited extent. Therefore the central leaders, whether they wanted to or not, were forced to constantly return to 'manual piloting', to central intervention.

These circumstances had affected employment policy and the labour market. Ostensibly to encourage risk taking and to revitalise economic competition as well as to better satisfy consumer demand, the economic policy supported the development of the second economy, primarily the 'auxiliary' activity of collective farms, as well as legal private small businesses. Simultaneously this policy led to an upswing in the semi-legal, tolerated activity of the 'the second economy'. As the second economy gained in strength it siphoned off a certain amount of manpower from the socialist sector. In terms of numbers this was at most two to three per cent of employment in the socialist sector, but the loss of this manpower to the second economy had an above-average effect on the large enterprises in industry and construction, particularly in those trades where the manpower shortage had anyhow been above average (lathe operators, masons, etc.).

The strengthening of competition in the labour market 'distorted' earning ratios. According to the target set by NEM, earnings of highly qualified specialists and managers should have increased by an above-average rate. In fact, however, differences in earnings continued to decline. The rise in the earnings of technical and economic specialists was less than average. In addition, the household plots dominant in the second economy, as well as moonlighting in construction and in certain branches of the service sector, reduced the interest of workers in the large-scale state-owned enterprises in fulfilling and overfulfilling workplace requirements.

Day-to-day experience and empirical studies seem to prove that enterprises suffer from a significant loss of work time, most of which is caused by organizational shortcomings, disruptions in the supply of materials, machinery and tools, but is also due to a lack of discipline. And this prompted the authorities to the view that the labour shortage was not 'real' but 'fictitious' and that enterprise management was being influenced by a 'labour shortage-psychosis'. Therefore they demanded that enterprises restrict their manpower demands and 'mobilize their internal reserves'.[21]

No matter how rational this position appeared from the formal-logical point of view, the enterprises were forced into a rational conduct of their own, based upon real interests, by the effect of the system of management and its environment. These factors strengthened unavoidably the trend to labour hoarding and made competition in the labour market even stronger. It is no wonder that under such circumstances the view surfaced – not only in everyday conversation but also in the press and even on television – that 'if we want order and discipline then we should make a little unemployment'.

Historical experience and analyses do not support this opinion. Not even in the capitalist system is there a political regime which 'wishes' for unemployment and it would be even more inconceivable and unacceptable for the government of a socialist country, all the more because the relationship commonly assumed between unemployment and economic efficiency does not really exist. As Keynes showed, even in the period of upswing, all unemployment in the advanced capitalist economies does not disappear; even then existential security is not 'complete' or 'absolute'. In the capitalist system unemployment is a consequence, not a precondition, of economic efficiency. Therefore it cannot be argued that, if there is unemployment or that if we 'make some', the result will be an improvement in efficiency and an upswing in the economy.

The criticisms of and appeals to labour economy by central leaders however, proved to be ineffective, and therefore they turned again to 'manual piloting', that is, to the application of administrative methods which had been used earlier in the period of administrative planning. The central intervention was intended on the one hand to mobilize the manpower reserves that were still free and available and on the other to limit manpower demand and achieve a planned reallocation of existing manpower.

In the early 1970s opportunities for pensioners to work were expanded while a special 'pension bonus' increased the level of pension for people who continued to work beyond retirement age. Transfer of workers from regions where manpower reserves were still available were financed from central and local funds. To mobilize these very same reserves many enterprises purchased or rented buses –

despite high costs – and transported workers between their home and their place of employment.

Simultaneously actions were undertaken to restrict 'unhealthy labour turnover'. Compulsory placement by employment agencies was again extended to the 'migratory birds'. The measure, which stopped the increase in administrative and managerial staff, was intended to alleviate the shortage of people in manual jobs. Actions were initiated to supervise the granting of disability pensions and the putting of persons on sick pay. Time off given to people continuing their studies while working was reduced. The activities of social organizations conducted during working hours was curtailed. There was even a transitional experiment to restrict the activity of the 'supplementary units' of collective farms as well as activity in the household plots and small private farms which still exist in Hungary.

None of these measures had any significant influence on the labour market but they did have undesirable side effects. The unfavourable consequences of the general labour shortage remained and were quite tangible on local markets. Under these conditions, the county political and government bodies came up with the idea of taking the 'organization' of the labour market into their own hands, of trying to curb labour demand and achieve a 'rational distribution' of available manpower. As part of these aspirations the county bodies classified all economic organizations operating under their jurisdiction into categories corresponding to their 'national economic significance'. Enterprises were obliged to submit economic plans in order to enable the county bodies to determine whether the planned manpower needs were justified. On this basis the county bodies endeavoured to achieve a 'planned distribution' of labour among those requiring it. This action, which began spontaneously and spread nationwide, was sanctified and formalized by a decree of the Minister of Labour.[22] In practice, however, it soon turned out that in the new conditions that had evolved since the economic reform and on a regional level, it was even less possible to 'supervise' enterprise plans and demands according to criteria of 'national economic significance' or 'economic efficiency' than it had been in the past under the system of administrative planning, when the National Planning Office and the sectoral ministries had tried to do this on a nationwide level. Thus, shortly after the appearance of the decree, the whole 'categorization' and 'manpower distribution' process died a quiet death. In this respect no favourable results came from the multitude of amendments to central earnings regulations either.

In the second half of the 1970s, due in no small extent to the increasingly depressing effect of the world economic crisis, the demand for a consistent continuation of NEM came again to the forefront. The new government positions, which were more definite and more farsighted than the earlier ones, as well as the low level of effectiveness (we might even say, the failure) of the employment policy actions in the 1970s, forced the steerers of employment policy to return to the employment policy concept that had been shaped during the period of the economic reform. Not only this, but it also became necessary to give an 'up-to-date interpretation' of full employment. The point of departure was the assumption that the modernization of the system of economic management would force the enterprises to use resources, including manpower, more efficiently, and that the number of workers transferred or dismissed by enterprises would increase. Finally it was taken into consideration that in the second half of the 1980s there would be a newer demographic wave which would increase the labour supply temporarily.

Because of all these factors the employment policy documents of the end of the 1970s stressed that the 'right to work does not mean the right to a given job'. The government would continue to care about full employment, but the worker would have to count on possible changes of jobs or even of occupation. For the moment the assumptions outlined are beginning to materialize only to a very small exent, at most in certain branches and micro-environments. In the major part of the country the majority of the enterprises are for the moment being characterized by the double bond of 'internal reserves' – 'external manpower shortage'. The contradictory requirement, of preparing for the future situation that is assumed to be coming and adjusting to current reality, is what has characterized the new phase of Hungarian employment policy that has been evolved in most recent years.

The regional councils' role in employment management and in the placing of employees has been changed fundamentally.[23] The councils have been relieved of the task of 'influencing the efficient employment of manpower' and of 'distributing manpower'. The placement role is geared not to the satisfaction of enterprise manpower demand but to the employment requirements of the population. In 1982 the system of 'retraining aid' was introduced, whose purpose is to compensate workers for losses in income during training and retraining because of changes in the structure of production or the regrouping of manpower. The funds come from the state budget.

Many restrictions on overtime and extra work have been relaxed, and the system of intra-enterprise partnerships[24] that allows enterprises to contract out work to their own workers to be performed outside of regular working hours has been firmly established. The prolonged maternity leave system has been extended and its users can collect benefits and take a part-time job at the same time. Information about up-to-date work time systems and opportunities for flexible or part-time employment is widely disseminated. The elaboration of a 're-employment aid'[25] system that is up-to-date and meets the requirements of the future is currently under way.

The measures outlined indicate that this newest era of employment policy is in harmony with the government intention to 'modernize' the system of economic management and with the latest measures introduced in 1985, whose main objective continues to be the evolution of a 'planned market economy'. Experience to date proves that employment policy can implement its specific targets to the extent permitted by the whole system of economic management.

**Notes**

1. In Hungary this means women between the ages of 15 and 54 and men between the ages of 15 and 59.
2. For more information see J. Adam, 'The Old Age Pension System in Eastern Europe', *Ost-Europa Wirtschaft*, no. 4 (1983).
3. Reality differs from what contemporary statistics show. The Central Statistical Office data exclude from the economically active those who undertake to work while receiving pensions. The fact is that two or three decades ago there were very strong restrictions on working if pensions were collected. In the meantime, due to manpower shortages, these restrictions have been gradually lifted. Thus, according to the latest data in 1984, there were about 430 000 people working and receiving a pension at the same time, of whom 170 000 worked full-time and 260 000 part-time. The number of average annual working hours for pensioners exceeded 1000, which is more than half of the work time input of people working full-time. Under conditions like this, keeping the old system of accounting is unjustified.
4. This special maternity leave (SML hereafter), which was introduced in Hungary in 1967, makes it possible for mothers whose maternity leave with full pay (6 months since January 1981) expires to continue to remain at home until the child reaches the age of 3 while their employment status and all social insurance rights are uninterrupted. During the time of this special leave (from 1985 on) they are to receive 75 per cent of their former earnings until the child reaches the age of one (minimum 2500 and maximum 5000 Frts) in a category called

'child-care fee', and after that, from the time the child reaches one until the age of 3 they are to receive 1340 Frts (per child) as 'child-care aid' at the expense of the central budget. The 'family allowance' is independent of this and is a sum of 710 forints per child (see *Magyar Közlöny*, 17 January 1985). To evaluate the sum given above it should be known that in early 1985 the monthly average earnings for persons employed in the industrial sector were almost 5800 forints.

Jan Adam gives a good overview of the regulation of the labour supply in 'Regulation of Labour Supply in Poland, Czechoslovakia and Hungary', *Soviet Studies*, no. 1 (1984) pp. 69–86. However, with respect to SML, he slightly simplifies interrelations when, in connection with the New Economic Mechanism (NEM), he concludes: 'Therefore they decided in 1967 to undertake several provisions against possible unemployment, and the introduction of a prolonged maternity leave programme was one of them' (p. 76). The concept of the SML arose in the early 1960s (for this see János Timár, *Planning the Labour Force in Hungary* (IASP, New York) 1966, p. 33: (Hungarian version, 1964). In 1965 the full programme of the SML had been approved and scheduled for introduction in 1967.

SML served to siphon off the temporary manpower surplus caused by the demographic wave, though its institution was exclusively motivated by a rational reconciliation of employment of women with children and the family burden.

5.  *Manpower Survey on Composition of Housewives and their Intentions to Seek Employment* based upon data collected in January 1983 (Central Statistical Office, 1985).
6.  M. Augusztinovics, *Közgazdasági Szemle*, no. 9 (1981).
7.  For latest debate information see P. Romány, *Valóság*, no. 1 (1984); M. Mentényi, *Közgazdasági Szemle*, no. 2 (1984).
8.  For more details see I. R. Gábor and P. Galasi, *A 'második gazdaság.' Tények és hipotézisek* (Budapest, 1981) p. 206, and I. R. Gábor, 'Second economy in socialism: lessons of Hungary', in E. L. Feigen (ed.), *The Unobserved Economy* (Cambridge University Press, forthcoming).
9.  J. Timár, *Time and Worktime*, in G. Fink (ed.), *Socialist Economy and Economic Policy, Essays in honour of Friedrich Levcik* (Vienna, Springer, 1985).
10. For more see *Mezögazdasági kistermelés*, 1981. Central Statistical Office, 1983; I. Oros and M. Schindele, *Statisztikai Szemle*, no. 10 (1985).
11. S. Szalai (ed.), *Idö a mérlegen* (Gondolat, Budapest, 1978) p. 137.
12. People with a full-time job who work part-time in the second economy as well as women with a full-time job working many hours in the household.
13. *Politikai gazdaságtan tankönyv* (Budapest, 1956) p. 566.
14. F. Böszörményi – J. Timár, *A foglalkoztatás távlati tervezésének tapasztalatai* (1961–75) (National Planning Office, March 1976) p. 8.
15. For more details see J. Kornai, *The Economics of Shortage* (North-Holland, Amsterdam, 1980), and I. R. Gábor, *Közgazdasági Szemle*, no. 2 (1979).

16.   T. Iván Berend, *Gazdasági útkeresés*, 1956–65 (Budapest, 1983).
17.   J. Timár, *Planning the Labor Force in Hungary*, op. cit., pp. 1, 3–4.
18.   For information see G. Kővári and J. Timár, 'Manpower – Performance – Stimulation', *Papers on Labour Economics*, no. 1 (1985) pp. 1–15.
19.   J. Timár, 'Problems of Full Employment', *Acta Oeconomica*, nos. 3–4 (1983) p. 221. To put it in a similar way, Keynesian full employment in the capitalist system 'is that special condition of the labour market in which the volume of labour supply is almost identical for short transitional periods and is generally somewhat larger than the demand for labour, i.e. the difference being the number of frictionally and structurally unemployed.'
20.   The significance of this thesis which today appears to be trivial can only be evaluated when compared with the ideological constraints of the preceding decade and a half. According to the earlier concept the socialist enterprise was expected to keep in mind the requirement of full employment in its manpower policy, i.e. in the employment and selection (dismissal) of labour.
21.   This shows what a mistake it is to make a mechanical comparison of the open unemployment in the capitalist economy with the 'hidden unemployment' of the socialist one. The work time losses and the lower than possible productivity cannot be identified either theoretically or practically, or, for that matter, cannot even be compared with unemployment according to the internationally accepted definition of the term, or even with the 'under-employment' appearing in the developing countries. The truth is that this phenomenon is caused by a variety of factors and is manifest in an unsatisfactory labour intensity and productivity.
22.   *Magyar Közlöny*, 10 April 1976.
23.   Instruction No. 103, 1982, National Wages and Labour Office, *Munkaügyi Közlöny*, no. 8 (1982).
24.   Certain groups of workers are allowed to establish quasi businesses whose purpose is to perform certain work which could not be done during the official work time. The restrictions of central earnings regulations do not apply to these groups, thus it becomes possible for the large-scale enterprises to provide workers who are very important to them with an additional income which ties them to the enterprise. For more information see J. Timár, 'Interest Enforcement in Hungary: Possibilities and Strategies', in *Work Organization, Incentive Systems and Bargaining in Different Social and National Contexts* (Institut für Sozialforschung, Frankfurt am Main) November 1984.
25.   Editor's note: This is a euphemism for unemployment benefits.

# Part II

Part II

# 6 Similarities and Differences in the Treatment of Labour Shortages*

## JAN ADAM

The reasons for labour shortages and their treatment in individual countries are discussed in other chapters. This chapter is intended to be of comparative nature; it discusses the similarities and the differences in the reasons for labour shortages and their treatment, and the extent to which they reflect similarities and differences in the systems of management of the economy and their subsystems in the countries under review.

It is obvious that a comparative chapter cannot treat problems related to the topic in great depth. In a sense this chapter is based on the assumption that many problems which are tackled generally in it are discussed in greater detail in the country studies.

The chapter is limited primarily to four countries: USSR, Poland, Czechoslovakia and Hungary.

## I.  REASONS FOR LABOUR SHORTAGES

### 1.  Demographic and related factors

Some of the reasons for labour shortages, such as various forms of underutilization of labour which will be discussed later on, are not

* I wish to express my gratitude to the Social Sciences and Humanities Research Council of Canada for the extended research grant which has enabled me to work on this chapter.

new; they came into being in the process of building of the so-called socialism. The negative effects of underutilization of labour are felt so strongly because all the countries under review have achieved very high, almost maximum, employment participation rates and are exposed to an unfavourable demographic development.

Very high participation rates mean that potential labour resources are almost fully absorbed in the labour force, and that no meaningful reserves (such as housewives) exist which could be attracted into the labour force. It means also that the further supply of labour depends on the growth rates of the working-age population. And these, as was already indicated in preceding chapters, tend to decline – a tendency which will continue for some time.

In some countries the labour supply is also unfavourably influenced by changes in the participation rates of some groups in the population. In most countries the participation rates of young people are declining due to the extension of time needed for education and professional training.

The statistics of the 1970s in Hungary and Poland showed a declining trend in the male participation rates in the age groups of 40–60.[1] The reasons for this phenomenon are not entirely clear, but no doubt one of them is the increasing number of disabled people. There is a mounting suspicion that one of the main reasons for the growing number of disabled and the consequent declining participation rates was the attractiveness of working in the second economy. In many cases a disability enables the pension to be supplemented by moonlighting in the second economy, which pays well.[2]

In Czechoslovakia, Hungary and Poland the female participation rate has been unfavourably influenced by the introduction of a prolonged maternity-care programme, which allows an employed mother to stay at home with her baby for a certain length of time and to collect an allowance without losing claim to her job.[3] Approximately 10 per cent of the female labour force takes advantage of this programme.

In all the four countries people of pensionable age play an important role in the labour force. Of course, their proportion of the labour force and the trend in their participation rate are different in different countries. Three factors are primarily decisive – age structure, the amount of the old-age pension and pension rules. In the USSR the proportion of working pensioners has increased (see Chapter 9), whereas in Hungary and Poland an opposite trend has asserted itself.

In Hungary the gradual reduction of the retirement age for collective farmers to the level of other segments of the population,[4] combined with other factors, has contributed to a large drop in the share of people past retirement age in the labour force. In 1960 their share amounted to 6.4 per cent of the total population; in 1983 to 2.5 per cent.[5]

In Poland, increases in old-age pensions and a temporary reduction of the retirement age in 1981 to the level in the other three countries (60 for men and 55 for women) increased substantially the number of retirees in 1981 and 1982. The extension of the pension programme to private peasants from July 1980[6] has worked in the same direction. It is of interest to note that the increases in the numbers of retirees and of women on prolonged maternity leave combined with an expansion of the private sector were the most important factors which averted the unemployment threatened by the economic crisis.

In the past, agriculture played a great role in providing manpower for the rapidly expanding sectors of the economy. However, the great exodus from agriculture to other sectors is now a thing of the past. This is not to say that agricultural employment has already declined everywhere to a level characteristic of highly advanced countries with an efficient agriculture. A major release of labour from agriculture would require changes in the methods of production (Poland),[7] investments and better youth vocational training (USSR).[8]

On the demand side there is an important factor which makes the labour market situation worse. In all the four countries there is a tendency – in one stronger than in the others – to channel more labour to some branches of the service sector which have long been undermanned. Plans for increases in the standard of living, including changes in lifestyle, are conditional on an expansion of the service sector.

## 2. Underutilization of labour[9]

Many economists believe that, despite all the unfavourable factors mentioned, labour shortages could be handled – at least numerically, if not structurally – if enterprises could be induced to improve the level of labour utilization. It is generally accepted that an improvement in the planning and organization of the production process in its different aspects and in the production techniques used, namely by mechanizing auxiliary processes and administration, and a tightening of labour discipline, could release enough manpower to bridge the shortages.

## (a)    Strategy of economic development

There are many reasons for the underutilization of labour. To really understand the present state of labour underutilization one must go back to the end of the 1920s and beginning of the 1930s, when the objectives and strategy for building socialism were laid down in the USSR. Only two objectives related to the present topic will be mentioned, one being to overcome economic backwardness in the shortest possible time, which led the Soviets to embark on an ambitious industrialization drive. The second objective was the desire to eliminate open and disguised unemployment,[10] which was regarded as a product of capitalism.

This is not to say that both objectives were seen to have the same urgency. It seems that the first was regarded as more urgent. But in order to achieve it, a strategy was chosen which enabled the second objective to be accomplished as well.

The Soviets were short of capital but had an abundance of jobless workers, mainly unskilled. Therefore they followed a policy of applying the most advanced production techniques accessible to them to the basic production processes, and labour-intensive methods to auxiliary production processes and administration.[11] The Soviet planners apparently believed that this strategy would enable ouput to be maximized. The strategy of 'extensive growth' was understandable and reasonable under Soviet conditions. What is questionable, and caused gross inefficiencies, was the pace at which this strategy was carried out and its impact on the demand for labour.[12]

The demand for labour was strengthened by the fact that most of the investment funds were channelled into the construction of new factories and only a little into the modernization of the existing ones,[13] a policy which was even strengthened in the further process of industrialization.

This strategy adopted in the 1930s in the USSR has survived in substance up to now;[14] after the Second World War it was embraced by the East European countries.

In addition to generating great inefficiency this strategy had other unfavourable consequences. It resulted in a policy of low wages, egalitarianism (this refers primarily to East European countries) and low labour discipline.

Under conditions of a massive influx of labour into the economy during the period of the first 5-year plans average productivity could not be high. Many of the newly employed could not be put to the most productive use,[15] partly because they had first to be trained even for the simplest jobs (it should not be forgotten that a great many of them were peasants who were not familiar with factory work and its rhythm) and partly because tremendous organizational problems arose in placing people in suitable jobs. (And these were also the reasons why the usually favourable effect on productivity of a shift of workers from agriculture, mainly to industry, was largely missing here.) Even if these initial difficulties were gradually overcome, the great army of auxiliary workers and administrators which came into being as a result of the chosen techniques and administrative methods continued to grow and unfavourably affected productivity.[16]

Such a strategy of choice of production techniques could result only in low wages[17] (relative to national income per capita). The policy of low wages was naturally supported by the planners' obsession with maximum economic growth which was reflected in the distribution of national income by high investment ratios and by treating consumption as a residual. Therefore, it is no wonder that in all the countries under review real wages in the period of the first medium-term plans dropped.[18] Even when real wages started to increase in the following 5-year plan periods a policy of letting wages lag far behind productivity has been followed as a matter of principle. Departures from this policy came about in periods of high political tension or their aftermath, or in periods of economic reforms.[19]

The policy of low wages – as has been mentioned – was a result of the industrialization strategy. However, it was also used in later stages of industrialization to mobilize labour reserves, mainly among housewives, and thus served as a stimulus for the expansion of employment. In this function the policy has turned out to be a two-edged sword as it has also led to pressure being put on the authorities to create job opportunities, often simply for social reasons.[20]

Low labour discipline – which is reflected in non-utilization of official working time, absenteeism, malingering, violation of technological rules, etc. – is a further reason for underutilization of labour. It is generally known that the actual work-time fund lags far behind the potential. If the time losses caused by workers themselves (disregarding losses caused by planners) could be at least halved, a whole army of 'new' workers could be gained.

*(b) Labour hoarding*

Underutilization of labour also results from the tendency of enterprises to hoard labour. A low-wage policy is one of the reasons for labour hoarding, because it is a disincentive to the substitution of capital for labour (this is mainly[21] true after the economic reforms of the second half of the 1960s when enterprises' role in the decision-making over investment increased) and to an increase in productivity.

Low wages, combined with narrow wage differentials, act as a disincentive to increases in productivity and are one of the inducements to managers to solve the problem of fulfilling higher output targets by expanding employment.

There are also other reasons for underutilization of labour and labour hoarding which have already been mentioned in the individual country studies. Some of them, such as the uneven spread of the workload during the year and the months, a tendency to conceal reserves including labour reserves and the reluctance of enterprises to rely on cooperation with other enterprises for the fulfilment of output targets are the result of the traditional Soviet system of economic management and planning. The same is true of the obsession with economic growth and the resulting high investment activities which necessarily led to ineffective use of machines and labour.

In this connection the question can be raised: has the new Hungarian economic mechanism (NEM), which is substantially different from the administrative system of management, brought about an important change in the behaviour of managers with respect to utilization of labour? Judging from Hungarian economic literature the answer must be negative.[22] Hungary, like other countries under review, suffers from the above-mentioned phenomena. It seems that the fact that systemic differences have not produced different results as is the case in many other fields is due mainly to three reasons: the original objectives of NEM were not consistently implemented, the obsession with economic growth has abated only recently and, finally, managers only slowly change their attitudes and ways of thinking.

An increased control over employment in enterprises is, of course, also an incentive to hoard labour, regardless of the system of management. Yet the controls themselves, as will be shown later, are influenced by systemic differences.

The wage regulation and/or incentive systems may also be an impetus to hoard labour, not only in a centralized but even in a decentralized system, as experience shows. This has been the case with the wage regulation system in the USSR and Czechoslovakia where overfulfilment of targets is rewarded by allocation of funds on top of the planned wage-bill. For many enterprises this is an attractive venture since it allows allocations to the wage-bill to be achieved which are much higher than the additional labour costs. In many cases the overfulfilment of targets depends on the availability of labour reserves; and hence the stimulus to hoard labour. In other cases, the overfulfilment of targets makes funds available for wage payments to internal labour reserves.[23]

If average wages are regulated by setting each enterprise a target, or by establishing a general ceiling, enterprises will respond by trying to circumvent the ceiling by hoarding unskilled labour or part-time workers (as long as they are counted as full-time for average-wage purposes) who can be paid wages below average. This happened in Hungary after the introduction of NEM when a 4 per cent ceiling on wage increases was imposed.[24]

The Soviet incentive system, mainly in its 1965 form, can be regarded as a classic example of an incentive system being a stimulus to hoard labour. In this system the normatives for increases in indicators (sales, profitability) were expressed in terms of a percentage fraction of the wage-bill. Obviously this was a built-in incentive for enterprises to strive for higher employment because in this way the bonus fund could be increased.[25]

In addition, there is another incentive to hoard labour which has to do with the wage system but which in systemic terms is neutral. This is the fact that the size of enterprises in terms of employment is an important factor in all four countries in the determination of basic salaries and bonuses for top managers.

At the conclusion of this section it is important to stress that despite differences in the system of management between the countries under review there have not been up to now important differences in the causes of shortages of labour in individual countries. It is necessary to wait and see whether the new Hungarian reform of 1985 will bring about a change in this respect.

## II. PROVISIONS FOR COPING WITH LABOUR SHORTAGES

In the deliberations on how to treat the methods used for coping with labour shortages the author has been confronted with a choice: to discuss how individual countries try to cope with individual causes of underutilization of labour or to discuss the methods used according to their systemic character. The latter alternative has been chosen since it is more in line with the author's approach to the topic and because it makes it easier to follow his expositions.

The format of the chapter does not allow discussion of all the administrative and non-administrative methods used; therefore attention will be confined to the most important.

## 1. Administrative methods

With the introduction of central planning, employment became an integral part of the planning process. At the level of enterprises planning meant assignment of employment limits. Originally the assignment of limits aimed at making enterprises cost-conscious; only later on did it also become a tool for coping with labour shortages. The reforms of the second half of the 1960s (in Poland 1973) brought the assignment of limits to an end for a short transitional period. Whenever administrative methods are applied they are usually directed primarily against white-collar workers.

In the USSR, in accordance with the resolution of the Party and government of July 1979 on the improvement of planning and the economic mechanism starting with 1980 (thereafter called the Decree of July 1979), binding numerical limits for employment expressed in annual averages are handed down to ministries which in turn disaggregate them for associations and the latter for enterprises.[26] With this provision enterprises have been deprived of the right given them by the economic reform of 1965 to make decisions about the number of employed and their skill mix.

To cope with the reluctance of enterprises to substitute capital for labour the Soviets are using direct methods since previous resolutions, campaigns and targets in the national plans have not brought the expected results.[27] Starting with the eleventh 5-year plan (for 1981–5) enterprises for the first time were assigned targets for the reduction of manual labour, primarily heavy labour.[28]

In Czechoslovakia numerical limits for employment have been again assigned to enterprises since 1970,[29] soon after Dubček's leadership was toppled. This provision was an integral part of the dismantlement of the decentralized system of management. The adopted provisions for the improvement of management for the seventh 5-year plan (1981–5) envisaged a change in the Czechoslovak employment policy in the sense that numerical limits were to be set in absolute terms instead of increments as they were before. It seems that the central planners wanted to shift to 'a zero budgeting' by basing employment limits gradually on 'scientific' data, on norms of labour consumption.[30] To the surprise of many economists in 1982 the government abolished mandatory limits for employment in the hope that the built-in incentive in wage regulation would induce enterprises to increase labour economy.[31]

In Hungary selective controls over employment were introduced in 1976 and applied up to 1981 to a minority of enterprises; to those which were not supposed to increase their workforce or which were scheduled for a major reduction in employment or for liquidation. The last category (major reduction or liquidation) was allowed to hire labour only through placement agencies. These provisions were abolished in 1981 mainly for two reasons. It has turned out that the categorization was a far cry from an objective undertaking due to a lack of reliable data and to political influences.[32] The recent trend to decentralization which culminated in the reform of 1985 made administrative controls over employment unacceptable. The 1985 reform namely gave enterprises a free hand in determining the size of the workforce and its structure.

In 1976 employment limits were introduced in Poland; they were, however, not set formally as limits.[33] The Polish reform of 1982 which is supposed to be based on three principles with regard to enterprises – independence, self-financing and self-management – gave enterprises the right to determine the size of the workforce and its structure.[34]

One of the reasons for labour shortages is that white-collar work absorbs a large share of the labour force. It is a widely held view in the countries under review that the work to be performed primarily by administrative and managerial staff could be accomplished with a much smaller labour force.

All four countries tried and some try even now to curb growth, primarily of the administrative and managerial staff, by administrative methods. Hungary and Czechoslovakia on the one hand, and Poland and the USSR on the other, used quite similar methods. Starting from 1977 in Hungary following a freeze on the hiring of administrative and managerial staff, the number of administrative workers was limited (probably until 1981) to the ratio achieved by the end of 1975.[35] In Czechoslovakia, following recent experiments with an administrative reduction of workers, the government has been experimenting with the introduction of some permanent mechanism. The annual plan for 1979 set binding targets for the employment of technical–administrative workers in the form of a ratio of the labour force in all organizations of industry and construction. Apparently this approach did not turn out to be successful since, for the quinquennium 1981–5, the government set targets for the reduction of the administrative and managerial staff.[36]

Poland used and the USSR uses very simple administrative methods. The former from time to time ordered reductions in the number of employed whereas the latter sets annual targets[37] for reduction in numbers and in rubles (for more details see Chapter 1).

The enforcement of direct methods is not an easy task. Enterprises can always find a loophole if they wish. Overfulfilment of plan targets may be an excuse for exceeding the employment limits. Reclassification of some of the white-collar workers as manual workers is a good way to achieve the target, or part of it, without great effort.

## 2.   Indirect methods

Indirect methods aim at inducing enterprises to better utilize labour resources and thus to release labour for other enterprises and/or reduce the demand for labour in enterprises. To accomplish the first goal countries use provisions which make labour more expensive. The second goal is pursued through taxes levied on increases in employment above certain limits. Wage-regulation and incentive systems are supposed to serve both goals.

To achieve the goal of releasing labour it is necessary to have not only the cooperation of enterprises, but also the willingness of the workers – who are to be released – to take jobs which should be filled preferentially. If the principle of freedom of choice of job is to be sustained, incentives must be used.

In this study only indirect methods applied to enterprises as a whole will be discussed.

### (a)   Increases in labour costs

To undo the adverse effects of the strategy of economic development a change in the strategy is needed. This requires channelling a much greater share of investment funds into modernizing existing capacities and gradually eliminating the techniques of production and methods of administration which have produced great armies of auxiliary and administrative workers. The most difficult problem is how to make enterprises follow this policy. Some countries try to tackle this problem by indirect methods, by reversing the price relativities for labour and machinery. Since wage increases which would make a meaningful change in the price relativities are not a viable solution, the same goal can be achieved by making labour costs to enterprises much higher, or by reducing the price of machinery. An increase in labour costs can be made by levying a tax on the wage-bill and/or by increasing the social security contribution paid by enterprises.

It is not surprising that only Hungary and Poland take advantage of the first possibility. (In the USSR and to a lesser degree in Czechoslovakia it would not make a great deal of sense, for reasons which will be shown later.) Both countries introduced the tax on the wage-bill as part of their economic reforms (in Hungary in 1968 and again in 1985,[38] and in Poland in 1973 and 1982).[39] Czechoslovakia, in connection with the reform of 1966, introduced a tax on gross income which at the same time was a tax on wages. In 1969, this tax was replaced by a tax on profit.[40] Czechoslovakia continued, however, to levy a small tax on wage increases up to 1978.[41]

All four countries make enterprises pay social insurance charges. The USSR had until recently the lowest charge (7 per cent of the paid-out wages).[42] The 5-year plan for 1981–5 envisaged an increase in charges.[43]

The provisions to make labour more expensive in order to encourage enterprises to substitute capital for labour have had little effect. Labour costs are mostly only a small percentage of production costs. The inclusion of the tax on fixed assets in production costs in some countries has reduced their weight even more. Therefore, to make enterprises change their behaviour would require a huge increase in labour costs. The tax rate introduced on the wage-bill and the set social security contribution have been too small (even in Hungary where it amounts to an equivalent of 40 per cent of the wage-bill) to have this effect.

### (b)  Taxation as a tool for controlling employment

This tool is similar to provisions for increasing labour costs in that it also increases the cost of labour. The difference is that the tax on the wage-bill, or an increase in the social insurance contribution, refer to the active workforce, whereas the tax which is going to be discussed is applied primarily in the case of the expansion of employment.

Till lately only Poland used something similar to a tax on employment increases. It was a charge introduced in 1975, limited only to enterprises which converted to the new system of planning and financing and, like the payment for wage increases (which will be discussed later in this chapter), it was payable to the branch reserve fund.[44]

Taxation for controlling employment was used for the first time among the Soviet bloc countries in Czechoslovakia during the reform of 1966–9. Its purpose was to regulate employment indirectly at a time when enterprises were given the right to make decisions about employment and its structure.[45]

Hungary also used such a tax for a short period of time (in 1970); with its aid it tried to cope with the detrimental labour hoarding which was brought about by the previously mentioned ceiling on wage increases.[46]

To make such a tax an effective instrument, costs must be a decisive factor in the financial position of enterprises, to put it generally (this will be discussed later in greater detail). In addition it is questionable whether it would be correct to apply such a tax a cross the board. Once it is accepted that it should be applied discriminately great problems arise, since to find an objective criterion is more difficult here than even in the case of taxes on wage increases.

### (c)  Wage regulation

In this chapter the author will concentrate on one of the crucial components of wage regulation, the regulation of the wage-bill at the level of industrial enterprises; he will also discuss the incentive system very briefly.

In all these countries, the planners, when designing the wage-regulation and incentive systems, took into consideration that they should serve as an instrument for encouraging enterprises to economize on labour. This is more true of the Hungarian and Polish systems, mainly the first, than the two others under review. It should be borne in mind that in Hungary, because of NEM and now of the 1985 reform administrative tools of the kind Czechoslovakia and the USSR use cannot be applied without undermining the decentralized system; therefore wage regulation is attributed a great role in the endeavour to improve labour economy.

One would expect that the incentive system would play an even more important role than wage regulation (in the sense here defined) in the effort to enhance utilization of labour. Yet the practice is different; the incentive system is more indirectly and generally geared to the labour-economizing function.

Due to systemic differences in the management system of the economy there are also differences in the wage-regulation and incentive systems, and hence in the labour-economizing function built in to them.

The various aspects of both wage-regulation and incentive systems with great stress on systemic aspects have been discussed by the author in other studies.[47] Therefore, only general, comparative information on the systems up to 1981 – to the extent needed to make their impact on labour economy more understandable – will be given here. Yet greater attention will be devoted to the changes in the wage-regulation system as instituted in the 5-year plans for 1981–5 and their possible impact on labour economy.

*Wage regulation up to 1981*. The USSR and Czechoslovakia had and have similar systems which could be characterized as direct. Up to 1981 in both countries the planned wage-bill was assigned to enterprises by supervising bodies; in the USSR mostly in absolute terms and in Czechoslovakia mostly in relative terms. The actual wage-bill depended on the fulfilment of output targets measured by gross indicators – in the USSR mostly by gross value of output and in Czechoslovakia as a share of marketed output. Overfulfilment of the targets was rewarded by an additional allocation to the wage-bill.

The Hungarian system could be characterized as indirect with some qualification; whereas the Polish could be characterized as a mixed system. Both systems (the Polish one is considered here in the form in which it existed before the crisis of 1980) were marked by similarities but they also contained important differences. In neither of them was the wage-bill of enterprises directly assigned from the centre as it was and is in the USSR and Czechoslovakia: instead its growth over the previous year depended on the increase in performance over the previous year. Performance was measured in Hungary in terms of value-added and in Poland by a similar concept – output-added. In both cases the indicators were net and sales (not output) indicators.

Since 1971 Hungary had been using taxation as a second defence line for controlling wage growth. The concrete application of taxation underwent many changes. The original wage-regulation system introduced in Poland in 1973 was supposed to rely only on the linkage of the size of the wage-bill to performance. Faced with fast increases in wages and employment the planners modified the system in 1976 by introducing a charge on wage increases above planned targets and on employment increases. This charge quasi a tax was payable to the branch reserve fund and could be used by ministries for wage increases.

The wage-regulation systems, despite systemic differences, had some common features. In all four countries the wage-bill was regulated (in a few Hungarian enterprises average wages were regulated) and targets for average wage increases were not set. One could expect that this arrangement would prompt enterprises to economize on labour as a way to achieve higher wages per employee. In addition, in all the countries the size of the bonus fund was and is dependent on earned profit and thus there is another incentive for labour economy.

Despite these incentives enterprises did not display eagerness to save labour. There was one important reason – apart from specific reasons for each country – namely the reluctance of planners until recently to allow enterprises to use much of the savings resulting from labour economy for average wage increases. The planners' stand was motivated by the fear that such a policy might fuel inflation, widen wage differentials and even cause unemployment in some areas. It seems that ethical considerations also played a role. Not all enterprises have the same preconditions for labour saving. Many of the enterprises achieved their favourable position by disregarding the planners' instructions, by hoarding labour and by concealing reserves. Questions were asked: should they be rewarded for quasi-illegal activities? Would a reward not be an encouragment of anti-social behaviour? Would this not undermine belief in the justice of the system in enterprises which followed the instructions of the planners? For all these reasons countries on the one hand made provisions to encourage labour saving and on the other hand applied measures which acted in a contrary direction. [48]

*Wage regulation since 1981.* In connection with the new 5-year plans in all the countries an effort has been made to turn the wage-regulation system into a more effective tool for economizing on labour without, of course, making any substantial systemic changes. This trend, for understandable reasons has been the strongest in Hungary.

Already in 1976 quite an important change in wage regulation had occurred in Hungary: average wage regulation was to a great degree replaced by wage-bill regulation (combined at a certain level with average wage regulation which served as a built-in brake). The planners came to believe that this new mode of wage regulation would make enterprises more willing to save labour since a reduction in the number of employees would create funds for higher average wages.

The economic reform of 1985 again overhauled the wage regulation system, this time more radically. Apart from the centrally-controlled wage regulation (which also existed in the past) the reform introduced two new methods, one entirely new and the second more traditional. Both are regulated by progressive taxes; in the new method, taxes are levied on the level of earnings (wages plus bonuses) of each employee separately (hereafter REL) and in the second, taxes are paid on increments in earnings compared to the previous year (REI). REL is more tied to produced profit than REI; enterprises applying the latter in contrast to the former can maintain earnings of the previous year even if they cannot spare profit for payment of taxes.[49]

It is hoped that REL primarily would encourage enterprises to practice labour economy. In contrast to the past when authorities set strict limits on the use of savings from workforce reduction for earnings purposes, it seems that new enterprises will be free to use the savings as they wish. However, under conditions of labour shortages, enterprises which have enough profit may appreciate more labour reserves than savings from workforce reduction.

Hopes of enhanced labour economy also result from the government's hints about its resolve to tackle overemployment. This is to be achieved by a division of responsibility between government and enterprises; the former is to take care of full employment and the latter is to be concerned with economic efficiency.[50]

The Polish reform gave enterprises the right to determine the wage-bill. However its growth was supposed to be controlled by a progressive charge to a special fund (used for among other things, job creation and labour training). In order not to lose control over wage increases the planners in 1983 tied the growth of the wage-bill to net output. For each percentage increase in net output enterprises are allowed to increase the wage-bill by 0.5–0.8 per cent without charges.[51] One way to avoid payments of charges is to reduce the workforce, and the planners hope that enterprises will take this route.

The changes in the wage-regulation system in the USSR and CSSR effective from 1981 are similar to a great degree; of course, the Czechoslovak planners follow the Soviet pattern. In both countries the wage-bill is planned for 5 years and individual wage targets are assigned by the known method of disaggregation for individual years. What is perhaps even more important is that both countries have finally decided to drop in most cases gross value of output as a wage growth regulator and replace it by net output.

In the USSR in most branches of industry the wage-bill of enterprises was to depend on the wage normative for one ruble of output and the value of output. The normative was supposed to be a long-term one (for 5 years), differentiated for individual years (probably diminishing from year to year) and its magnitude determined by the planned productivity.[52]

Long-term normatives imply stability for a longer time preferably during a five-year plan. Such stability has a chance if at least the production plan and wholesale prices do not change. Therefore it is no surprise that the Soviets did not manage to maintain the long-term normatives, described above.[53]

Starting with 1984, the Soviets are experimenting with a slightly different system of wage-bill regulation. The growth of the wage-bill compared to the previous year depends on increases in an indicator, usually net output. The normative by which the increase in the wage-bill is determined is supposed to be stable.

The new normatives are different from the old in the sense that they are no longer linked to *planned* increases in output and productivity. In addition, what is interesting is that increases in the wage-bill are not linked to increase in output per employee (or to another productivity indicator). The only limitation is that the basic wage-bill (i.e. of the previous year) can be maintained only if labour productivity in the planned year is at least of the average level for the last five years.[54] In other words, the wage-bill can be stable if productivity does not decline. This also means a stimulus to reduction of the workforce since in this way more funds per employee are available for remuneration.

In Czechoslovakia, the relative system of wage-bill formation (wage-bill as a percentage share, now in net output) has been preserved. What is of importance for this study is that the absolute form of wage-bill formation has been expanded at the expense of the relative form; it is to be applied in all enterprises where the emphasis is on reduction in the labour force.[55]

Both the Soviet system (including the one in experimenting enterprises) and the Czechoslovak have built-in incentives for labour saving. In the Soviet system fund savings can be used for wage increases.[56] In the Czechoslovak system since 1982 all savings resulting from labour economy, regardless of whether they were planned or not, have belonged to enterprises.[57]

Whether the applied systems of wage regulation in the USSR will really provide the momentum for labour saving will depend to what extent and how the promised rewards are implemented[58] and how the normatives are handled. If the normatives change often, according to the considerations of the supervising authorities, as was the case in the past,[59] then no noticeable change in the behaviour of enterprises can be expected. The same is true of the Czechoslovak system with regard to the relative system of wage-bill formation, which is also based on a normative.

## (d)   Some remarks on the indirect methods

All the indirect methods have been partly evaluated already. Here some additional observations will be made which have a more general validity.

The willingness of central planners to allow enterprises to use a great part of the savings resulting from a better utilization of labour resources for wage increases is an important precondition for an improvement in labour economy but not a sufficient one. Even such willingness on the part of the planners may be frustrated if enterprises can find easier ways to achieve higher average wages. Keeping labour reserves at the given low labour costs still has its advantages.

In the author's opinion another precondition is no less, perhaps even more, important; this is the creation of an environment in which enterprises will be pushed to pursue efficiency to a much greater degree than they are at present. A close linkage of wage increases and bonuses to profit earned is essential in this regard but not decisive. (Of the four countries under review, Hungary and Poland fulfil this precondition and Czechoslovakia and the USSR have come closer to it with changes in the wage-regulation system in 1981.) What is more important is the extent to which enterprises' financial conditions are really dependent on their performance; that is, the extent to which enterprises are genuine autonomous economic units. And more precisely, with regard to our topic, this implies primarily two things.

Firstly it implies that the profit earned is quite a genuine reflection of performance. If enterprises can increase their profit without great effort, which is possible even in Hungary,[60] then it cannot be expected that a close linkage of wage growth and the size of the bonus fund to profit will really encourage enterprises to utilize labour more rationally.

Secondly, it implies that enterprises are allowed to use net profit according to their own consideration within the centrally set regulations, and the surrender rate of profit is such that it leaves profit for major investment. If enterprises must surrender the 'free remainder' of profit to the state as in the USSR,[61] or even if there is no carry-over of profit to the next year as it was in Czechoslovakia up to 1981,[62] then the linkage of wage growth and/or the size of the bonus fund to profit cannot act as a strong stimulus for labour economy. Needless to say, under such conditions a tax on the wage-bill in order to make labour more expensive, or a tax for increasing employment, cannot have a great impact on the behaviour of enterprises either; therefore the Soviets are correct in not using these methods. The Hungarian, Czechoslovak and Polish authorities set a tax on gross profit in advance and the remainder can be used by enterprises in the framework of existing regulations. Since 1976 Hungarian enterprises have been allowed to distribute net profit according to their own consideration, taking into account tax provisions.[63]

In the USSR and Czechoslovakia, and to a lesser degree in Poland, enterprises' decision-making about investment is quite limited.[64] In Hungary enterprises have formally a greater jurisdiction over investment decisions. Since the amount of profit remaining with enterprises was usually small for major investment projects, loans were sought from the National Bank. But these were available only with the consent of the supervising ministry, which in practice meant a limitation of the autonomy of enterprises.[65] It is necessary to wait and see how the greater autonomy given to enterprises in the 1985 reform will work out in practice.

The achievement of these two preconditions, particularly the first (the profit earned is a genuine reflection of performance), is impossible without a rational price system. None of the four countries has one nowadays (though Hungary in particular is making efforts in this direction) and this is also one of the reasons why the Hungarian system, though decentralized, cannot produce much better results in the area discussed than other countries.

## III.  CONCLUSION

It has been shown that the methods individual countries use for coping with labour shortages differ, but even where they are the same they vary in their application. In brief, the methods used no doubt reflect systemic differences in economic management. But as to the effectiveness of the methods there are no noticeable differences. None of them is very effective; the Hungarian methods have not proved to be much superior to the Soviet which reflect the most consistent traditional approach to the solving of economic problems. This is interesting since in many other spheres differences in methods are mostly coupled with differences in results.

From what has been said it is clear that the main key to the solution of the problems of labour underutilization and thus labour shortages lies in two areas, on the one hand – to put it generally – in making enterprises genuine autonomous economic units in the sense that their financial condition is solely dependent on their performance, a task almost unrealizable under existing conditions. On the other hand, timid efforts to change the strategy of economic growth must be replaced by more forceful ones in those aspects which have brought about the huge armies of auxiliary and administrative workers. And this is possible only as a result of a joint effort by the central authorities and enterprises on the basis of a well-thought-out plan. To turn such a plan into practice requires a new set of incentives not only for enterprises but also for employees who will be affected by these changes.

It is worthwhile noting that all the countries could ease labour shortages by raising the retirement age, which is relatively low in the East compared to the West, and by shortening the prolonged maternity leave programmes where such exist. A rise in the retirement age would be very unpopular politically, and it is doubtful whether the political leaders would want to take the risks involved. It seems that the central authorities prefer the use of incentives which have the advantage that they can be designed in a way to keep at work those people beyond retirement age who are needed in the labour force.

As is known, all the countries experience a period of substantial decelerated economic growth. This refers more to the small countries than the USSR. Labour shortages are only one of the reasons for this phenomenon; an even more important one is that small countries are forced to curtail imports because of balance-of-payments troubles (due to worsening terms of trade and indebtedness). It will require new research to find out how this new development will be reflected in enterprises' behaviour with regard to utilization of labour.

**Notes**

1.  L. Pongrácz, *Munkaügyi Szemle*, Supplement II (1977) and Panel discussion; *Gospodarka planowa*, no. 7–8 (1975) p. 411.
2.  J. Timár, *Közgazdasági Szemele*, no. 2 (1977) p. 132.
3.  J. Timár, 'The level of employment and its equilibrium in socialism', *Acta Oeconomica*, 4(2) (1969); L. Pachl, *Plánované hospodářství*, no. 12 (1976) and M. Kabaj, *Praca i zabezpieczenia spoleczne*, no. 1 (1980).
4.  See *A társadalom biztosításáról mindenkinek* (Budapest, publication of Népszabadság, no publication year is given).
5.  *SE, 1978*, p. 28; *Magyar Statisztikai Zsebkönyv*, 1983, p. 29.
6.  See M. Kabaj, *Życie gospodarcze*, no. 41 (1979) and Z. Glapa, *Gospodarka planowa*, no. 6 (1979).
7.  M. Kabaj, in a Polish panel debate on employment, *Gospodarka planowa*, no. 7–8 (1975).
8.  L. Sbytova, *Voprosy ekonomiki*, no. 6 (1979).
9.  Underutilization of labour – characterized by M. Bornstein as disguised unemployment or underemployment ('Unemployment in capitalist regulated market economies and in socialist centrally planned economies', *American Economic Review*, May 1978) – is not only a property of centrally planned economies.
10. See L. M. Danilov, in A. P. Volkov (ed.), *Trud i zarabotnaia plata v SSSR* (Moscow, 1975) pp. 160–3.
11. See also M. Ellman, 'Full employment – lessons from state socialism', *De Economist*, no. 4 (1979).
12. In the USSR in 4 years (1929–32) the total number of employed workers almost doubled; compared to the original 5-year plan it increased almost $2\frac{1}{2}$ times (see M. Dobb, *Soviet Economic Development since 1917* (London, 1966) pp. 239–40). Of course, such a rapid increase in employment dramatically reduced unemployment.
13. This policy was partly reversed in the last decade.
14. See also H. H. Höhmann and G. Seidenstecher, in H. H. Hohmann (ed.), *Arbeitsmarkt und Wirtschaftsplannung* (Cologne, 1977) p. 41.
15. A Polish economist talking about the first 6-year plan in Poland mentions that in many cases enterprises hired workers in such great numbers that the marginal value of output of the newly hired workers was very often less than the cost they incurred. W. Baka, *Gospodarka planowa*, no. 6 (1979).
16. E. L. Manevich (*Ekonomika i organizatsiia promyshlennogo proizvodstva* – henceforth *EKO* – no. 2, 1978) asserts that according to Soviet managers who visited West Germany, the productivity of basic workers in enterprises is equal in the Soviet Union to the German or even superior. But the level of productivity is reduced by the excessive number of auxiliary, service and technical personnel.
17. See also G. Kruczkowska, *Egalitaryzm a place* (Warsaw, 1979) p. 147.
18. The effects of the policy of low wages were mitigated by high employment opportunities.
19. See J. Adam, *Wage Control and Inflation in the Soviet Bloc Countries* (London, Macmillan, 1979) pp. 40–3.

20. Kruczkowska, op. cit., p. 148.

21. Even before the economic reforms enterprises had at their disposal some funds for so-called small, technical–organizational improvements. Had they been interested in the mechanization of auxiliary work, some progress could have been achieved.

22. F. Munkácsy, *Munkaügyi Szemle,* no. 8 (1978).

23. N. Gorovskii, *Sotsialisticheskii trud,* no. 2 (1980) p. 12.

24. L. Pongrácz, *Társadalmi Szemle,* no. 4 (1973) and A. Kemény, *Práce a mzda,* no. 3 (1971).

25. For more see J. Adam, 'The incentive system in the USSR', *Industrial and Labor Relations Review,* no. 1 (1973).

26. Gorovskii, op. cit., pp. 9 and 10.

27. See M. Ia. Sonin, *EKO,* no. 4 (1977); N. Rogovskii, *Planovoe khoziaistvo,* no. 9 (1977).

28. Gorovskii, op. cit., p. 13, and K. Golinowski and N. Grzeszkowicz, *Gospodarka planowa,* no. 12 (1979).

29. M. Bartos, *Práce a mzda,* no. 10 (1970) and V. Bakajsa, *Práce a mzda,* no. 9 (1976).

30. See Supplement to *Hospodářské noviny,* no. 11 (1980).

31. K. Ujházy, *Plánované hospodářství,* no. 8 (1982).

32. See *Munkaügyi Szemle,* supplement i–ii (1976); *Magyar Közlöny,* no. 7 (1976); *Magyarország,* no. 2 (1977) and J. Czender and P. Mátyás, Munkaügyi Szemle, no. 2 (1981).

33. M. Rybak in A. Sajkiewicz (ed.), *Ekonomika pracy* (Warsaw, 1977) p. 81, and A. Kierczynski, *Swoboda decyzji w organizacjach przemysłowych* (Warsaw, 1979) p. 181. K. Golinowski (*Gospodarka planowa* no. 9 (1977)) maintains that there are no limits in the material sphere.

34. W. Baka, *Hospodářské noviny,* nos. 51–52 (1984).

35. E. Vincze, *Munkaügyi Szemle,* no. 12 (1976) and *Munka,* no. 1 (1977).

36. For more see J. Adam, *Employment and Wage Policies in Poland, Czechoslovakia and Hungary since 1950* (London, Macmillan, 1984, and New York, St Martin's Press, 1984), p. 183.

37. *Ekonomicheskaia gazeta,* no. 10 (1980) p. 16.

38. In 1985 the tax was set at 10 per cent of the wage-bill payable from profit after taxation. See *Magyar Közlöny,* no. 47 (1984).

39. In 1982 the tax was set at 20 per cent of paid out wages. See *Dziennik Ustaw,* no. 7 (1982).

40. See J. Valach, *Finance a finanční rozhodování průmyslových podniků* (Prague, 1972) p. 142.

41. M. Pick, *Finance a úvěr,* no. 4 (1978).

42. See V. Sitnin, *Chistii dokhod* (Moscow, 1974) p. 172.

43. Decree of July 1979, Supplement to *Hospodářské noviny,* no. 34 (1979) p. 14.

44. B. Gliński *et al., Zmiany w systemie zarządzania* (Warsaw, 1975) p. 59.

45. For more see J. Adam, *Wage, Price and Taxation Policy in Czechoslovakia, 1948–1970* (Berlin, 1974) pp. 154–7.

46. J. Bokor, *Pénzügyi Szemle,* no. 12 (1973).

47. J. Adam, *Wage Control ...,* op. cit., pp. 57–102; 'Systems of wage

regulation in the Soviet Bloc', *Soviet Studies*, no. 1 (1976); 'The present incentive system in the USSR', *Soviet Studies*, no. 3 (1980).

48.  The measures have been discussed by me in greater detail in the following papers: 'Labor shortages in Hungary and their treatment', *Osteuropa Wirtschaft*, no. 1 (1981); together with J. Cekota, *Revue d'etudes comparatives Est-Ouest*, no. 4 (1980), and Employment and Wage Policies in Poland, Czechoslovakia and Hungary since 1950, op. cit.

49.  R. Borlói, *Munkaügyi Szemle*, no. 11 (1984); L. Pongrácz, in M. Pulai and F. Vissi (eds.), *Gazdaságirányitás 1985*, (Budapest, 1984).

50.  See A. Rácz, *Figyelö*, no. 27 (1984).

51.  M. Kabaj, *Ekonomika i Organizacja Pracy*, no. 5 (1984).

52.  See 'Methodological guidelines for the determination of long-term normatives for wages in one ruble of production', *Sotsialisticheskii trud*, no. 2 (1980).

53.  V. Rzheshevskii, *Planovoe khoziaistvo*, no. 6 (1984).

54.  V. Rzheshevskii, *Sotsialisticheskii trud*, no. 5 (1984).

55.  For more see *Práce a mzda*, no. 11–12 (1980) pp. 571–6.

56.  See Decree of July 1979, Supplement to *Hospodárské noviny*, no. 34 (1979) p. 14.

57.  E. Moravec, *Plánované hospodářství*, no. 9 (1981).

58.  If the Shchekino experiment is any indication, the chances are not good. As Iu. Margulis (*Finansy SSSR*, no. 1 (1979)) indicates, some ministries used part of the savings of enterprises working according to the Shchekino method to cover the overdraft of the wage-bills of other enterprises.

59.  I. Slavnyi, *Dengi i kredit*, no. 3 (1980) p. 41.

60.  L. Gyetvai, *Figyelö*, no. 19 (1980).

61.  *Ekonomicheskaia gazeta*, no. 23 (1980).

62.  See supplement to *Hospodářské noviny*, no. 11 (1980).

63.  O. Gadó. *Közgazdasági szabályozó rendszerünk* (Budapest, 1976).

64.  It is not yet clear how the provisions of the 1982 reform in Poland will manifest themselves in practice.

65.  R. Nyers and M. Tardos, 'Enterprise in Hungary before and after the economic reform', *Acta Oeconomica*, **20** (1–2) (1978).

# 7 Displacement by Technological Progress in the USSR (Social and Educational Problems and their Treatment)

ANNA-JUTTA PIETSCH,
HEINRICH VOGEL
GERTRUDE SCHROEDER

## I. INTRODUCTORY REMARKS

The labour force of industrialized nations is subject to a constant process of restructuring. This is true for Western industrialized societies as well as for the Soviet Union. The origins of this process are to be found in two interrelated developments:

(1) Technological progress leads to an increase in labour productivity. This means that the same quantity of goods is produced with fewer workers because the output capacity of capital equipment is increased, or certain jobs are no longer needed due to mechanization and automation.
(2) The increasing national product brought about mostly by rising labour productivity is, as a rule, not used in the same way as the national product generated in the past. As individual and collective prosperity of the nation increases, the structure of demand for goods and services changes likewise.

Under ideal circumstances, the jobs lost as a result of the two processes described above are compensated by the creation of new jobs in the same or other production units. In most cases, however, this process does not run smoothly. In Western industrialized nations, demand cannot expand fast enough to keep up with the increase in

149

labour productivity. This gives rise to structural unemployment. In the Soviet Union quite the opposite is the case. The rhythm of labour displacement,[1] defined as the number of workers set free by technological change in relation to total employment per annum, lags behind the demand of expanding factories and branches for additional manpower.

Characterized by an increasing labour shortage, this peculiar Soviet situation, which will be aggravated by the fact that the growth rate of the civilian labour force is going to drop in the 1980s by approximately 50 per cent in comparison with its level in the 1970s, allows two hypotheses to be formulated:

(1) The rhythm of displacement is very slow in the Soviet Union compared with other industrialized countries;
(2) The rhythm of displacement is constantly overestimated by ambitious Soviet planners.

In order to test these two hypotheses an attempt is made in the first section of this chapter to analyse the magnitude of manpower displacemet in the Soviet Union. The displacement process deserves our interest, however, not only with respect to its dimensions, but also because of its social effects. Section II of the chapter, therefore, is dedicated to the organizational and legal framework developed in the Soviet Union to protect workers against the possible negative effects of this process and to guarantee their employment if they are dismissed from their enterprise.

Social effects of technical change are not, however, limited to concrete cases of displacement. Technical change in the long run affects the working conditions of the labour force as well as the qualifications needs of the society. These effects will be analysed in the third part of the chapter, which will deal in particular with educational problems related to technological progress and their solution in the Soviet Union.

## II. QUANTITATIVE ASPECTS OF MANPOWER DISPLACEMENT IN THE SOVIET UNION

In the USSR, unlike most Western countries, there are no representative empirical studies on the overall rate of displacement.[2] In the Soviet case we only find some analyses of regional coverage as well as studies on individual enterprises. One of the best-known, cited by Aitov[3] and Baranenkova[4], was done in the Bashkir region. It was based on interviews with 1002 displaced workers, the documentation being organized by the respective enterprises which were selected from several industrial branches. According to this study the annual rate of displacement in 1968 was 1 per cent. However, Aitov does not consider this result representative of industry as a whole. In view of this lack of representative studies one can gain some insight into the dynamics of displacement by looking at changes in sectoral occupation and in the structure within industry. This is done in Tables 7.1 and 7.2.

*Table 7.1*   Employment trends by sectors in the USSR (manpower per sector as percentage of total manpower)

|  | 1913 | 1940 | 1950 | 1960 | 1965 | 1970 | 1975 | 1980 |
|---|---|---|---|---|---|---|---|---|
| Primary sector (agriculture) | 75 | 54 | 48 | 32 | 31 | 25 | 23 | 20 |
| Secondary sector (industry and construction) | 9 | 23 | 27 | 35 | 36 | 38 | 38 | 39 |
| Tertiary sector (services, including trade and transport) | 16 | 23 | 25 | 33 | 33 | 37 | 39 | 41 |

*Source:* Authors' calculations based on *NK 1980* and *1967*.

Table 7.1 shows that in the Soviet Union, as in all industrialized countries, employment in the primary sector has been decreasing in favour of the secondary and tertiary sectors. Compared with employment trends in industrialized Western countries, employment in agriculture is still quite high in the Soviet Union (21 per cent of all persons employed versus 5.5 per cent[5] in the FRG in 1979), whereas occupation in the secondary and tertiary sectors is relatively low (39 and 40 per cent), with the corresponding figures for the FRG being 45 and 50.5 per cent in the same year. The high proportion of the working population in agriculture indicates a relatively abundant displacement potential for the coming decades. It should be remembered, however, that because of its structural peculiarities and its different role in the international division of labour, the Soviet Union

*Table 7.2*  Employment trends by branches of Soviet industry

| | Employment in 1980 (1960 = 100) | Branch-employment as percentage of total industrial employment | |
| --- | --- | --- | --- |
| | | 1960 | 1980 |
| All industries | 163 | 100 | 100 |
| 1. Branches with high increases in employment (more than 50%) | | | |
| Chemical and petrochemical | 241 | 3.5 | 5.2 |
| Machine-building and metalworking | 215 | 31.9 | 41.9 |
| Electric power | 197 | 1.8 | 2.1 |
| 2. Branches with moderate to low increases in employment (10–50%) | | | |
| Food industry | 146 | 9.6 | 8.6 |
| Construction materials | 145 | 7.0 | 6.2 |
| Light industry | 137 | 17.1 | 14.4 |
| Ferrous metallurgy | 133 | 4.6 | 3.8 |
| 3. Branches with stagnating or decreasing employment (10% and less) | | | |
| Timber, woodworking, and pulp and paper | 103 | 11.9 | 7.6 |
| Fuels | 100 | 6.9 | 4.2 |

*Source:* Computed on the basis of S. Rapawy *Civilian Employment in the USSR: 1950 to 1983*, Center for International Research, Bureau of the Census, U.S. Department of Commerce, Washington D.C., CIR Staff Paper No. 10, August 1985, p. 3.

cannot be expected to follow the same development patterns as the FRG. In particular, employment in agriculture may only go down slowly if the Soviet Union continues to try to reach and maintain autarchy in food production. Indeed, the share employed in the primary sector was the same in 1983 as in 1980.

As we can see from Table 7.2, the only industrial branch with decreasing employment was the fuel sector (due to the reduction in coal-mining); all other branches experienced increasing employment. This branch, however, accounts for only a small proportion of total employment.

Looking at industry as a whole, one would expect much displacement there. Yet aggregate industry is far too global a concept to permit any accurate appraisal. Displacement takes place not only in branches with decreasing employment; branches with expanding employment also release manpower as a result of technological change. In order to analyse the process of displacement on a more disaggregated level, it seemed useful to adopt a model developed by Lutz and Weltz.[6] Using the census data on changes in the employment structure of the FRG, they calculated how many jobs had been eliminated between the censuses of 1951 and 1960, also taking into account the regional decline in jobs, in so far as this was not reflected in the change in employment structures in the national average. (The increase in jobs on the national average may be made up, for example, of a decrease in jobs of this type in region A and a more than compensating increase in region B.) The total number of jobs actually lost is then related to the total working population and converted into annual rates.

The same process can be applied to the Soviet Union for the period 1959–70. Unfortunately the latest census of 1979 still cannot be included because the data on the occupational structure are not yet published for this year. With respect to the accuracy of the displacement rate calculated by this method two caveats are necessary. Because census data are usually collected every 10 years, only long-term changes in the employment structure can be traced. This may be of minor importance in the case of the Soviet Union which up to now has not had a record of unemployment cycles. The second and more serious caveat regards the job classification used in Soviet census material. Some of the trade categories cover individual trades such as smiths, carpenters and the like. Other categories, however, comprise a group of individual trades as, for example, 'railway repair workers'. An increase in the number of employees in this group could be made up, for instance, by a decrease in the number of maintenance mechanics and a greater increase in the number of maintenance electricians. This means that one gets only a minimum rate of displacement by using census data. But even this minimum rate might be interesting, especially when compared with the non-representative rates of displacement one can find in Soviet studies or with rates calculated for other countries. Comparability in the latter case may, however, exist only in a very limited way.

If one looks at the loss of jobs on the basis of the census statistics of 1959 and 1970,[7] it is striking that branches with declining employment were not the only ones affected. Even rapidly growing sectors such as mechanical engineering displaced manpower. This displacement is, however, more than compensated by the creation of new jobs. Of course, the highest displacement figures were attained in agriculture (as already shown in Table 7.1), which accounted for 71 per cent of all jobs eliminated. Second place, after a wide margin, is held by the group of transportation workers without any specialized skills. The jobs lost in this sector of the economy made up 7 per cent of the overall job reduction. The same percentage was covered by the reduction in traditional handicrafts such as blacksmiths, carpenters, coopers, weavers, tanners, furriers, saddlers, millers and cobblers. Manpower displacement in all other trades was relatively insignificant.

Adding together the figures for all these declines in employment, we find that on the average for the entire Soviet Union approximately 18.5 million jobs were eliminated between 1959 and 1970.[8] If further regional manpower displacement is taken into account, which was not included in the above average, a total figure of 20.3 million cases of lost employment[9] can be obtained.

Relating this figure to the average working population in the period under consideration, one obtains an annual displacement rate of 1.72 per cent. This rate is somewhat higher than the 1 per cent cited by Aitov, and may confirm his warning not to consider his study to be representative. If one tries to compare the Soviet rates with figures calculated by the same method for the FRG it turns out that they are within the same order of magnitude. The figures for the German displacement process are given as 1.3–1.5 per cent for men and 2.0–2.2 per cent[10] for women. They cover the period between 1950 and 1961. An American study based on a representative sample of interviews undertaken in the late 1960s arrived at an annual rate of displacement of 2–3 per cent of the labour force.[11]

It seems, therefore, that the rate calculated for the Soviet Union is in no way extraordinary even if in reality it must have been higher, for the reasons mentioned above.[12] Whether, as Baranenkova argues,[13] this displacement rate can be increased significantly does not depend so much on additional investment. According to an econometric study by R. Uffhausen,[14] a change in the sectoral investment pattern would have only a very marginal displacement effect. On the other hand a further increase in the already extremely high Soviet investment quota of roughly 25 per cent of the national income is not feasible.

An increase in the manpower displacement process is conceivable, if at all, only as the result of a fundamental transformation of the system of economic planning and management, the incentive system, labour organization, etc.[15]

Summarizing our findings about the quantitative aspects of the displacement process in the Soviet Union we can state that it is not particularly low in comparison with other countries, such as the United States, which are already experiencing increasing unemployment with similar rates of displacement. Thus labour shortages in the Soviet Union cannot be explained by low rates of displacement in absolute terms. This gives even more credit to the opinion already mentioned that the reasons for Soviet labour shortages must rather be looked for on the demand side, a point we cannot deal with in this chapter.

## III. PROBLEMS RESULTING FROM DISPLACEMENT FOR WORKERS AND ENTERPRISES

The rate of displacement mentioned above does not appear dramatically high with respect to the labour force affected by it, if we consider the intergeneration exchange and the high level of voluntary labour turnover in the Soviet Union. In the period under consideration, in many of the declining occupations there was a higher than average proportion of elderly workers in 1959[16] (agriculture, service sector, handicrafts). If one adds the maximum number of employees that could possibly have left the declining occupations because of age, we arrive at a total of 9.5 million people, which implies that about half the work force displaced could have coincided with persons retiring from working life.

The amount of displacement seems even less problematic if we compare it with the high rates of labour turnover[17] in the Soviet Union. In Soviet industry they reached 19.6 per cent in 1959, 21 per cent in 1970 and 18.9 per cent in 1975. In construction the turnover rate averaged 27 per cent, for the service sector a figure of 25 per cent has been quoted for 1974.[18] Voluntary mobility is thus many times higher than that caused by economic and technological necessity.

Another point contributing greatly to the alleviation of displacement problems is the fact that a high percentage of the workers set free by technological change can get new jobs in the same factory, mostly after retraining. In the study of displacement in the Bashkire region already mentioned, Aitov indicates this proportion as 80 per cent.[19] Sonin[20] refers to the displacement process organized by the

Ministry of Ferrous-metal processing between 1971 and 1975, when only 40 per cent of the displaced workers remained on in the same factory, as a highly untypical instance, stating that normally the great majority of displaced workers continue to work in the same factory.

All the same, manpower displacement problems are not solved of their own accord in the Soviet Union. The workers affected by displacement need not necessarily be identical to those who will retire or have decided to change jobs anyway; and even those getting new jobs in the same factory sometimes have to accept less favourable conditions especially with respect to wages. Thus Baranenkova[21] refers to the case of the Kuybishevski rubber factory where 18.2 per cent of those displaced but staying in the same factory did less qualified work after displacement. In Aitov's example, 33.8 per cent[22] of the workers displaced suffered a wage reduction in their new jobs. This happened especially with workers who had done very strenuous physical work before displacement for which they had received extra payments to compensate for bad working conditions. Workers could do better,[23] if they changed factories; but some, especially displaced women who mostly do unskilled work,[24] cannot move easily because of their families.

On the whole one can see that Soviet literature on displacement concentrates much more on the question of how displacement can be increased, than on the problems arising for workers through this process. This attitude corresponds to the neglect in Soviet legislation of financial compensation for displaced workers. Allowances are paid only in case of retraining in the same factory during a maximum period of 6 months. This allowance, however, does not take into account premium, bonuses, or fringe benefits related to the old job.[25] Those who are assigned to new enterprises are paid only the equivalent of 2 weeks' average wages plus moving expenses.[26] They will also suffer a reduction in premiums, bonuses, and additional pension payments and extra holidays to which they are entitled after a certain number of years worked without interruption in the same factory.[27]

Since only poor financial compensation for displaced workers is offered, labour regulations and comments in legal literature[28] are quite strict about the obligations of the management which wants to displace workers as a consequence of rationalization. It is the managers' obligation to look for new positions first within the same enterprise, to ensure programmes of retraining and of increasing qualification of workers in coordination with the Labour Offices.[29] The necessity of rationalization measures which result in displacing workers has to be proved in detail.[30] The termination of employment contracts is considered legal only if:

(1) the displacement of trades by technological progress, mechanization and automation is economically justified;
(2) the worker to be displaced has no preferential rights according to legal regulations;
(3) the management has offered retraining in the enterprise and this has been refused by the respective worker or employee;
(4) the executive committee of the enterprise's labour union organization has agreed;
(5) there is no vacancy in the enterprise or the worker declines to change to the new post;
(6) the Local Labour Office offers a new job in a new enterprise.

These regulations leave the enterprises with a heavy burden, especially considering that the network of exchange offices which should assist management in finding new jobs for displaced workers is far from satisfactory.

It was only at the end of the 1960s that the Soviet authorities realized that leaving the reallocation of manpower to the spontaneous action of displaced employees was highly inefficient under conditions of an increasing demand for skilled labour. With workers being granted the right of free choice of the job the arrangement for placement of labour remains within the competence of individual enterprises. Planning and supervising institutions set the conditions for planning manpower and wage-funds. Under the economic reform of 1965 a new approach became necessary: a decree of the Council of Ministers of December 1966 instituted a 'State Committee for the Utilization of Labour Resources' which for the first time was to monitor and control placement arrangement on the republican level with regional sections (Otdeli) and local offices (Biuro po trudoustroistvu i informatsii naseleniia). In 1977 the number of local offices (in the USSR mostly towns with over 100 000 inhabitants) reached 372.[31] The total number of towns of this size in 1979 was 277, of which 45 had more than 500 000 and 22 more than 2 million inhabitants.[32]

The reallocation of labour displaced by rationalization and related measures is explicitly mentioned as one of the major tasks of the new State Committee.[33] In practice, however, the effectiveness of this work suffered substantially from the lack of specialized personnel, the

limitation of the Committee's jurisdiction and insufficient information from enterprises.[34]

A reform in 1976 not only changed the appellation of the (republican) State Committees – now 'State Committees for Labour' – but
also put them under the direction of the All-Union 'State Committee
for Labour and Social Problems' (Goskomtrud). The previous sections are renamed 'Labour Administrations', the local offices are now
called 'Offices for Labour Redistribution'. The authority of the new
State Committees was expanded in the field of controlling actual
utilization, including mechanization and rationalization measures,
retraining of workers whose trades have become obsolete, and participation in setting up plans of social development (social'noe planirovanie).[35] The Administrations have the right to interfere directly where
hiring and displacement of labour are inadequate or run counter to
obligatory regulations and plans regarding manpower utilization or
social conditions of the population. The main thrust of these
measures is to reduce turnover in the number of workers and the
enticement of labour from one enterprise to another, but at the same
time new responsibilities for the reallocation of displaced labour are
assumed.

The publication of a Standard Statute for the Offices of Labour
Redistribution in April 1979[36] marks the beginning of a phase of
consolidation. The tasks of the Offices are enumerated, their powers,
including the right of inspection irrespective of the organizational
subordination of the production unit or administration under investigation are defined in great detail. Though displacement is not
explicitly mentioned in the Standard Statute, the Offices are 'to
participate in all activities of executive committees of the local
councils of deputies [soviety deputatov] aiming at the perfection of the
reallocation of labour'.

As a rule the activities of the Offices are limited to arrangements
within their regional competence. The Standard Statute does not even
mention procedures for interregional coordination with other offices.
If there is such a thing, the regional and interregional redistribution
by means of the new labour administration obviously takes lengthy
ways due to their vertical bureaucratic structures during the planning
procedures.

In view of the still underdeveloped organizational structures and
fragmentary legal framework for redistribution of displaced manpower it is not surprising that managers prefer to keep displaced
workers within the factory even in cases where they are required for

vacancies in expanding sections of production.[37] This behaviour of the managers is, however, strongly criticized in Soviet literature. Time and again Shchekino is held up as a positive example to managers, most of whom are reluctant to set workers free. But there is a whole complex of organizational, technical, economic and psychological problems which must be solved before the Shchekino model can be generally introduced. Baranenkova[38] mentions, for example, the fact that the level of management remuneration still depends on the number of workers, and bonuses on overfulfilling the plan for realized output, and that scientific work norms must be introduced before the model is adopted, etc. Therefore the famous experiment launched in 1967[39] has since spread to only about 2000 other enterprises.[40] The general economic reform Decree of July 1979 has attempted, apparently without notable success, to spread the principles of the Shchekino experiment throughout industry and to other sectors of the economy.

## IV. TECHNICAL PROGRESS AND QUALIFICATION REQUIREMENTS

Repercussions of technical change, generating the displacement process, go far beyond the problems of reintegration of displaced workers. Technical change affects the working and living conditions of the labour force in the broadest sense. For this reason, great importance has been attached in all industrialized societies to the question concerning the direction of this change, since major decisions in the field of social and educational policy are contingent upon this question being answered. In the postwar years, in Western industrialized nations as well as in the Soviet Union, it was taken for granted that technological progress would lead to qualitative improvement in working conditions and to an increase in skill requirements.[41] In the 1970s this appraisal was shaken in many Western nations. Empirical studies of the working environment in industry[42] had established an increase in unskilled repetitive work for a large part of the labour force. Only for a small proportion of the working population (repair and maintenance personnel) had the level of skills needed been raised. The results of these studies also noted the fact of structural unemployment even among qualified manpower, who were graduating from colleges and universities in great numbers as a result of educational expansion. This led to a less optimistic view of the effects of technological progress as a means of improving working conditions.

In the Soviet Union, however, the dominant opinion[43] continues to be that technical change has positive effects on working conditions and qualification requirements. From this appraisal the conclusion was drawn that it was necessary to expand education in order to prepare the labour force for increasing qualification requirements.

The expansion of education, as in most Western countries, primarily took the form of a rapid increase in general education, whereas vocational education for the skilled workers' level, as provided in the so-called vocational-technical schools, was neglected. This educational policy in the meantime led to a growing discrepancy between the career plans of the better-educated younger generation and the occupational possibilities offered to them. However, this situation has not generated fundamental doubts about the positive effects of technical change. Instead the problems were attributed to an overly pronounced orientation of the younger generation to university studies, and to the fact that vocational training and orientation had been weak points in the Soviet educational system. At present, attempts are being made to correct this structural imbalance.

If one tries to form an independent opinion of the qualification trends in technical change in the Soviet Union there are, as in most countries, only few reference materials to study. Very illustrative but not representative are the few examples which show qualification structure and qualification needs before and after displacement.

In the Aitov example already mentioned, we learn that the majority of displaced workers had done unskilled manual work before displacement and that the transition to less qualified jobs after displacement is really a rare phenomenon.[44] Less favourable is the case quoted by Baranenkova,[45] in which 18.2 per cent of the displaced workers performed less skilled work afterwards. However she concentrates on those workers who stayed in the same factory after displacement. Had she made a wider sampling of displaced workers, the overall picture might have been more favourable.

These cases, however, are not representative. If one looks for overall data on changes in the qualification pattern one has to confine oneself to data on the occupational structure derived from census data. Studying changes in the occupational structure, H. Wiegmann[46] discovered that between 1959 and 1970 the educational level of workers doing mainly manual work was below average in declining occupations[47] while it was above average in expanding occupations.[48]

Less clear-cut were the results obtained for the category of employees doing mainly intellectual work. Part of the expanding occupations in this category are not occupations requiring above-average education.[49] Yet this category, which as a whole shows a much higher level of education than the category of mainly manual work, is increasing its share in total occupations, with the result that the average educational level of the total labour force is augmented. Assuming that the educational level can be considered an indicator for the qualification level, which is normally accepted,[50] the overall effect of technological change as reflected by the occupational structure has been in favour of higher skill levels.

It might be interesting to note that West German scientists[51] obtained similar results for the period between 1950 and 1961. Since 1960, however, the German development has become more heterogeneous. It has been characterized by a strong increase in unskilled auxiliary jobs, whereas among declining occupations jobs with a high qualification level, such as management personnel and company accountants, can be found. It therefore seems possible that the Soviet Union in the years under consideration went through a period which is comparable with the pre-1961 phase in the FRG. However, this point would have to be corroborated by further studies. It will be especially interesting to investigate occupational changes between 1970 and 1979 after publication of the census data for 1979, but such data had not been published as of the end of 1984.

On the whole, Soviet development thus corresponded to the opinion held by Soviet scientists as to the positive effect of technical change on qualification needs, at least in that period.

As Soviet education policy was based on this appraisal, it is striking that the problem of discrepancy already mentioned between the educational and the occupational systems should have arisen. This phenomenon would become clearer if one could compare the pace of change in the educational level with that of the occupational structure. This, however, is rather difficult to do. The figures published by the Central Bureau of Statistics regarding changes in degree of mechanization of jobs in industry and construction give some indication about the situation in trades. These figures (see Table 7.3) show a surprisingly high proportion of jobs requiring purely manual labour (Group 4). This proportion decreases very slowly while the share of Group 1 increases at about the same pace. As to the qualifications required in these two large groups: as the numbers in Group 4 decrease, so does heavy physical labour that requires very low or no

*Table 7.3* Jobs in industry and construction by degree of mechanization (shares of total employment in percentages)

| | (1) Employees working on machines or supervising automatic equipment (%) | (2) Employees engaged in repairing, fitting and maintaining machinery (%) | (3) Manual work with machines (%) | (4) Manual work without machines (%) |
|---|---|---|---|---|
| INDUSTRY | | | | |
| 1959 | 36.0 | 9.5 | 9.0 | 45.5 |
| 1965 | 40.3 | 11.2 | 7.9 | 40.6 |
| 1972 | 44.3 | 12.6 | 7.1 | 36.0 |
| CONSTRUCTION | | | | |
| 1959 | 20.3 | 1.3 | 8.4 | 70.0 |
| 1965 | 27.3 | 2.8 | 9.4 | 60.1 |
| 1972 | 34.2 | 3.6 | 10.0 | 52.2 |

*Source:* E. V. Klopov *et al.* (eds), *Sotsial'noe razvitie rabochego klassa SSSR* (Moscow, 1977) p. 238.

qualifications at all.[52] The increase in Group 1 is linked to different requirements of qualifications. On the one hand, there is an increase, within this group, of monotonous repetitive piecework requiring few or no skills.[53] On the other hand, this group also includes skilled workers, who must necessarily have completed training in the trade.[54] However, the increase in the relatively sparse Group 2 means added skill requirements, since the work in this group can only be done by well-trained specialized workers. Group 3 comprises mainly semi-skilled occupations that are not particularly demanding.

Processes of dequalification can hardly be deduced from this development, particularly since it is possible to draw upon the reserves of unskilled labour in Group 4 in order to cover the monotonous jobs in Group 1. These workers consider the transition from heavy physical labour to the so-called clean assembly-line jobs an improvement in working conditions. However, the real problem is the slow decrease in Group 4, so that, in fact, there has been an absolute increase in this type of job. At the same time the group of workers with a very low educational level, who therefore must be the most willing to take on work of this type, is decreasing rapidly.

Unfortunately the Central Statistical Office does not provide figures on the educational level of workers occupied in the different groups; therefore no exact comparison is possible. Yet certain information can be gained from data on education obtained in the census.

In Table 7.4 these figures on the proportion of those employed in

*Table 7.4* Decrease of unskilled manual labour compared to the decrease of workers with little schooling

|  | Proportion of workers doing unskilled manual labour* | | Proportion of workers with less than 7 years' education | |
|---|---|---|---|---|
|  | % | 1959 = 100 | % | 1959 = 100 |
| **INDUSTRY** | | | | |
| 1959 | 45.5 | 100 | 51.7 | 100 |
| 1972 | 36.0 | 79 | 36.8 (1970) | 60 |
| **CONSTRUCTION** | | | | |
| 1959 | 70.0 | 100 | 68.2 | 100 |
| 1972 | 52.2 | 75 | 45.9 (1970) | 67 |

*Refers to Group 4 of Table 7.3.

*Sources:* Table 7.3 and *Itogi vsesoiuznoi perepisi naseleniia 1970 godu*, vol. VI (Moscow, 1972).

industry and construction and having less than 7 years' education are compared with the decrease in the number of workers belonging to Group 4.

This table shows that in the late 1950s the number of workers prepared to accept modest unskilled jobs corresponded to, or even exceeded, the proportion of such unskilled jobs in Group 4. This number had decreased by the early 1970s at a faster pace than the proportion of unskilled jobs. In all probability this development continued into the 1970s. In that decade a major thrust in education took place, as shown in Table 7.5. Even though these figures refer to the population as a whole, and not just to the group of workers discussed above, it is clear that the reserve of unskilled labour is decreasing rapidly. This is due not only to efforts to increase the educational level of the labour force, but also to the fact that a large

*Table 7.5*  Percentage of population aged 10 years and older related to levels of education*

|  |  | *General education* |  |  |  |
| --- | --- | --- | --- | --- | --- |
| *Year* | *University* | *Technical high school* | *10 years* | *7 years* | *Less than 7 years* |
| 1959 | 2.3 | 4.8 | 6.1 | 21.8 | 65.0 |
| 1970 | 4.2 | 6.8 | 11.9 | 24.1 | 53.0 |
| 1979 | 6.8 | 10.7 | 20.7 | 24.1 | 37.7 |

*No data available for percentage of population with vocational–technical education.

*Sources:* 1979 data, *Vestnik Statistiki*, no. 2 (1980) p. 21; 1959 and 1970 data, *Itogi ... 1970 godu*, vol. III, p. 6 *et seq.*

proportion of workers with low levels of education will reach retirement age. Young workers who enter the labour force have a high level of education and job expectations. Thus it is predicted in the Soviet Union[55] that it will be very difficult to fill unskilled job vacancies, especially if one considers that manpower growth will drop by nearly 50 per cent in the 1980s.[56] This means that young workers will be able to be choosy about what jobs they will accept.

Workers are not the only ones affected by the growing gap between job expectations inspired by the educational level they have achieved and the job opportunities offered to them in reality. This can also be seen in the growing number of so-called specialists (people with degrees from universities and technical high schools) working in blue-collar jobs (cf. Table 7.6). This indicates a certain amount of over-qualification, even if one considers that on the other hand a good many specialist jobs are occupied by 'praktiki' who do not have the formal education required.

Thus, as within the period under observation, technological advancement in the Soviet Union has not brought about a noticeable dequalification process, so also have improvements in working conditions and the rise in qualification requirements not kept pace with the job expectations of the younger generation; expectations that were generated by the expansion of the Soviet system of education. This expansion was mainly directed towards raising the level of general education, as well as technical and university education, while vocational training at the skilled labourer level was sadly neglected.

*Table 7.6*  Specialists in blue-collar jobs in different industrial branches

| Branches of industry | Percentage of specialists in blue-collar jobs of the total number of specialists in the branch concerned | |
| --- | --- | --- |
| | 1968 | 1973 |
| Electroenergy | 15 | 23 |
| Chemicals | 23 | 33 |
| Non-ferrous metallurgy | 22 | 34 |
| Ferrous metallurgy | 28 | 39 |
| Oil extraction | 35 | 44 |
| Machine building | 12 | 18 |
| Mining | 13 | 23 |

*Source:* Rutkevich and Filippov, op. cit., p. 68.

Such neglect of practical training has a long tradition in the Soviet Union.[57] It dates back to the time of the first 5-year plan when it was thought that there were not enough funds available to teach the workers in the production process more than they could learn by routine. This decision had a detrimental effect on the organization of work. In order to begin the integration of the masses of unskilled workers into the production process, the work process was subdivided into particularly narrow routines. At the same time the worker in the production process was subjected to strict bureaucratic regimentation and control. He thus found himself in a particularly menial position. This in turn generated a strong reluctance on the part of young workers to take any interest in jobs in production, or go through the skilled-worker training required for such jobs.

Thus the vocational–technical schools had difficulty filling their training vacancies. As a result, a top-heavy educational hierarchy developed which heightened the expectations and aspirations of the younger generation, but not so much its concrete occupational proficiency. As a reaction to this situation an attempt has been made to upgrade vocational education (creation of vocational–technical schools which entitles graduates to apply for university study if they wish). It is doubtful whether this upgrading will succeed in bringing the level of aspirations of the young workers more into line with the on-the-job reality. Unless this is accompanied by changes in the organization of work, the workers who, having passed through the new type of vocational–technical schools, will have not only a broad-based general education but also training as skilled workers, will be even less satisfied with jobs which are not up to their standard of knowledge.[58] At the same time the upgrading and expansion of skilled-worker training are also essential preconditions for an extension of the margin of competence of the workers. Considerations along these lines have given rise to a series of interesting experiments with integrated professions, rotation, job-enrichment, the creation of complex brigades, etc.[59] The main course of present-day changes in the organization of work appears, however, to be in the opposite direction towards more regimentation and control (introduction of scientific norms).[60]

## V.   CONCLUSION

1.   The process of technical change, leading to displacement by eliminating certain jobs and creating new ones with different characteristics, is rather slow in the Soviet Union, if not by objective standards, then without doubt as far as the expectations of the Soviet authorities, scientists and the labour force itself are concerned. This is true with respect to economic as well as social and political aspects. Recognition of this situation led the Party and government in mid-1983 to launch a wide-ranging program to speed up the introduction of new technology throughout the economy and to cope with the potentially disruptive consequences.[61]

From the economic point of view the unrealistic expectations which planners have hitherto shown towards displacement possibilities has led to an ever-increasing labour shortage, which could be relieved not so much by investment as by organizational improvements in the use of this scarce factor. This fact is recognized in the Soviet Union and has sparked a broad discussion on measures to be taken in an attempt to bring about some relief. However, the measures implemented so far can eliminate only some of the causes because of production units' reluctance to displace manpower. To bring about a substantial change in the behaviour of enterprises would require a radical economic reform and this is politically unfeasible at present.

2.   Besides these fundamental questions, the improvement of the poor set of tools in use today, and the consequent increased ability to manage a more voluminous process of displacement and replacement

of manpower, would be preconditions for the enhancement of this process without grave social consequences.

3.    Analysing the qualitative aspects of technical change in the Soviet Union we find that the improvement of working conditions and the escalation of qualification requirements are unable to keep pace with the hopes awakened in the younger generation by Soviet educational expansion. One of the main reasons for this is that the educational expansion was oriented too exclusively towards general education and to the college and university level. This situation, which will be corrected to some extent in the near future by the expansion of secondary vocational–technical schools, has led to considerable frustration for young workers who react to unsatisfactory work conditions with high absenteeism and high turnover.

It is, therefore, reasonable to say that in the Soviet Union it is not so much technological progress which has given rise to sociopolitical problems as over-estimation of the effects of that process, the reaction to which in the education sector has, furthermore, been too one-sided and isolated.

The most recent attempt to deal with these complex problems is a major reform of the entire educational system, to begin with the 1984/5 school year and to extend over more than a decade.[62] The reforms, which add one year of schooling, aim to upgrade the political/ideological content of the curriculum, while requiring substantial amounts of 'socially useful labour' from all children as part of their formal education. Ultimately, all secondary students will spend their summer vacation working in production, and all schools will be linked directly with enterprises. Secondary school graduates are to be streamed into various kinds of vocational–technical schools in much larger proportions than at present. It remains to be seen whether this mammoth undertaking will resolve some of the current problems, or even can be carried out in the face of likely resistance from many quarters.

## Notes

1.    Displacement can, but need not necessarily, result in dismissal. The latter is only the case if the factory in question cannot offer the displaced worker a new job in a different expanding sector of its production. In reality, this happens to a rather high degree in Soviet enterprises, as we will see later on.

2.   This rate must not be confused with the potential rate of displacement, deduced for many countries by input–output analysis (e.g. D. M. Gallik *et al.*, 'The 1972 input–output table and the changing structure of the Soviet economy', in *Soviet Economy in a Time of Change* (Washington, DC, 1979) pp. 423–71). These studies indicate the number of workers who would be displaced by technical progress if production remained constant. This figure is compared with manpower needs resulting from the expansion of output calculated for constant technology. However, the difference between the two figures does not correspond to the real amount of displacement, because in reality the two processes are correlated. The increase in labour productivity brought about, e.g., by the introduction of a more productive machine need not result in any displacement at all, if production of the corresponding goods is expanded simultaneously.

3.   N. A. Aitov, *Tekhnicheskii progress i dvizhenie rabochikh kadrov* (Moscow, 1972) p. 21.

4.   T. A. Baranenkova, *Vysvobozhdenie rabochei sily i uluchshenie ee ispol' zovaniia pri sotsialisme* (Moscow, 1974) p. 105.

5.   Author's calculations based on the *Statistical Yearbook for the FRG*, 1980 edition.

6.   B. Lutz and F. Weltz, *Der zwischenbetriebliche Arbeitsplatzwechsel* (Frankfurt Main, 1966) p. 67.

7.   *Itogi vsesoiuznoi perepisi naseleniia 1970 g.*, vol. 6 (Moscow, 1973) pp. 14–23. *Itogi vsesoiuznoi perepisi naseleniia 1959 g., SSSR* (Moscow, 1962) pp. 132–41.

8.   A. J. Pietsch, in W. Gumpel (ed.), *Arbeits-und Sozialpolitik in der Sowjetunion* (Munich, 1976) p. 102.

9.   This was calculated by using census data for the individual republica, corrected for differences in their dimensions. For details cf. Pietsch, op. cit., pp. 103–7.

10.  B. Lutz and E. Weltz, op. cit., p. 89.

11.  E. Mueller *et al., Technological Advance in an Expanding Economy: its Impact on a Cross Section of the Labour Force* (Ann Arbor, 1969) p. 10.

12.  This result may be striking because in Soviet publications we learn much about the reluctance of Soviet firms to release manpower. So one should expect displacement rates to be lower than in Western countries. Taking into consideration, however, the high rates of labour turnover in the Soviet economy, it becomes evident that part of the displacement needs of Soviet firms can be met by people leaving voluntarily. Certainly displacement would be increased significantly by a fundamental transformation of the system of economic planning and management. Measures to this end – rather than technical change – could have a strong but non-recurring effect on displacement.

13.  Baranenkova, op. cit., p. 105.

14.  R. Uffhausen, *Die Auswirkungen der demographischen Entwicklung auf das Wirtschaftswachstum und die Effizienz der sektoralen Arbeitskrafte-Allokation in der Sowjetunion* (Research paper of Osteuropa-Institut no. 76) (Munich, 1981).

15.  this can be seen in a very interesting table given by Baranenkova, op.

cit., p. 65, which shows that the highest displacement effect per ruble can be achieved by improving standardization (Normierung), whereas the least effect per ruble is achieved by improving working conditions, such as mechanization and automation.

16. Cf. *Itogi ... 1959.*

17. The annual rate of labour turnover is defined as the percentage of resignations and dismissals in the average number of employees in a given year.

18. These data based on different Soviet sources were given by A. McAuley and A. Helgeson, 'Soviet labour supply and manpower utilization 1960–2000' (unpublished manuscript) p. 38a.

19. Aitov, op. cit., p. 25.

20. M. Sonin, *Sotsialisticheskii trud*, no. 3 (1977) p. 100.

21. Baranenkova, op. cit., p. 118.

22. Aitov, op. cit., p. 24.

23. Ibid.

24. Ibid.

25. V. Sozinov, *Sotsialisticheskii trud*, no. 10 (1976) p. 91.

26. V. I. Terebilov, *Kommentarii k zakonodatel'stvu o trude* (Moscow, 1975) p. 93.

27. Sozinov, op. cit., p. 91.

28. Cf. A. I. Stavceva, *Pravovye voprosy pereraspredeleniia trudovykh resursov* (Moscow, 1974) p. 17.

29. 'Reallocation plans' are developed on the basis of plans for the introduction of labour-saving measures into the enterprises and from individual interviews with the workers liable to displacement (cf. B. D. Breev, *Methods of Planning Employment in the USSR* (Moscow, 1979) pp. 57–9).

30. Already in 1975 the proportion of charges against displacement in the total number of legal cases because of termination of employment before the respective courts was 16.9 per cent (cf. O. Luchterhandt, *UN-Menschenrechtskonventionen, Sowjetrecht – Sowjetwirklichkeit* (Baden-Baden, 1980) p. 43).

31. A. E. Kotliar and V. V. Trubin, *Problemy regulirovaniia pereraspredeleniia rabochei sily* (Moscow, 1978) pp. 38–40.

32. *NK 1978*, pp. 18–23.

33. *Vosproizvodstvo rabochei sily i povyshenie effektivnosti ispol'-zovaniia trudovykh resursov* (Moscow, 1971).

34. P. Stiller, 'Probleme und Methoden der Arbeitskraftelenkung' (unpublished manuscript, Munich, 1980).

35. E. Smirnov, *Sotsialisticheskii trud*, no. 3 (1978) p. 110.

36. *Biulleten Goskomtrude SSSR*, no. 8 (1979).

37. Baranenkova, op. cit., p. 151.

38. Baranenkova, op. cit., pp. 109, 110, 154.

39. J. Delamotte, *Shchekino, entreprise sovietique pilote* (Paris, 1973).

40. *Regionalnye problemy naseleniia i trudovye resursy* (Moscow, 1978) p. 28. *Voprosy ekonomiki*, no. 2, 1983, p. 59. Radio Liberty Research Report RL337/83.

41. For example, R. Blauner, *Alienation and Freedom* (Chicago/London,

1964); A. Touraine, *L'evolution du travail ouvrieur aux usines Renault* (Paris, 1955).

42.     H. Kern and M. Schumann, *Industriearbeit und Arbeiterbewusstsein* (Frankfurt/Main, 1970).

43.     For example, S. Ia. Batushev. *Sovetskaia pedagogica,* no. 8 (1971) pp. 11 *et seq.*; W. N. Turtshenko, *Sowjetwissenschaft, Gesellschaftswissenschaftliche Beitrage,* no. 8 (1973) pp. 11 *et seq.*; M. N. Rutkevich and F. P. Filippov, *Sotsial' naia struktura razvitogo sotsialisticheskogo obshchestva v SSSR* (Moscow, 1970).

44.     Aitov, op. cit., p. 23.

45.     Baranenkova, op. cit., p. 118.

46.     H. Wiegmann, *Die Entwicklung der sowjetischen Berufsstruktur,* Research paper of the Osteuropa-Instituta, Munchen (1975).

47.     Soviet census data of 1970 give two categories of activities: those requiring mainly manual work, and those requiring mainly intellectual work.

48.     Wiegmann, op. cit., pp. 67, 71.

49.     Ibid., p. 84.

50.     Cf. e.g. G. M. Safranov, *Trudovye reservy* (Kisinev, 1972) p. 56.

51.     M. Baethge *et al., Produktion und Qualifikation* (Hannover, 1976) p. 112.

52.     V. A. Jadov, in M. Yanowitch (ed.), *Soviet Work Attitudes* (New York, 1979) p. 8.

53.     V. G. Aseev, *Preodelenie monotonnosti truda v promysh'lennosti* (Moscow, 1974) p. 7.

54.     Jadov, op. cit., p. 8.

55.     Rutkevich and Filippov, op. cit., p. 52.

56.     M. Feshbach, 'The structure and composition of the Soviet industrial labour force', *The USSR in the 1980's* (Brussels, NATO, 1978) p. 59.

57.     A.-J. Pietsch, *Die Interdependenz von Qualifikarionsbedarf und Arbeitsorganisation,* Research paper for Osteurope-Institut, Munchen, no. 63 (1980).

58.     Studies carried out in Leningrad have already shown that graduates of intermediate vocational schools in jobs that are not commensurate with their qualifications have a poorer performance record than the less highly qualified graduates from the traditional type of vocational–technical schools (cf. O. O. Shkaratan, O. V. Stakanova and O. V. Filipovna, *Sotsiologicheskie isledovaniia,* no. 4 (1977) pp. 39 *et seq.*).

59.     Cf. M. Tatur, in *Leviathan,* no. 3 (1979)

60.     Cf. M. Tatur, 'Vergleich der Politiken zur Modernisierung der Arbeitsorganisation in der UdSSR, Polen und der CSSR' (unpublished manuscript, 1980).

61.     *Pravda* 28, August, 1983.

62.     The basic Guidelines for the school reform are published in *Pravda,* 14 April, 1984. Initial Implementing Resolutions are published in *Pravda,* 29 April, 15, 19 and 23 May, 1984.

# 8 Regional Employment Policies in East European Countries

## HANS-ERICH GRAMATZKI

## I. INTRODUCTORY REMARKS

Country studies of employment mostly neglect regional aspects or deal with them only in a very global or general manner. This contribution will, therefore, try to offer some research findings to complement these studies. First, the decision-makers in East Europe look for regional labour force reserves which they either try to 'mobilize' themselves, or want regional institutions to do so. The second, and still more important, activity focuses not on the goal of increasing the number of gainfully employed, but on their more rational use, on a better intra- and inter-regional division of labour, i.e. on higher labour productivity.

One of the reasons for the low level of both total productivity and regional productivities of labour and capital is the inefficient coordination between sectoral and regional institutions. The need to improve sectoral–regional coordination has been discussed constantly in the East European literature during the past 20 years. Even if the past has been characterized by an improvement on the legal and institutional side, this improvement is proceeding very slowly and is being carried out only half-heartedly – and the legal provisions do not establish a clear division of authority between sectors and regions. This, along with the traditional economic power of the sectors, is responsible for the large gap between the normative–legal and the real situation in the fields of regional policy and regional planning, as is most clearly shown by the 1980–81 Polish discussion about economic reform needs.

This study includes only East European countries: the GDR, CSSR, Poland and Hungary. If, for analytical reasons, we divide the tasks of regional policy and planning into only two fields, development and coordination, then we can say that in the USSR regional development policy (Far East, Far North, Central Asia) still dominates, whereas in the smaller East European countries the improvement of coordination is of primary importance for overall production and productivity growth, even if there are some differences between the more highly developed GDR and CSSR on the one hand and Poland and Hungary on the other. Poland and Hungary have not only lower development levels but also larger regional differences.

What is meant by regional employment policies? It is necessary to define these first with regard to space, second with regard to problems. The first task is easier than the second. On the one hand almost every aspect of employment policy has its regional implications. On the other hand the *administrative-type mesoregion* (county-level region) clearly has to be at the centre of the analysis, because this type of region represents both the basic statistical unit for employment and the basic unit for decisions in the areas of employment policy and regional policy. The existing *macroregions* (see Table 8.1) are solely

*Table 8.1*　Regionalisation of the CSSR, GDR, Hungary and Poland

| | Macro-regions | Meso-regions (countries)* | Area (km²) | Population (millions) 31 December 1983 | Average population sizes (millions) Macro-regions | Meso-regions |
|---|---|---|---|---|---|---|
| CSSR | — | 12 (10) | 127 877 | 15.44 | — | 1.29 (1.54) |
| GDR | 4 | 15 (14) | 108 180 | 16.70 | 4.18 | 1.11 (1.19) |
| Hungary | 6 | 20 | 93 036 | 10.68 | 1.78 | 0.53 |
| Poland | 9** | 49 | 312 683 | 36.75 | 4.08 | 0.75 |

*The country-level region is 'kraj' in the CSSR, 'Bezirk' in the GDR, 'megye' in Hungary, and 'województwo' in Poland; the data in parentheses do not treat capitals as separate units. The table was compiled by the author on the basis of data from the Statistical Yearbooks of the four countries.
**In 1982 the macroregion Centre was divided into two macroregions: the (new) central macroregion (with Łódź) and the capital macroregion (with Warsaw).

for planning purposes, primarily for long term planning. *Economic regions* (regions delineated according to economic criteria), not to speak of special *employment regions* (which are intended to stabilize employment in regional labour markets, i.e. prevent a larger interregional labour turnover), play a secondary role and, for statistical, planning and political reasons, even the macroregions represent only the sum total of administrative (meso)regions. The problems which are of primary importance are the general problems of intraregional and interregional specialization and cooperation, as well as the special problems of small towns (unemployment, underemployment), small villages with heavy out-migration, small enterprises, commuting, different problem regions, etc.

Section II of this study analyses the regional employment structures of the four countries, the statistical labour force reserves of the regions, their actual availability (settlement structure and infrastructure restrictions for labour force use), and also their quality (qualification restrictions). Regional demographic differences determine the future regional distribution of employment. Section III deals with regional problems and problem regions, and Section IV with regional policy and planning from the point of view of employment. Section V summarizes the main conclusions of the study.

## II. REGIONAL STRUCTURES

### 1. Regional development strategies

After the Second World War the regional development policy and strategies of the four countries were clearly determined (restricted) by accelerated industrialization (in Poland and Hungary), restructuring of the sectoral structure (GDR), integration of new territories (Poland), rebuilding of facilities destroyed during the war, filling up of territories which had experienced population losses (western parts of Poland and the CSSR), etc. Thus, the altered regional structures were not primarily a result of regional development concepts, but of the above-mentioned determinants. Only Czechoslovakia, immediately after 1948, started a regional equalization policy in favour of Slovakia. But the motivation for this policy was complex. Czechoslovakia was the only country with two ethnic groups, both of political importance; Slovakia had an extremely low level of industrialization and relatively large labour reserves (the Czech Lands had lost 3 million inhabitants after 1945) and there were also strategic and foreign trade arguments for an industrialization of Slovakia. The development gap between the Czech Lands and Slovakia can best be shown by statistics indicating industrial employment per thousand inhabitants for 1948; CSR 158 and SSR 67.[1] At the end of 1983 the figures were 181 (CSR) and 140 (SSR).[2] The investment share for the SSR (1951–83) was 33.2 per cent, with the SSR population rising from 27.9 per cent (1950) to 33 per cent (1983) of the total population.[3]

The most important aspects of the regional development policies or strategies of the other three countries are the following: *Poland* went through different stages of regional–strategic thinking.[4] the 1950–60 period was dominated by the 'principle of equal industrialization of the country', which was intended to contribute to the strengthening of political power (enlarged working class), to an improvement of the social situation (reduction of unemployment) and the economic potential (heavy industry). The 'principle of economic activation of neglected regions' during the years 1960–70 was the logical consequence of the 1950–60 model, which was doomed to failure because of limited resources and which represented too strong a political–ideological approach. Typical of the second decade was the large share of investments going to the larger cities where however – because of an extreme neglect of infrastructural development and housing – labour force deficits soon became acute. This was at least one reason for the development of the 'principles of deglomeration and selective development' (1965–70), in the context of the 'activation principle'. Deglomeration meant use of the available labour force in smaller cities (transfer of whole enterprises and/or establishment of regional branch enterprises). Selective development focused on larger industrial centres. Finally, the last decade was characterized by the 'principle of moderate polycentric concentration' (1970–9). This principle is known from Western countries: a combination of an equalization policy (decentralization) with the concentration of resource use in certain growth centres or central places. But the strongly heavy-industry based 'second industrialization' of the Gierek era gave no chance for a 'moderate'.

*Hungary*'s regional development policy, according to Gy. Enyedi, can also be described in terms of stages:[5] the 1950s (the phase of accelerated industrialization), the transition period between 1958 and 1968, and the New Economic Mechanism period (NEM) since 1968. The first Five-Year Plan had already stressed the need to industrialize the Great Plains, but this, according to Gy. Enyedi, had to remain 'a pious wish', because 'regional planning did not exist'. Therefore, labour had to leave the agricultural areas with their labour surpluses, especially the Great Plains, and go to Budapest or to new industrial areas in the Hungarian Middle Mountains. During the second period from 1958 to 1968 'the objectives and framework of a comprehensive regional development policy'[6] were formulated for the first time. Regional development policy was then identified with industrialization because of continued serious employment difficulties in the Great Plains and Transdanubian Hills. Central elements of the new policy were the beginnings of industrial decentralization with regard to Budapest and a growth pole strategy for the five largest cities of the countryside or periphery (Miskolc, Debrecen, Szeged, Pecs, Györ). But settlement restrictions for Budapest could then not prevent employment from increasing there (due to an increase in commuting). The NEM also brought industrial employment to the Great Plains. Regional decentralization of industrial locations was promoted by the growth of enterprise decision-making power; the enterprises in the capital could use the labour available in small towns and larger villages by establishing small plants using primarily unskilled female labour.[7]

In the *GDR* one will hardly find a sequential development of regional strategic thinking comparable to Poland and Hungary or which can be seen in the stages of its own economic policy. Regional policy was discovered very late, is still dealt with in an extremely normative manner,[8] and focuses primarily on 'territorial rationalization', i.e. the coordination aspect (cf. Section IV).

## 2. Regional demographic structures

Different degrees of industrial development and urbanization on the one hand and migrations (changing regional age and/or sex structures) on the other are responsible for regional demographic differentiations in the four countries. We find the most remarkable differences in *Czechoslovakia*, where they are due to differnces between the two large ethnic regions of the Czech Lands (CSR) and Slovakia (SSR). The SSR had 28 per cent of the total CSSR population in 1950 and 33.1 per cent in 1983, but it accounted for 54.6 per cent of all population increases from 1950 to 1983. Corresponding to this is the difference in the age structure. In 1982, 23.5 per cent of the CSR population, as opposed to 26.2 per cent of the SSR population, were younger than 15 years, while 17.2 per cent and 13.9 per cent, respectively, were older than 60.[9] In the Czech area Prague has by far the worst demographic structure, while Northern Moravia, a region with a strong industrialization drive in the immediate past, has the best. In Prague, in 1978 persons of 'post-productive' age accounted for 12.7 per cent of total employment.[10] In the SSR this group only represents a small proportion of the total population. The demographic differences can also be shown by the average age of the employed in the socialist sector. The difference between Prague and Eastern Slovakia was 4 years in 1978.

*Poland*, which has experienced an extremely favourable overall demographic development in the past, has greater regional demographic differences due to large postwar migrations into former German territories and migrations induced by different industrial regions, especially Katowice. The Northern and Western voivodships have the best demographic conditions. There, as a rule, not more than 10 per cent of the total population is of 'post-productive' age (Poland 11.8 per cent). On the other hand, there are rural voivodships with about 14 per cent, mostly in the Central and Middle-East macroregions. The percentages of persons of preproductive age are also strongly differentiated regionally. Lódź (22.9 per cent) and Warszawa (23.3 per cent) have the most unfaviourable shares, the average value for Poland being 29.2 per cent.[11]

The migration pattern in the past showed two immigration areas with regard to the inter-macroregion migrations, the South and the old Centre, and five out-migration areas – Middle-East, North-East, South-East, Middle-West and South-West. But due to the Polish economic crisis interregional migration was sharply reduced from 1980 to 1983. In 1980 Katowice and Warsaw had net immigrations of 26 800 and 13 100 persons, in 1983 of only 9200 and 6800.[12]

To a large extent the regional demographic situation of *Hungary* is determined by Budapest, i.e. by its negative influence on the goal of establishing a more balanced settlement structure (a hierarchical system of central places) and its unfavourable natural increase rate. With regard to natural population growth, Budapest had none during the 1970–80 decade, and had large negative rates in the 1980s (1982 − 4.6 and 1983 − 5.4 per cent).[13] On the other hand – as there is still a large amount of immigration into Budapest and county Pest. From 1975 to 1983 Hungary had a population growth of 178 000 and the Central Region's share in this growth was 52.8 per cent (in 1983 its share of the population was 28.5 per cent). In the Central Region, of the increase from 1970–80 only 35.0 per cent was due to natural growth. the principal 'losers' in this migration process were the more highly developed Northern Region and the two less-developed Great Plains regions (particularly the extremely poorly developed Szabolcs

Table 8.2  Regional employment, production and demographic structure of Czechoslovakia, 1983

| | Area in % | Population[a] in % | Employment in the socialist sector[b] 1982 in % | Population of working age[b] in % | Participation rates[c] | Industrial employment per 1000 inhabitants[d] | Industrial employment Shift coefficient* | Industrial employment in %[f] | Industrial gross production[f] in % | Investment[g] in % | Population development (natural increase/decrease)[h] in % |
|---|---|---|---|---|---|---|---|---|---|---|---|
| Czechoslovakia | 100.0 | 100.0 | 100.0 | 100.0 | 47.4 | 168 | | 100.0 | 100.0 | 100.0 | 2.8 |
| Czech Area | 61.7 | 66.9 | 68.6 | 66.8 | 48.5 | 181 | | 73.2 | 71.6 | 66.6 | |
| Slovakia | 38.3 | 33.1 | 31.4 | 33.2 | 45.0 | 140 | | 26.8 | 28.4 | 33.4 | |
| Prague | 0.4 | 7.7 | 9.1 | 7.5 | 56.0 | 195 | 1.11 | 9.0 | 8.5 | 10.0 | −4.0 |
| Central Bohemia | 8.6 | 7.4 | 7.0 | 7.3 | 44.6 | 154 | 1.34 | 6.9 | 8.7 | 6.4 | −2.4 |
| (Central Bohemia + Prague) | 9.0 | 15.1 | 16.1 | 14.8 | 50.4 | 175 | | | 17.2 | 16.4 | |
| Southern Bohemia | 8.6 | 4.5 | 4.4 | 4.5 | 46.6 | 137 | 1.24 | 3.7 | 4.3 | 4.0 | 0.6 |
| Western Bohemia | 8.5 | 5.7 | 5.8 | 5.8 | 47.9 | 148 | 1.25 | 5.1 | 4.3 | 5.5 | 0.9 |
| Northern Bohemia | 6.1 | 7.6 | 8.0 | 7.7 | 49.4 | 224 | 1.31 | 10.1 | 11.0 | 9.3 | 2.3 |
| Eastern Bohemia | 8.8 | 8.1 | 8.5 | 7.9 | 49.5 | 187 | 1.26 | 9.2 | 8.3 | 6.3 | −0.3 |
| Southern Moravia | 11.8 | 13.3 | 13.1 | 13.2 | 46.7 | 160 | 1.28 | 12.9 | 11.2 | 12.5 | 0.9 |
| Northern Moravia | 8.6 | 12.6 | 12.8 | 12.9 | 47.8 | 214 | 1.43 | 16.3 | 16.2 | 12.6 | 3.0 |
| Bratislava | 0.3 | 2.6 | 3.7 | 2.7 | (67.3) | (276) | 1.28 | 3.6 | 5.9 | 4.8 | 7.0 |
| Western Slovakia | 11.3 | 11.1 | 9.5 | 11.1 | (40.8) | (104) | 1.41 | 6.7 | 6.1 | 11.1 | 5.5 |
| (Western Slovakia + Bratislava) | 11.6 | 13.7 | 13.2 | 13.8 | 45.9 | 136 | | 10.3 | 12.0 | 15.9 | |
| Central Slovakia | 14.1 | 10.1 | 9.7 | 10.2 | 45.6 | 173 | 1.44 | 10.2 | 9.9 | 9.3 | 7.7 |
| Eastern Slovakia | 12.6 | 9.3 | 8.5 | 9.3 | 43.2 | 115 | 1.48 | 6.3 | 6.5 | 8.2 | 10.6 |

*The shift coefficient is the ratio of the total number of workers in the shift system divided by the number of workers employed on the shift with the largest number of workers.

Sources: [a] SRC 1984, p. 98; [b] SRC 1984, p. 180; [c] SRC 1984, p. 98; [d] SRC 1984, p. 180; [e] SRC 1984, p. 98 and Statistické přehledy, no. 4 (1984) pp. 118, 120; [f] Statistické přehledy, no. 4 (1984) pp. 118, 120; [g] SRC 1984, p. 357; [h] SRC 1984, p. 98.

Table 8.3 Regional indicators of Poland

| Macroregions | Area in %[a] | Population in %[a] | Distribution of investment | | | | Industrial employment | | | | |
|---|---|---|---|---|---|---|---|---|---|---|---|
| | | | Industrial[b] | | Total[a] | | in %[c] | | | per 1000 inhabitants[d] | |
| | 1978 | 1978 | 1961-5 | 1971-5 | 1978 | 1983 | 1965 | 1978 | 1983[a] | 1979 | 1983[a] |
| South | 8.0 | 17.6 | 31.0 | 29.3 | 22.8 | 18.9 | 29.2 | 26.5 | 27.1 | 209 | 187 |
| South-East | 13.8 | 15.4 | 17.4 | 13.7 | 13.8 | 13.8 | 11.7 | 13.6 | 13.7 | 122 | 108 |
| South-West | 12.9 | 11.7 | 12.5 | 12.3 | 11.0 | 11.0 | 13.6 | 13.4 | 12.9 | 160 | 135 |
| Capital | 10.4 | 12.3 | 8.3 | 9.7 | 12.0 | 11.8 | 10.3 | 10.2 | 10.0 | 113 | 99 |
| Centre | 7.0 | 8.4 | 7.7 | 9.0 | 8.0 | 9.5 | 11.3 | 10.0 | 9.3 | 162 | 135 |
| Mid-West | 15.4 | 13.6 | 11.7 | 11.0 | 11.8 | 13.2 | 11.4 | 11.7 | 11.8 | 119 | 106 |
| North | 12.6 | 9.8 | 6.2 | 9.1 | 12.2 | 10.1 | 7.2 | 7.8 | 7.9 | 111 | 98 |
| North-East | 12.6 | 5.8 | 1.9 | 2.9 | 4.6 | 5.9 | 2.6 | 3.5 | 3.7 | 82 | 78 |
| Mid-East | 7.3 | 5.4 | 3.3 | 3.0 | 3.8 | 5.8 | 2.7 | 3.3 | 3.6 | 83 | 81 |
| Poland | 100.0 | 100.0 | 100.0 | 100.0 | 100.0 | 100.0 | 100.0 | 100.0 | 100.0 | 136 | 122 |

Sources: The data for the macroregions were aggregated by the author according to the voivodship data of the following sources:
[a] RS 1984, pp. LVI, LVIII.
[b] A. Mykaj (ed.) Procesy inwestycyjne w gospodarce przestrzennej Polski w latach 1961–1975 (Warsaw, 1978); RS 1979, p. 119.
[c] M. Opałło, Przemiany w strukturze przestrzennej przemysłu w-35 leciu, Rada narodowa ..., 1979, no. 12, p. 34.
[d] Mały Rocznik Statystyczny 1980, p. XLV.

Table 8.4 Regional employment and demographic structure of Hungary

| Macroregions, regions | Area (%) | Population (%) 1983 | Regional shares of industrial employment | | Industrial employment per 1000 inhabitants | | | Population development 1970–80 (%) | | | Natural decrease/decrease 1983 (%) |
|---|---|---|---|---|---|---|---|---|---|---|---|
| | | | 1970 | 1983 | 1970 | 1979 | 1983 | Natural increase | Migration difference | Population difference | |
| North Transdanubia | 20.6 | 17.4 | 18.6 | 20.5 | 188 | 175 | 164 | | | 5.0 | |
| Fejér | 4.7 | 4.0 | 3.4 | 4.7 | 153 | 162 | 165 | 7.2 | 0.2 | 7.4 | 0.6 |
| Győr-Sopron | 4.3 | 4.0 | 4.5 | 4.6 | 195 | 182 | 158 | 5.9 | 1.5 | 7.4 | -0.3 |
| Komárom | 2.4 | 3.0 | 4.2 | 4.1 | 240 | 211 | 187 | 6.2 | -0.6 | 5.6 | -0.8 |
| Vas | 3.6 | 2.7 | 2.5 | 2.7 | 154 | 157 | 138 | 3.2 | -1.0 | 2.2 | -2.2 |
| Veszprém | 5.6 | 3.7 | 4.0 | 4.4 | 172 | 170 | 167 | 6.2 | -1.6 | 4.6 | 0.5 |
| South Transdanubia | 18.8 | 12.8 | 9.3 | 11.9 | 121 | 137 | 128 | | | 2.6 | |
| Baranya | 4.8 | 4.1 | 3.7 | 4.5 | 152 | 161 | 152 | 3.5 | -0.9 | 2.6 | -2.0 |
| Somogy | 6.5 | 3.3 | 2.0 | 2.2 | 98 | 98 | 90 | 1.1 | -0.8 | 0.3 | -4.2 |
| Tolna | 4.0 | 2.5 | 1.7 | 2.2 | 114 | 126 | 124 | 2.7 | — | 2.7 | -1.8 |
| Zala | 3.5 | 2.9 | 1.9 | 3.0 | 131 | 162 | 141 | 2.6 | 0.7 | 3.3 | -2.0 |
| Northern Region | 14.4 | 12.9 | 13.2 | 15.5 | 171 | 177 | 165 | | | 3.5 | |
| Borsod | 7.8 | 7.5 | 8.1 | 9.6 | 182 | 188 | 179 | 6.1 | -2.1 | 4.0 | 0.4 |
| Heves | 3.9 | 3.2 | 2.9 | 3.3 | 150 | 156 | 138 | 2.9 | 0.3 | 3.2 | -3.0 |
| Nógrád | 2.7 | 2.2 | 2.2 | 2.6 | 164 | 173 | 158 | 3.8 | -1.7 | 2.1 | -1.4 |

*Table 8.4 cont.*

| | | | | | | | | | | | |
|---|---|---|---|---|---|---|---|---|---|---|---|
| Northern Great Plain | 19.1 | 14.8 | 8.3 | 12.1 | 94 | 115 | 113 | | | 3.2 | |
| Hajdu | 6.7 | 5.2 | 3.1 | 4.2 | 102 | 115 | 112 | 6.8 | -1.3 | 5.5 | 0.9 |
| Szabolcs | 6.4 | 5.5 | 2.0 | 3.9 | 63 | 95 | 99 | 8.5 | -4.5 | 4.0 | 2.0 |
| Szolnok | 6.0 | 4.1 | 3.2 | 4.0 | 125 | 142 | 132 | 3.8 | -2.7 | 1.1 | -2.0 |
| Southern Great Plain | 19.7 | 13.6 | 10.5 | 11.7 | 126 | 131 | 119 | | | 0.5 | |
| Bács-Kiskun | 9.0 | 5.3 | 3.6 | 4.2 | 111 | 120 | 110 | 2.4 | -1.9 | 0.5 | -2.7 |
| Békés | 6.0 | 4.0 | 3.0 | 3.6 | 120 | 133 | 123 | 1.8 | -3.2 | -1.4 | -3.2 |
| Csongrád | 4.6 | 4.3 | 3.9 | 3.9 | 153 | 143 | 126 | 1.8 | 1.6 | 3.4 | -3.4 |
| Central Region | 7.4 | 28.5 | 40.1 | 28.3 | 244 | 181 | 137 | | | 5.3 | |
| Pest | 6.9 | 9.2 | 5.8 | 5.7 | 115 | 104 | 85 | 5.9 | 3.8 | 9.7 | -1.2 |
| Budapest | 0.6 | 19.3 | 34.3 | 22.6 | 298 | 218 | 162 | 0.0 | 2.9 | 2.9 | -5.4 |
| Hungary | 100.0 | 100.0 | 100.0 | 100.0 | 170 | 158 | 139 | | | 3.8 | -2.0 |

*Sources: SE 1978*, p. 487; *SE 1976*, p. 436; *SE 1979*, p. 433; *Statisztikai szemle*, no. 4 (1980) pp. 417, 418; *SE 1983*, pp. 349, 350; *Statistical Yearbook 1982*, pp. 370, 371.

County which lost more than 50 per cent of its population increase from 1970 to 1980 and 90 per cent from 1976 to 1979). In the Northern Region the county Borsod – including Miskolc, the most important industrial 'counterpole' to Budapest – lost a third of its natural increase between 1970 and 1980, and more than 50 per cent from 1976 to 1979.[14] Borsod grew only from 793 000 (1975) to 800 000 (1984), i.e. by less than 1 per cent. (Budapest + Pest by 3.2 and Hungary by 1.7 per cent.) The more highly industrialized North Transdanubia and the agricultural macroregion Northern Great Plains exhibit better demographic conditions. South Transdanubia and the Southern Great Plain region, both industrially less developed, have – along with Budapest – the least favourable demographic conditions.

A demographic North–South gap corresponds to the South–North gap of industrial development in the *German Democratic Republic*. As can be clearly proved by all demographic indicators in Table 8.5, the agrarian counties of the Northern macroregion and Frankfurt and Cottbus in the Central macroregion have a better demographic structure than the GDR, on the average, and especially than the old industrial regions of the Southern macroregion. Regional differentiations in the demographic situations are also clearly shown by the population growth data. The GDR lost 2.8 per cent of its population from 1960 to 1983. Of the overall population loss of 487 000 more than 100 per cent occurred in the Southern counties, which lost 7.8 per cent of their population. The South-West counties ( + 0.4 per cent) and the Northern counties ( + 0.1 per cent); the Central counties even had a small population gain ( + 1.7 per cent) because of the immigration into Berlin, Frankfurt and Cottbus.[15]

## 3. Regional employment structures

Different regional indicators such as employment participation rates (for overall employment and especially female employment), industrial employment per thousand inhabitants, regional shift coefficients and other indicators clearly show regional differences in employment in the four countries. There are regions with labour reserves, and others – above all highly industrialized agglomerations – with tight labour markets. In short, in all countries there are imbalances in the overall labour market from the macro- and mesoregional points of view. In all four countries there are still stronger macroregional

**Table 8.5** Regional employment, production and demographic structure of the GDR, 1983

| Zone/macroregions/counties | Area (%) | Population (%) | Total partici-pation rates | % of regional employment 1960 | 1978 | 1983 | Regional shares 1978 | 1983 | Per 1000 inhabitants 1978 | 1983 | Gross industrial production (1970 = 100) 1975 | 1983 | 1975–83 | Population in 1000 1960 | 1983 | in 1000 (in %) 1960–83 |
|---|---|---|---|---|---|---|---|---|---|---|---|---|---|---|---|---|
| North | 61.4 | 43.4 | 50.0 | | | | 32.1 | 33.3 | 138 | 147 | | | | 7 182 | 7 269 | +87 (+1.2) |
| Northern Counties | 24.5 | 12.6 | 49.2 | | | | 7.2 | 7.6 | 106 | 114 | | | | 2 107 | 2 109 | +2 (+0.1) |
| Rostock | 6.5 | 5.4 | 50.1 | 20.1 | 24.2 | 24.5 | 3.3 | 3.5 | 116 | 123 | 136 | 195 | 59 | 832 | 896 | +64 (+7.7) |
| Schwerin | 8.0 | 3.5 | 48.3 | 15.1 | 23.7 | 24.1 | 2.1 | 2.2 | 108 | 116 | 147 | 199 | 52 | 623 | 592 | −31 (−5.0) |
| Neubrandenburg | 10.0 | 3.7 | 48.2 | 9.6 | 20.0 | 20.4 | 1.8 | 1.9 | 90 | 98 | 153 | 208 | 55 | 652 | 621 | −31 (−4.8) |
| Central Counties | 36.9 | 30.8 | 50.4 | | | | 24.9 | 25.7 | 151 | 160 | | | | 5 075 | 5 160 | +85 (+1.7) |
| Magdeburg | 10.7 | 7.5 | 51.1 | 29.1 | 33.0 | 33.0 | 6.6 | 6.6 | 160 | 169 | 138 | 198 | 60 | 1 377 | 1 259 | −118 (−8.6) |
| Potsdam | 11.6 | 6.7 | 47.2 | 25.0 | 30.5 | 31.2 | 4.9 | 5.2 | 136 | 147 | 139 | 204 | 65 | 1 161 | 1 122 | −39 (−3.4) |
| Berlin | 0.4 | 7.1 | 54.9 | 30.2 | 25.6 | 24.8 | 4.9 | 5.1 | 135 | 136 | 131 | 185 | 54 | 1 072 | 1 186 | +114 (+10.6) |
| Frankfurt | 6.6 | 4.2 | 44.1 | 30.2 | 29.0 | 29.1 | 2.7 | 2.8 | 121 | 128 | 152 | 254 | 102 | 658 | 709 | +51 (+7.8) |
| Cottbus | 7.6 | 5.3 | 51.3 | 35.3 | 41.7 | 42.6 | 5.8 | 6.0 | 203 | 219 | 151 | 212 | 61 | 807 | 884 | +77 (+9.5) |
| South | 38.6 | 56.6 | 51.1 | | | | 67.9 | 66.7 | 220 | 226 | | | | 10 007 | 9 434 | −573 (−5.7) |
| South-West counties | 14.1 | 15.1 | 51.3 | | | | 17.7 | 17.9 | 218 | 225 | | | | 2 521 | 2 532 | +11 (+0.4) |
| Erfurt | 6.8 | 7.4 | 51.0 | 35.1 | 41.6 | 41.4 | 8.1 | 8.2 | 204 | 211 | 141 | 211 | 70 | 1 249 | 1 239 | −10 (−0.8) |
| Suhl | 3.6 | 3.3 | 53.6 | 41.8 | 50.0 | 49.5 | 4.6 | 4.6 | 261 | 264 | 141 | 211 | 70 | 545 | 550 | +5 (+0.9) |
| Gera | 3.7 | 4.4 | 50.3 | 43.5 | 43.3 | 43.2 | 5.0 | 5.1 | 212 | 217 | 148 | 245 | 97 | 727 | 743 | +16 (+2.2) |
| Southern counties | 24.5 | 41.5 | 51.0 | | | | 50.2 | 48.8 | 221 | 227 | | | | 7 486 | 6 902 | −584 (−7.8) |
| Halle | 8.1 | 8.1 | 51.1 | 42.6 | 45.2 | 45.0 | 13.1 | 13.0 | 220 | 230 | 134 | 184 | 50 | 1 970 | 1 810 | −160 (−8.1) |
| Leipzig | 4.6 | 8.3 | 50.7 | 41.6 | 39.8 | 39.6 | 8.9 | 8.8 | 194 | 201 | 131 | 172 | 41 | 1 519 | 1 393 | −126 (−8.3) |
| Dresden | 6.2 | 10.8 | 50.8 | 43.6 | 43.7 | 43.5 | 12.6 | 12.4 | 215 | 221 | 131 | 196 | 65 | 1 885 | 1 796 | −89 (−4.7) |
| Karl-Marx-Stadt | 5.6 | 11.4 | 51.1 | 51.9 | 49.7 | 48.4 | 15.6 | 14.6 | 248 | 247 | 134 | 189 | 55 | 2 112 | 1 903 | −209 (−9.9) |
| GDR | 100.0 | 100.0 | 50.6 | 36.0 | 38.2 | 37.9 | 100.0 | 100.0 | 185 | 192 | 137 | 196 | 59 | 17 188 | 16 701 | −487 (−2.8) |

*Source: SJD, 1979 and 1984.*

development differences and regional differences in the use of the labour force. The GDR has a South–North development gap, the same can be said about Poland, the CSSR has more highly developed Western areas, and Hungary has a North–South gap.

Again, we will begin with *Czechoslovakia*. In accordance with the demographic differences between the CSR and SSR, employment growth in both parts was quite different in the past. From 1961 to 1978 the able-bodied population rose by 6.9 per cent in the CSR and by 23.6 per cent in the SSR. From 1975 to 1983 the able-bodied population rose by 0.87 per cent in the CSR and by 6.18 per cent in the SSR (employment rose by 3.51 and 11.0 per cent).[16] Because of the more favourable demographic situation, rapid industrialization and rising employment participation, as well as the socialization of agriculture, employment in the SSR's regions in the socialized sector rose to within the range of 53–70 per cent during the period form 1961 to 1978, the increases in the CSR ranging from 13 to 24 per cent. The additional industrial employment of 126 000 persons during the years 1970–5 was distributed as follows: + 88 000 for Slovakia; + 32 000 for the two Moravian regions; and only + 6000 for the Bohemian regions, Prague included.[17] From 1970 to 1980 the employment figure for the CSSR went up from 7.03 to 7.22 million (industrial employment from 2.66 to 2.78 million). But there was a gain only for the SSR. Its employment rose by 251 000, its industrial employment by 142 000.[18] Compared with the CSR the SSR still has relatively low industrial employment per thousand inhabitants, the participation rates are lower, and the shares represented by female employment are smaller. According to the data the highest actual labour reserves and the best future supply can be expected in Eastern Slovakia.

*Poland* has a strong territorial concentration of industrial employment. Even the macroregional data still show an extremely large gap between the more highly developed macroregion, South, and the two underdeveloped macroregions, North-East and Mid-East. No county in the other three countries has such low figures for industrial employment per thousand inhabitants as the North-East (78) and Mid-East (81) of Poland (cf. Table 8.3). The strong regional economic polarization of industrial employment can best be shown by the fact that in 1983 the industrial employment share of the macroregion South (27.1 per cent) was as high as that of the macroregions Mid-West, North, North-East and Mid-East together (27.0 per cent). The industrial employment share of the voivodship Katowice (19.0 per cent) was higher than that of the three least developed macroregions –

North, North-East, and Mid-East as large as Capital and Centre shares together. Whether the Polish regionalization into 49 voivodships has an economic rationale will be briefly discussed in Section IV.

Private agriculture is a special Polish problem. There are still rural labour reserves in some voivodships, but labour deficits already exist in some other areas. Only a greatly reformed agricultural policy which offers better professional and economic prospects to younger persons can prevent the excessive out-migration of young people and growing regional disproportions in the rural labour supply.[19]

In its spatial dimension the employment structure of *Hungary* is determined by the high concentration of employment in Budapest, especially in some industrial branches, by severe infrastructural and settlement structure restrictions for regional reallocation of labour, the difficulties other cities have in competing with the attractiveness of Budapest, the poor global demographic situation, the negative overall economic situation, etc. Limited resources, the need to use existing facilities, and personal or organizational preferences in location choices tend to favour a transfer of labour to capital or result in employment patterns with too little qualified labour in some areas. The 'deindustrialization' policy towards Budapest was quite success-ful, as shown by the fact that industrial employment decreased there from 623 000 persons in 1970 to 334 000 in 1983 (from 34.3 to 22.7 per cent of Hungarian industrial employment).[20] Budapest's reduction in industrial employment was much higher than it was for all of Hungary. The Great Plains gained in industrial employment, and its agriculture – which benefits from good conditions for large-scale farming – 'became economically dynamic'.[21]

The *GDR* employment structure shows employment reserves in the Northern macroregion and tight Southern regional labour markets. The extremely high figures for industrial employment per thousand inhabitants in the South show that here 'territorial rationalization' and modernization are needed. Due to the settlement structure, in the Northern counties it is only possible to establish smaller and medium-size plants, above all for female workers and also for the seasonally unemployed in agriculture.

R. Hauk stresses some mistakes the GDR has made in the past with regard to economic development of the North.[22] In locational choices regional or local labour reserves often have been overestimated, and not nearly enough manpower has been available for the 'service' branches. The still existing but (spatially) highly dispersed labour reserves in the North can only be used more efficiently if workers can be convinced to migrate, more transportation investments are made, and more of the building industry's capacity is transferred to the new industrial locations. According to R. Hauk the primary task now is not so much to utilize extensively the still-existing reserves of the North, but rather to 'consolidate' the activities of the immediate past.

## III. REGIONAL PROBLEMS AND PROBLEM REGIONS

The sectoral principle of management in the USSR and East Europe has led to sectoral and regional structures which must be considered suboptimal. They have led to 'extensive' use of labour, and to unused potentials for raising labour productivity. The author wants to outline the main problems in a given region, i.e. intraregional problems, as follows: product mix, parallel activities, enterprise size structure, and linkages. Sectoral management has led to 'empire-building', i.e. to too-large product mixes (insufficient specialization), and to too much small-scale production in the sectors and in the regional units. Particularly in auxiliary production we had and still have too little specialization, too small economies of scale, and an overly 'extensive' use of the regional labour force. So one reason for the existence of parallel activities in the production field (too many enterprises with the same production in a given region) has been the traditional branch policy aiming at a high degree of self-sufficiency in material–technical supply. Other reasons for parallel activities are historical structures and lack of financial means or bureaucratic and/ or enterprise inertia in regard to restructuring production.[23]

The aspect of enterprise size structure is a subject of discussion, especially in Hungary and Poland. One criticism of enterprise mergers in East Europe is that these mergers, sometimes criticized as 'giganto-mania' (for example, in Poland in the current reform discussion, and for some time now in Hungary),[24] destroy small-scale enterprises or their relative autonomy and lead to enterprise size structures which are unfavourable, especially when no adequate specialization follows. Mergers are criticized because they cause deficits in certain products or product parts (formerly produced by small independent enterprises), sometimes raise average costs of certain products, and weaken local or regional economies or their consumer food supply. They also have negative implications for regional labour markets when the new enlarged sectoral units do not sufficiently take into account the structures of regional labour markets according to the quantity and quality of their labour force. The interest of regional decision-makers often differ from sectoral interests with regard to regional development and the use of the regional labour force. Furthermore, there must be interest conflicts as long as there are so many sectoral decision-makers in a given region and both the regions' planning and decision power and their financial and material resources to realize central or regional goals are extremely limited. The current Polish reform discussion demands enlarged political and economic power for the regions,[25] which are also the natural entrepreneurs for managing small-size enterprises.

Release of labour and labour productivity growth are also prevented by insufficient intersectoral/interbranch linkages and cooperation. In sharp contrast to the strategic concept of complex regional development, there is not enough cooperation and integration between industrial branches and/or enterprises and between industry and agriculture. Insufficient cooperation is also responsible for seasonal unemployment or underemployment in rural areas.[26]

A second group of general problems is of *interregional character*. There is suboptimal interregional specialization with regard to the capital–labour and land–labour ratios. To quote some examples: labour is used 'extensively' in labour-deficit regions, new labour-intensive industries are constructed in regions which lack labour, old fixed capital with low productivity is combined with new high-quality human capital. Often in these agglomerations labour is tied up in industry by obsolete machines which should either be transferred to other regions or scrapped. The depreciation policy of the East European countries is another factor; it not only contributes to overall labour scarcity, but also to regional misallocation of labour. If, in a certain region, labour is more scarce than in others, then – other things being equal – the depreciation period should be shorter so that machines can be replaced earlier. Normally, other factors are not equal, because in agglomeration centres the labour force is on the average more qualified so that innovations should be introduced more rapidly. On the other hand, the result of this wasting of qualified labour – shown by very high figures for industrial employment per thousand inhabitants in many industrial agglomerations – does not permit enough innovative capacity in the tertiary sector.

As far as the land–labour ratio is concerned, there is not enough regional specialization in the agriculture of the East European countries, even if the problems may be less serious there than in the Soviet Union. The reasons for overly diversified regional economies in the field of agricultural production can be: the risk for the central authorities of restructuring production with regard to supply patterns and sale channels, lack of knowledge on the part of regional administrations about the relative advantages of agricultural production, lack of price or profit incentives for specialization, unwillingness of the regions to enter into a supply risk for certain products because of transport problems or extreme undersupply in the case of bad overall harvests, etc.

*Problem regions* in Eastern Europe are not to be defined by unemployment rates as in market economies, but by infrastructure and settlement structure deficiencies that create instabilities in regional labour markets. This applies above all to Hungary with its extremely large number of tiny villages and its lack of central places on different hierarchical levels. The second determinant of the existence of problem regions and employment instability is certainly economic policy. Here the neglect of agriculture can be cited. Above all, the agricultural policy of the Polish leadership not only caused food supply problems, but also regional disproportions in the rural labour supply.

## IV. REGIONAL POLICY AND REGIONAL PLANNING

So far, the East European countries are far from realizing their normative goal of comprehensive regional development which must include employment from the very beginning of the planning process. Planning reality with regard to labour was often quite different in the past. The bargaining of the enterprises with their superiors for investment and material resources has led to a kind of sequential planning in which the provision for labour force resources by the enterprises has followed the central allocation of material resources. This has also been largely responsible for imbalances in regional/local labour markets (the other primary reasons for imbalances being incorrect central planning or insufficient intersectoral coordination). In the past enterprises/ministries often did not devote enough attention to the (limited) potentials of regional labour markets, which led to under-used capacities or low shift coefficients or to unplanned out-migration and commuting from neighbouring regions. This created problems either for the transport system or housing, or employment disproportions and deficits in the out-migration regions.[27]

## 1.  Regional policy

Even if in every economic system regional policy has important coordinative functions – supplementing or correcting market coordination – its coordinative role is much more imporant in the centrally planned economies because of the insufficient horizontal coordination linkages in this system. So, to a certain extent, regional coordination is a surrogate for market coordination. The legal status of the regions has gradually improved in Eastern Europe during the last 15 years; further improvements are demanded and can be expected. On the other hand, the economic mechanisms – Hungary excepted – have not been dramatically changed nor sectoral powers widely reduced. Furthermore, the mergers on the enterprise level have created large, economically powerful organizations. Thus, it is surely realistic to suppose that the goodwill of the large sectorial units is more important for cooperation and coordination than the strengthened legal status of the region. True, the regional party secretary still remains the strongest actor. His importance is constantly stressed, even in scientific literature.[28] But even if the 'Soviet prefect' may substantially help his region, this can hardly be a substitute for 'integrated' sectoral–regional planning.

There is a constant trend towards formalizing the informal elements of coordination. This can best be shown by the GDR's policy of 'territorial rationalization' (territoriale Rationalisierung),[29] which uses regional coordination by 'fraternal help' and coordination by agreement (on a contractural basis). Territorial rationalization is intended to rationalize the use of all resources in a given region, human capital included. Until now this concept has focused primarily on capital productivity.[30] Better use of regional capital stocks is to be achieved by raising the regional shift coefficients. The so-called 'bank of reserves of productive funds', a data bank that shows interested enterprises which machines in which other enterprises are under-used, could become an important instrument for improving capital use in the future.[31] The regional or town executives' decisions based on data bank information can lead to labour productivity increases by means of inter-enterprise labour force exchanges, transfers of workers from old technology to modern equipment and also to the establishment of cooperation centres with the most productive technology and three-shift machine utilization, etc. Territorial rationalization also aims to improve specialization and build up linkages between centralized and regional industry. Above all, it encourages centralized enterprises to provide various forms of assistance to regional enterprises: transfers of equipment, use of research and development facilities or results, transfers of management personnel, training of qualified workers and managers, professional education of youth, etc. On the regional or city level special organizations are established to promote closer cooperation and coordination: working groups for technology, working groups for repair work, councils for professional education, etc.[32]

How should we evaluate this new development in regional coordination which is still in the experimental stage? What motivational or incentive backing is there to push territorial rationalization forwards in its development? This regional coordination follows the lines of traditional central planning, is still continuing to increase complexity, and relies too little on economic interests and instruments.

There are different incentive instruments aimed at influencing the behaviour of the workers, but so far there is no concept of also using economic levers to influence enterprise behaviour in order to promote rational regional allocation of labour and capital. Only economic and not administrative instruments would – according to Orlov and Shniper – be able to improve coordination between sectoral and regional planning. They do not consider it possible to end resource waste (labour included) by purely administrative means.[33] Improved regional coordination will primarily require the strengthening of regional and local budgets, thus giving them more financial (self-financing) power and reducing their dependence on the enterprises, especially for financing infrastructure investments.

'Reform economists', however, do not see at all how the traditional central planning system can cope with the technical problem of enlarging the system of indicators by a regional component and how a sectoral–regional balance of power can be realized in an administrative system. They demand an essential increase in political and economic power for the regions,[34] and J. Jasieński stresses the need not only to enlarge the decision-making and control power of the regions with regard to all enterprises in their territory, but above all with regard to their entrepreneurial regional activities. An industrially more highly developed region has more prospects than smaller, less-developed peripheral regions of developing regional enterprises and getting better assistance from centralized enterprises, in particular when it has capacities for innovation (especially large universities).

Regional and local entrepreneur activities are above all small-scale firm activities. Future mergers need more careful analysis. In Poland the legal basis for small industry has just been strengthened and in

Hungary, at the beginning of 1981, about 75 medium-sized enterprises were freed from central management and subordinated to counties.

Conflicts of interest in employment between regions and sectors remind us of the Western labour market segmentation approach, which stresses the existence of a (primary) high-wage and a (secondary) low-wage sector, good and bad jobs, and job instability in the secondary labour market. M. I. Dolishniy sees negative labour market developments in the Soviet Union similar to those described by Western labour market segmentation theory.[35] His criticism is that branch enterprises in small and medium-sized towns (considered in general to be a valuable organizational form for linking branch and regional planning interests) have too many bad jobs and the pay is, on average, significantly lower. Branch enterprises are sometimes not well organized and rarely specialized; the average qualifications needed, and the average wage categories, are essentially lower than in the main enterprises. Some ministries have solved the establishment of branch enterprises in small and medium-sized towns only 'in a formal way, transferring to them "unfavourable" kinds of products'. And Enyedi has criticized the use of regional labour reserves by centralized enterprises in Hungary.[36]

In East Europe, until now, the existing incentive system has not put enough pressure on the main enterprises to help branch enterprises to specialize. The regions have too few incentive possibilities to induce the main enterprises to transfer more innovation and more highly qualified work to the branch enterprises. In addition, the region may not be very interested in helping the branch enterprise of a 'foreign' entrepreneur. The low level of mechanization and automation in industry means there is a great need for less qualified workers.

## 2.  Regional planning

Regional planning in Eastern Europe needs better organization (larger staffs and better specialized economists) and improved instruments as well as information. If regions are to help reduce costly labour turnover, they can only do so with better information and regional statistics which, in turn, require better information from the enterprises (sectors). The regional labour balances represent the most important contribution to employment planning by the regions.[37] A better regionalization of labour balances is essential. In other words, balances are also needed for smaller levels and for economic regions instead of just for administrative ones. V. Churakov emphasizes two other more general deficiencies of the balance system.[38] Since the balances do not include indicators from work-places, they do not answer the question about how the sectors, the regions and the country as a whole are supplied with labour. In addition, the average data for a year do not allow larger seasonal variations in employment to be taken into account. One of the aims of the use of regional labour balances is simply to better utilize seasonally free labour and to achieve a better exchange between sectors during the season. For this reason Churakov proposes monthly balances of labour.

An interesting investigation of regional labour balances was made in Poland.[39] The voivodship planning commissions were asked by the State Planning Commission about the quality of the balances (a set of 28 questions). The answers (from 41 of 49 commissions) most often focused on (1) the need to have regional balances below the voivodship level, (2) the development of voivodship balances for qualified labour, and (3) the introduction of town–countryside disaggregations of the voivodship balances. Other proposals referred to balances for young workers, sectoral disaggregation (more than 'agriculture–outside of agriculture') and the disaggregation of the balance for agricultural workers and the inclusion of the commuting structure.

All countries attempt to increase the control that regional administrations (subordinated either to a central organization or to the regional executive) exert over enterprise utilization of labour.[40] The main tasks are to reduce labour hoarding by the enterprises, control enterprise demands for additional labour, and allocate the scarce additional regional labour force according to certain priorities. It seems that control over labour limitations imposed on the enterprises can be exerted more effectively in the smaller countries (GDR, CSSR) than in the USSR, where the Union ministries are extremely powerful, ministerial egoism is still more pronounced and local self-management has never existed. There are many restrictions on the effectiveness of the employment agencies – lack of staff and above all lack of qualified staff. They have to cope with a multitude of functions. They are expected to act as an information agency, manage transfers to other regions, do job counselling for young people, be controllers of the enterprises, etc. As long as the situation in the overall labour markets remains as tight as it is now, the state employment agencies in Eastern Europe will gainly only limited influence. The enterprise directors will not help the regional employment agencies to become 'overly efficient'.

One 'link' between regional policy and employment policy is the concept of an *employment region* (labour market region). The goal of regional employment stability is not in conflict with the goal of regional labour force mobility, but one of its determinants. Neither regional employment stability (trying to avoid in particular a deterioration of regional qualification structures) nor regional mobility is an end in itself. Both are determined by a range of conditions in the four countries. Leaving aside unfavourable overall economic and demographic conditions, dispersed settlement patterns and institutional factors which weaken regional policy, there are problems of conceptional choice. In every system regional policy is a matter of political power. The county level regions, for instance, are on the average extremely small in Poland and Hungary, the least developed of the four countries. This weakens the power of the regional 'prefects'. It is doubtful whether the Polish decision on 1 June 1975, to enlarge the number of voivodships from 22 to 49, was wise economically.[41] It is not even certain that it strengthened regional policy from the developmental point of view (there is danger of too much regional dispersion of resources); at any rate the coordination power of the voivodships, which is so necessary in a central planning system, was weakened.

## V.   CONCLUDING REMARKS

In view of the tight overall employment situation in East Europe, regional labour force reserves play a role and surely an increasingly significant one. But the 'intensive' use of the part of the population already employed, the labour productivity aspect, is much more important than the 'extensive' use of regional reserves. More than that, too much emphasis on regional reserves can delay rationalization processes in the agglomeration centres. And 'mobilizing' regional reserves to the last degree can be costly not only in demographic terms but also economically, leading to additional costs for infrastructure and settlement structure. The danger is extremely great that individual (enterprise) calculations are incomplete with regard to the social costs of regional development.

The increase in regional labour productivity has to be the primary goal for the planners and decision-makers. This is closely linked to what the author calls the coordination aspect of regional policy, and as long as 'parametric' steering or the use of economic instruments (levers) plays no role in regional policy, the political strength of the regional 'prefects' is essential. This strength can only exist if regions are not too small. In every system there is competition between the regions and the enterprises located in their areas at least for qualified personnel. Thus, the tight overall labour market situation in the centrally planned economies is highly detrimental to the regional allocation of qualified labour. As the experiences of the immediate past show, even in centrally planned economies the given distribution of economic power can lead to labour market segmentation phenomena.

### Notes

1. J. Kende, *Der ökonomische und soziale Ausgleich zwischen der CSR und der SSR als zentrales Problem der tschechoslowakischen Regionalpolitik*, Diplomarbeit FU Berlin (Berlin–West), 1979) p. 102.
2. *Statistické prehledy*, no. 4 (1984) p. 118; SRC 1984, p. 98.
3. Kende, op. cit., p. 108; *SRC 1984*, p. 98; *Statistika*, no. 7 (1984) pp. 299–308.
4. See H. E. Gramatzki, 'Territorialplanung in sozialistischen Ländern: Das Beispiel Polen', *Regionale Aspekte der Wirtschaftsplanung in den mitteleuropäischen RGW-Staaten* (Marburg, 1983) pp. 55–76.
5. See Gy. Enyedi, 'Economic Policy and Regional Development in Hungary', *Acta Oeconomica*, no. 1–2 (1979) pp. 113–25.
6. Ibid., p. 115.
7. Ibid., pp. 118, 119. For Enyedi the 'dispersed location of industry in the countryside' – which was widely criticized – 'brought basically good results', introducing industrial culture.
8. See for instance the leading textbook, R. Bönisch, G. Mohs and W. Ostwald (eds.), *Territorialplanung* (Berlin–East, 1976).
9. Kende, op. cit., p. 97; *SRC 1984*, p. 91.
10. *Statistika*, no. 8–9 (1980) p. 347.
11. Concerning the above data see *RS 1984*, p. 39.
12. *RS 1984*, p. LVII.
13. *Statisztikai Szemle*, no. 4 (1980) p. 417; *SE 1978*, p. 487; *SE 1979*, p. 485.
14. *SE 1979*, p. 485; *Statistical Yearbook 1982*, pp. 370, 371; *SE 1983*, pp. 349, 350.
15. *SJD 1984*, pp. 65–94; see also Table 8.5.
16. *SRC 1980*, p. 91; *SRC 1984*, pp. 178, 179, 183, 184.
17. *Plánované hospordárství*, no. 1 (1978) p. 50.
18. *SRC 1972*, p. 128; *SRC 1982*, pp. 202–4.
19. The average private farm had a mere 6.3 ha in 1978, but two-thirds of all private farms have 5 ha or less.
20. *SE 1983*, pp. 349, 350; sources of Table 8.4.
21. Enyedi, op. cit., p. 117.

22.  R. Hauk, *Wissenschaftliche Zeitschrift der Hochschule für Ökonomie 'Bruno Leuschner'* (Berlin–East, 1979) no. 3, p. 36.

23.  R. Bönisch, *Zur Planung der territorialen Produktionsstruktur, Beiträge zur territorialen Produktionsstruktur* (Leipzig, 1976) p. 23; cites East-Berlin and Karl-Marx-Stadt.

24.  See R. Evstigneev, *Voprosy ekonomiki,* no. 10 (1979) pp. 90–8; RFE-RL *Hungarian Situation Reports,* 12 April 1978 and 31 January 1980; *Rada Narodowa Gospodarka Administracja,* no. 9 (1979) pp. 1–4 and no. 11 (1979) pp. 20–5.

25.  See Podstawowe zatozenia reformy gospodareczej (projekt), *Zycie gospodarcze,* 18 January 1981, p. 8.

26.  This refers to the fact that a better general linkage between industry and agriculture and special organizational forms for transferring seasonally free labour to the capital, or vice versa, are needed.

27.  For an improvement in regional labour-balancing with reference to planning of migration and commuting see R. Dittmann, *Effektive Nutzung des gesellschaftlichen Arbeitsvermögens* (Berlin–East, 1974) pp. 32–40.

28.  See *Die örtlichen Organe der sozialistischen Staatsmacht* (Berlin-East, 1978).

29.  See R. Bönisch, *Wirtschaftswissenschaft,* no. 9 (1977) pp. 1341–53. Much is published in the weekly *Die Wirtschaft,* often dealing with pioneering counties and districts.

30.  Some authors demand that the innovation aspect be emphasized more than the reallocation of the given capital stock.

31.  A bank of reserves was established by the city of Dresden, for example.

32.  See A. Zimmermann, *Territoriale Rationalisierung als Intensivierungsaufgabe* (Berlin–East, 1978).

33.  A demand for such economic levers was already made in 1969 by the Soviet economists B. O. Orlov and R. I. Shniper, *Ekonomicheskaia reforma i territorial'noe planirovanie* (Moscow, 1969) pp. 45–56. Today it is chiefly the Polish economists who press for them; see for instance J. Jasienski, *Problemy ekonomiczne* (Krakow) no. 4 (1980) pp. 25–32.

34.  See Jasienski, op. cit., pp. 25–7.

35.  M. I. Dolishnyi, *Formirovanie i ispol' zovanie trudovykh resursov* (Kiev, 1978) pp. 122, 123.

36.  See Enyedi, op. cit., p. 118: '. . . the production lines of the plants located are not connected to each other'.

37.  Concerning the regional labour balances see Dittman, op. cit., especially pp. 32–40; V. Churakov, *Problemy regional'nogo balansa trudovykh resursov* (Moscow, 1977); J. Meller, *Gospodarka planowa,* no. 9 (1978) pp. 450–3 and *Gospodarka planowa,* no. 11 (1978) pp. 555–9.

38.  Churakov, op. cit.

39.  Meller, op. cit.

40.  Because of the wide range of problems involved, it was impossible to discuss here the legal, institutional, and functional aspects of the regional employment offices in the four countries.

41.  With regard to the overall polarized allocation of economic activities

(Katowice, Warsaw), the limited power of the macroregion, the extreme development differentials even between these macroregions and the present extreme economic difficulties, a 'dispersion policy' favouring so many small voivodships and/or their capital is no longer possible, in the opinion of the author.

# 9 Manpower Constraints and the Use of Pensioners in the Soviet Economy

DAVID E. POWELL

The population of the Soviet Union, like that of other advanced industrial societies, has been growing older. The number of persons of pension age (55 and above for women, 60 and above for men) increases with each passing year, and today they constitute a significant proportion of the country's total population. On the eve of World War II, only 8.9 per cent of the men and women living in the USSR were of pension age. By 1959, this figure had risen to 12.7 per cent by 1970 to 15 per cent and by 1979 to 15.5 per cent.[1] As of 1 January 1984, some 37.2 million Soviet citizens were receiving old-age pensions, an astonishing seven-fold increase from the 1961 number of 5.4 million.[2]

The reasons for this development are not hard to find. Probably the most important underlying cause is the sharp reduction in the birth-rate that has been observed in most parts of the USSR over the past several decades.[3] This phenomenon, in turn, is largely a consequence of the two great traumas of the 1930s and 1940s – Stalin's terror and the Second World War. While we are unlikely ever to have a statistical breakdown comparing the relative suffering of different population groups during these two lengthy episodes, it is clear that an enormous number of young males (and, to a lesser extent, young females) perished before they had a chance to raise families. Large-scale urbanization has also contributed to the decline in birth-rates in both urban and rural areas, and thus to the ageing of Soviet society.[4] Crowded housing, together with the different life-style characteristic of urban dwellers, have conspired to keep the number of births in the cities down; at the same time, the loss of younger, more fertile men and women from the USSR's villages has produced a reduction in the number of children born in the provinces.

The second major factor contributing to the 'greying' of the Soviet population is the fact that people are living longer now than they were earlier. Before the Revolution, life expectancy among women in Russia was 33 years; today it is about 74. Among men, too, the figure has risen dramatically – from 31 in 1896–7 to a high of 66 in the mid-1960s.[5] In the main, this increase can be attributed to achievements in the fields of public health and sanitation, i.e. bringing under control the diseases that formerly decimated infants and young children, eliminating epidemics and certain debilitating diseases, and similar developments. Until very recently, it has been expressed in lowered mortality levels among virtually all population groups.

Recent years, however, have witnessed an increase in both infant mortality and adult male mortality. During the period 1955–65, for example, the infant mortality rate fell steadily and rapidly; thereafter, it continued to fall, but at a less rapid rate, reaching its lowest level (22.9 per thousand live births) in 1971. At that point, however, it began to rise, reaching 27.9 in 1974. Responding to this troublesome circumstance, the Soviet statistical authorities simply decided not to publish any additional information on the subject, so we do not know how matters stand now.[6]

A similar pattern can be observed with regard to male life expectancy. After reaching a peak of 66 years in 1966–7, the figure dropped to 65 and then to 64. After 1971–2, new data concerning life expectancy disappeared from the standard Soviet reference books. According to Murray Feshbach, a leading American demographer, the situation has continued to deteriorate: even though the relevant tables no longer appear in *Narodnoe khoziaistvo SSSR* (*The National Economy of the USSR*), Feshbach estimated in 1983 that male life expectancy was only 61.9 years.[7] The reasons for this negative development are shrouded in secrecy. None the less, they appear to be the result of growing alcohol abuse, smoking, environmental pollution, and a deterioration in nutritional standards.[8]

However interesting and important the 'greying' of the Soviet population is in its own right, it is vital to understand its crucial implications for the country's manpower situation. In as much as this ageing process is expected to continue for the next several decades at least (a fact which both Soviet and non-Soviet specialists accept),[9] the prospects for continued economic development may well be severely threatened. The ageing of the population has led to the ageing of the Soviet labour force. Furthermore, greater numbers of pensioners will place greater burdens on the nation's resources, while lower birth rates will reduce the supply of badly needed manpower for industry, construction and farming. If, as the sociologist V. D. Shapiro has remarked, 'The economy's growing need for labour demands that additional manpower be brought into social production',[10] the question becomes, Where will these workers come from?

## I. IS THERE A MANPOWER SHORTAGE?

For more than a decade, Soviet planners and scholars have expressed concern about an 'inevitable' and 'increasingly acute' labour deficit. Some argue that there already is such a deficit, while others predict with varying degrees of urgency that the shortage will begin to make itself felt in the near future. Whether these fears are unreasonable is by no means clear, however. The evidence is contradictory, as is the testimony of expert witnesses both in the USSR and abroad.

As early as 1973, one Gosplan official complained of 'the growing deficit in labour resources', warning that additional sources of manpower 'have begun to run dry'.[11] A year later, the economist A. Tarasov spoke out even more forcefully, declaring that 'limited labour resources are now a fact, and the more rational use of these resources is becoming a burning question'.[12] Even former General Secretary Leonid I. Brezhnev expressed concern about the manpower problem on more than one occasion. Speaking at the October, 1975 plenary session of the Party Central Committee, for example, the Soviet leader remarked, 'Our need for labour resources will grow, both in the production and the non-production [i.e. service] sectors. At the same time, the effects of demographic factors connected with the long-term consequences of the war will lead in the 1980s to a sharp decline in the growth of the able-bodied population.'[13]

Western experts, too, have pointed out that the Soviet labour force has been expanding at a slower and slower rate. According to Murray Feshbach and Stephen Rapawy, the rate of increase during the period 1970–90 will be only one-third of the rate which prevailed during the period 1950–70.[14] The distinguished economist Abram Bergson has drawn a similar contrast between the 1970s and the 1980s. During the earlier decade, he has written, the labour force grew by roughly 1.7 per cent per annum; during the current decade, it will increase by only 0.4 per cent each year.[15] A high-ranking Central Intelligence Agency official, Henry Rowen, has drawn a somewhat less pessimistic picture. The net increment to the work force was about 19 million during the time period 1971–81, he estimated in 1982; for the decade 1981–91, however, he predicted an increase of 9 million, less than half the number added during the previous decade.[16] The important point here is not whether one or another set of estimates is more nearly correct; what is crucial is the fact that net increments to the labour force have become smaller and smaller with each passing decade. This is a matter of considerable interest to Western analysts, but it is a source of immense concern to planners in the USSR.

Whether or not these developments and projections testify to a genuine manpower shortage is a very different question. Because the Soviet economic system seems incapable of efficiently allocating labour resources (it is no less wasteful of land and capital), the 'shortage' of workers may be more apparent than real. A number of specialists in the USSR have raised precisely this question. For example, in 1975, the well-known sociologist A. Aitov remarked that 'our labour resources are completely adequate, but they are utilized irrationally'.[17] Other commentators, while admitting to regional shortages or a lack of *skilled* workers, deny that these circumstances imply the existence of 'an absolute shortage of able-bodied persons'. To quote an official of the Job-Placement (Labour Exchange) administration of the RSFSR State Committee for Labour, 'the task at the present time is not to increase the number of workers, but rather to make correct use of available labour resources'.[18] Still other authorities have dismissed the whole idea of a manpower shortage as 'imaginary' and 'fictional'.[19]

Even Western experts who argue that the demographic picture offers 'disturbing prospects for the future availability of manpower' also point to the 'poor utilization of available manpower and material resources' as an equally powerful source of concern. Low labour productivity, the inefficient use of the workforce, the 'hoarding' of workers by enterprise managers and a number of other factors conspire to limit the economic contribution of men and women in the labour force today.[20] Indeed, given the widespread waste and inefficiency involved in 'spontaneous' (i.e. inadequately regulated) population migration, the high rates of labour turnover that prevail in most sectors of the economy, inefficiencies associated with the system of planning, incentives and rewards, the lack of automated machinery and equipment, the poor quality of most vocational guidance programmes, and the loss of work time brought on by alcohol abuse, poor labour discipline, absenteeism and similar problems, one wonders just how real the manpower shortage is.

Still, planners and enterprise managers alike continue to look for more workers. And unless the Gorbachev regime introduces some sort of basic, structural reform of the economic system, this quest will go on indefinitely. Where will they look? Soviet sources reveal that, as recently as 1950, more than one-fourth (26 per cent) of the population was not engaged in 'social production' or involved in full-time study. A decade later, the figure had fallen only slightly, to 22 per cent, but today it has dropped to a mere 8 per cent.[21] In the past, additions to the work force could be secured through recruiting women who were engaged in household work or rural dwellers who devoted their time to farming their private plots.[22] At the present time, however, these 'reserves' have essentially disappeared, and this fact lies at the root of official concern.

A proportion of the total population of the USSR that is currently employed is unusually high by international standards, and the prospects for bringing additional housewives, students, military personnel or other men and women into the labour force are not very good. As a 1977 CIA study noted, 'The share of females in the primary working age group 20 to 54 years that is employed is already about nine-tenths and probably cannot be maintained in the face of rising family income levels. Reducing the school-leaving age or demobilizing some of the armed forces would yield only one-time windfalls and would not reverse the downward trend in employment growth.'[23]

Soviet planners have placed increasing reliance on young people who have just entered the labour force. During the Seventh Five-Year Plan (1961–5), young people provided 29.1 per cent of the annual increment in manpower levels, but during the Eighth Five-Year Plan, this figure rose to 57.3 per cent and in the Ninth Plan period (1971–5), it went above the 90 per cent level. But this approach can no longer provide a panacea, and one of the major considerations leading to the 1984 education reform was the desire to channel more teenagers directly into production.[24] Demographic forces are working against the authorities, however. The relatively small generation that was born in the 1960s has already begun to enter the work force; clearly, it will not be sufficiently numerous to replace the much larger generation born during the 1920s, which is now leaving the labour force.[25] Fewer persons will be reaching working age, while more will be reaching the age of retirement. Indeed, in the 1980s, there will be a downturn in the number of persons added to the able-bodied age bracket to just over one fifth of the number added in the first half of the 1970s; the increments in the latter half of the decade will be only slightly larger.[26] Additional manpower supplies, it is clear, will have come from some other source.

## II. PENSIONS AND PARTICIPATION IN THE LABOUR FORCE–A BRIEF HISTORY

One potential source of manpower is the large number of pensioners in the country. At the present time, more than 37 million Soviet citizens are old-age pensioners, and each year betweeen 1 and 1.5 million more are added to the rolls.[27] Many of these men and women have specialized training, and all have accumulated considerable life experience – traits which make at least some of them attractive to enterprise managers in need of more workers. As two leading scholars in the field of labour economics have put it, 'their [retirees'] experience and skills are, of course, capital which we value most highly, and our society is vitally interested in continuing to use it in the future.'[28]

The idea of utilizing in the public sector the labour of men and women who are of pension age is by no means new, however. Old-age pensions[29] were first introduced in the USSR on 5 January 1928, when a special programme for workers in the textile industry was introduced.[30] Then, as now, eligibility for women began at age 55, while for men the figure was set at 60. The only other eligibility requirement was that the individual had to have been employed for at least 25 years. A year later, on 15 May 1929, pension benefits were extended to other groups and, 'with a view to stimulating retirement', a system of regulations linking benefits to seniority, sex and working conditions was established. A law promulgated on 28 September 1929 authorized miners and others employed in dangerous or difficult occupations to retire at 50, and they needed to have given only 20 years of service to do so.

Pension benefits were set at 50 per cent of the individual's average monthly wage, although in no case could they exceed a level of 112.5 rubles per month. Policy-makers were anxious not only to reward 'labour veterans' and provide them with an opportunity to take life easy: they also wanted to have older workers retire in order to make room for younger men and women, people with greater skills, energy and (it was thought) political reliability.[31]

When the pension system was first being introduced, there was still considerable unemployment in the country. Thus, it is not surprising that the first programmes were put into effect precisely in those sectors where labour supplies were especially abundant, especially the textile industry.[32] The regime's objective was to prod older, 'superfluous' workers to drop out of the labour force. As B. Bykhovsky, the man who apparently drafted the 15 May 1929 decree, put it, 'The specific purpose of the law is to eliminate old people from production . . . The new law has great importance for our unemployed youth, who will have an opportunity to take the jobs vacated by old people.[33] Towards the end of 1929, however, and even more so in 1930, labour shortages began to appear. As a result, older workers were urged *not* to retire, but to remain instead at their jobs or to switch to another position that would require less skill and/or experience, even if it would also be less remunerative.[34]

Throughout most of the 1930s, planners held out two kinds of incentives to individuals who had reached or who were approaching pension age. One involved continuing to pay them their regular wage, but supplementing it with a full or partial pension. (These additional benefits could increase a person's income up to 100 per cent.) A second scheme offered those who remained in the labour force higher pension benefits once they actually retired; as a rule, someone's pension was set 20 per cent higher for every two years of additional work. In addition, more elaborate and remunerative programmes were devised for special categories of workers, e.g., those who were employed in the Far North, Siberia or the Far East, as well as coal miners and others engaged in arduous or hazardous labour.

The postwar situation only served to intensify efforts to keep as many men and women as possible on the job. In view of the overwhelming human and material losses which the USSR suffered during the war years (not to mention the losses sustained earlier during collectivization and during Stalin's 'war against the people'), it is not surprising that the postwar era witnessed further efforts to persuade people of pension age to continue working. During the period 1947–56, pension benefits were raised sharply: the maximum wage on which benefits were calculated had been frozen in 1932, so that even though wages had increased dramatically since that time, pensions had not kept up with them.[35] Once again, pensions were set at a level equal to 50 per cent of the individual's former wages – except in the case of high-ranking administrators, who were permitted to receive 65 per cent of their former pay.

But the 1947 reforms did not affect the entire labour force. Only one-third of all blue- and white-collar personnel were granted the right to increased pensions; for everyone else, the regulations established in 1932 still applied. The death of Stalin and the promulgation of Khrushchev's de-Stalinization programmes gave rise to more changes, however, the most important of which was the sweeping reform introduced in 1956. The number of those eligible was increased, and precise regulations were draw up to aid in computing monthly payments. The individual's age, the number of years he had worked, his health, his family status, the working conditions that prevailed at his place of employment, and the region of the country in which he had worked were all weighed in the final calculation. For the first time, the law provided special supplements for those with a lengthy and unbroken work record (*nepreryvnyi stazh*), and it also established partial pensions for those who had not worked long enough to be eligible for a full pension.

All of these 'progressive' steps, however, were significantly under-cut by the introduction of one genuinely retrograde measure: the drastic curtailment of the citizen's right to receive *both* a pension and a monthly wage. Low-income workers (i.e., those whose wages did not exceed 100 rubles a month), as well as miners and other people employed in hazardous occupations, were permitted to receive up to 50 per cent of their pension along with their current wages. But all other pensioners who wanted to work were forced to choose between receiving their wages and receiving their regular pension benefits.[36] As we shall see, the policy of increasing pension benefits, while sharply limiting the system of combining wages and pensions, quickly led to a reduction in employment among pensioners.

By 1964, the pendulum had swung back in the other direction. Various decrees, laws, regulations and 'instructions' issued in that year and afterwards once again authorized working pensioners in blue-collar occupations to receive not only their pay, but a substantial part of their pensions as well.[37] The consequences for labour partici-pation rates were dramatic; indeed, the proportion of pensioners who were employed has continued to rise steadily in the past two decades (see Table 9.1).

The year 1964 witnessed one other major change in Soviet pension law: collective farmers were finally brought into the system. However, in much the same way that industrial workers were encouraged not to retire, *kolkhozniki* on the eve of retirement were given various financial incentives to stay at their jobs. In fact, the law granted collective farmers the right to receive *full* pensions in addition to their regular wages.[38] To be sure, in the years before 1964, some *kolkhozy* managed to set up their own pension systems, while others (probably most) 'helped their aged members in other ways'.[39] But their resources were, by and large, meagre, and retired *kolkhozniki* had to make ends meet by tending their own private plots and/or by receiving assistance

*Table 9.1* Working pensioners as a
percentage of old-age pensioners

| Year | % |
| --- | --- |
| 1956 | 59.0 |
| 1960 | 11.7 |
| 1962 | 9.2 |
| 1965 | 12.5 |
| 1970 | 19.0 |
| 1975 | 24.2 |
| 1979 | 27.8 |
| 1981 | 30.6 |
| 1984 | 34.2 |

*Sources:* Stephen Sternheimer, 'The Graying
of the Soviet Union', *Problems of
Communism*, vol. XXXI, no. 5
(September–October, 1982), p. 83;
*Sotsial'noe obespechenie*, no. 5 (1984) p. 3.

from their relatives. In a number of ways, the system introduced in
1964 was highly discriminatory: male collective farmers could become
eligible for pensions only at age 65 (women at age 60), and pension
allotments were so low as to lead Lazar Volin, a leading Western
expert on Soviet agriculture, to term them 'paltry'. Despite these
serious shortcomings, however, one cannot but agree with Volin's
conclusion: 'The 1964 law, for all its faults, [was] still a modest step
toward greater security.'[40]

But providing greater financial security for one or another group of
citizens sometimes brought about contradictory results, including
developments that the authorities found extremely distressing. Evidence from various Western countries, including the United States,
suggests that increasing pension benefits often leads individuals to
withdraw prematurely from the work force. In the USSR, the
improvements introduced in 1956 had only a limited impact, primarily because older men and women could not count on receiving a
pension supplement if they remained on the job after reaching
retirement age. The fact that the number of working pensioners
plummeted from almost 60 per cent of all old-age pensioners in 1956
to only 9.2 per cent in 1962 was a direct result of the Soviet
government's new approach.[41] Evidently, more people felt that they

could afford to retire – i.e., to leave the work force without experiencing serious privation – since pensions were increased. At the same time, other men and women presumably decided that they no longer had any real incentive to remain in the labour force, so they, too, chose retirement.

The outcome of the 1964 reform was more predictable; as we have seen, it brought about a dramatic *rise* in the proportion of the pension-age population who chose to continue working. For the country as a whole, the figure more than doubled between 1964 and 1971; in the RSFSR, it increased fourfold. While 11 per cent of all old-age pensioners were employed in 1964, the percentage in the USSR today is more than three times that level – 34.2 per cent as of 1984.[42] To be sure, not all of this increase can be attributed to the legal changes introduced in 1964. Since 1 January 1980, men and women of pension age have had the option of having their pension raised by 10 roubles per month for every additional year they work after becoming eligible to retire. (The new law does, however, place a ceiling of 150 rubles on pension benefits for individuals who choose this scheme.)[43] Persons who have maintained an unbroken record of employment at any enterprise for 15 years are eligible for a 10 per cent increase in their pensions, while anyone with 25 or more years of un-interrupted service may receive an additional 20 per cent, on top of the 10 per cent granted for 15 years of uninterrupted work. Women with children are eligible for the extra 20 per cent if they put in 20 or more years without interruption at the same plant.[44]

The principal factor inducing men and (to a lesser degree) women to continue earning money today is the promise of more income. The desire (or need) to continue earning money is cited by slightly more than half the males questioned in several surveys; the figure for women ranges from about a quarter to two-fifths. In contrast, the decision *not* to work seems to hinge on non-financial considerations. The most important of these is the desire to avoid heavy physical labour, but the lack of opportunities to work part-time or to work at home also pushes people toward retirement as soon as they become eligible. Not surprisingly, women approach the work–retirement decision with a very different attitude from that of their male counterparts. In particular, women tend to retire in order to deal with family responsibilities, e.g., to take care of grandchildren, or to liberate children and/or grandchildren to study, work or enjoy additional leisure.[45]

## III. USING PENSIONERS IN THE LABOUR FORCE TODAY

We have already noted that more than 30 million individuals – 'enough to populate an entire country!', the editors of one Soviet newspaper exclaimed[46] – presently receive old-age pensions. By the end of this century, the number is likely to be twice as large; this circumstance, in turn, makes it almost inevitable that the government will call upon these people for additional efforts 'on the labour front'. For a number of years, analysts have been urging a 're-evaluation of our image of the role of people of pension age in the development of the country's economy and culture.'[47] Although pensioners have been used in the work force for many years, it is increasingly clear that they will be called upon to make a more substantial contribution. Given the present situation and the expected course of future economic development, one sociologist has written, the idea of 'using the labour of pensioners in social production has acquired special significance'.[48] That is, 'Society will be forced to utilize more fully this additional source of manpower.'[49]

Not everyone agrees with this point of view, however. Indeed, opinion about the wisdom (and even the possibility) of recruiting older people into the work force is divided. There are some who see any such programme as difficult to implement and, at best, capable of making only a marginal contribution to the national economy. For example, V. Kostakov argues that the labour potential represented by old-age pensioners 'has obviously been exaggerated. What has been lost sight of is the fact that in material production, with its rapidly changing technological base, the widespread use of the labour of these people is incompatible with efforts to update production techniques, and in the service sphere it lowers the quality of service to the population, largely because of the low educational level of the overwhelming majority of these people, who are beyond the able-bodied age.'[50] Even A. G. Novitskii, who has been in the forefront of efforts to bring pensioners into the labour force and to keep them there, acknowledges that older men and women are 'the least mobile, in both the social and geographical senses, and also have a low educational level in comparison with the able-bodied population'.[51]

This is a distinctively minority position, however. The great majority of analysts – and, more important, government decision-makers[52] – consider it imperative that pensioners who are physically and mentally competent participate actively in the labour force. They argue that such a policy is, on the one hand, in the economic interest of the state and, on the other, beneficial to the workers themselves – promoting their physical well-being, making them feel useful and needed, and providing them with additional income.

However strong the economic self-interest of the state is – and, as we have already indicated, official policy is largely a response to real and/or perceived labour shortages – most of the public discussion is cloaked in language emphasizing the government's benevolent attitude towards the citizenry, its solicitude for the needs of older men and women, and similar expressions of parental concern. For example, Novitskii, while noting the economic benefits to be derived from utilizing 'the accumulated experience, the creative skills' and the feelings of 'responsibility to society' supposedly manifested by most older men and women, emphasizes that staying on the job or returning to work 'is in the interest of the pensioners themselves. Doing whatever work they can is a way to prevent ageing; it makes one healthy and helps one to live longer.'[53] Similarly, Shapiro underscores the need 'to improve the living conditions and everyday life' of these people. 'The essence of social security,' he contends, 'amounts to more than a simple payment of pensions. The lofty and humane goal of social policy with respect to ageing people under a socialist system involves careful attention to their needs, the creation of those conditions necessary to organizing their lives in a rational manner, maintaining their social activity, and providing support for their feelings of social optimism – and, as a result of all of this, guaranteeing them a long and valuable life.'[54]

At the present time, more than one of every three pensioners is employed. Almost all of these individuals decided to continue working without interruption, even though they could have retired; only a handful left the labour force, reconsidered their decision, and returned to work. More important, the group as a whole consists largely of people who have only recently reached pension age, i.e. men who are 60–64 years of age and women who are 55–59.[55] Planners and scholars accept this circumstance and do not regard individuals who are much older as a significant manpower reserve.[56]

Of course, older pensioners are not necessarily less healthy, less energetic or less anxious to work than their younger counterparts. As the eminent Soviet gerontologist V. P. Belov has observed, 'by itself, age cannot serve as an absolute criterion for determining who is, and who is not, fit to work. The rates at which people age are strictly an individual matter.'[57] Indeed, as recently as a decade and a half ago, the great majority of pensioners were considered fit to work. One study carried out by Belov in the early 1970s found that 72 per cent of all men and women of pension age were able-bodied; another 19.5 per cent were deemed capable of doing some work, and only 8.7 per cent were unable to work at all.[58] Other surveys conducted at about that time in various areas of the country produced similar findings.[59]

But the situation has changed dramatically in the years since these studies were carried out. The decrease in male life expectancy that we noted earlier has served to limit the number of men over the age of 60. Furthermore, the quality of medical care available to the population as a whole has deteriorated; as a result, those who reach retirement age generally find it difficult to work for more than a few years. The usual infirmities of old age appear much earlier in the USSR than they do in North America, Western Europe or Japan. Because premature ageing is so common in the Soviet Union, Belov's conclusions are now out of date.[60]

At the same time, the fact of premature ageing has helped to reinforce a key finding that emerged from earlier investigations: it is all but impossible to persuade non-working pensioners to re-enter the work force. For example, after carrying out a far-ranging study of men and women of pension age in Moscow in the 1970s, Shapiro argued that the potential economic contribution of non-working pensioners was not very great. 'Most pensioners, having made the decision to retire, have evaluated the situation thoroughly, and having passed through a period of adaptation to their new living conditions, are even less inclined to resume working.'[61] Novitskii has made precisely the same point, asserting that, 'It is far easier to persuade people of pension age not to retire than to induce them to return to work once they have gone on pension.'[62] The deterioration in public health levels during the past 10–15 years has made the task of recruiting the so-called 'old-old' back into the work force even more difficult.

Virtually all pensioners who want to continue working after 'retirement' have had to take full-time jobs, either staying on at their regular place of employment or seeking a position elsewhere. Very few have the opportunity to work part-time, whether a few hours a day or a few days a week. Various surveys of pensioners with jobs have put the number of those working at home at less than 1 per cent of the overall sample; even fewer – between 0.3 and 1 per cent – enjoy a reduced working day or working week.[63] According to one estimate, only 9000 out of a total of 2 000 000 working pensioners in the Russian Federation – i.e. less than half of one per cent – are employed part-time.[64] A more comprehensive and detailed survey of Muscovites, carried out in 1973–5, drew a picture that was only slightly more encouraging. According to the investigators, fully 86 per cent of all working pensioners in that city had to put in a full day, even though 58 per cent of the sample expressed a desire to work part-time.[65] Soviet scholars and officials are candid in admitting that existing programmes do not meet the needs of older men and women.[66]

Of course, the government has taken a number of steps to increase the role of 'labour veterans' in the work force. Besides the most important message – permitting them to receive their regular wages in addition to a large portion of their pensions – some attempt has been made to provide such individuals with special working conditions, lighter work loads, special sections and shops that are exclusively (or chiefly) staffed by pensioners, reduced output norms (without a reduction in wages) and longer paid vacations.[67] But there is frequently a disparity between the kinds of jobs pensioners would like to have and the kinds of jobs they ultimately get. For example, fully one-third of all employed pensioners work as guards or watchmen – sedentary and boring jobs that are hardly in keeping with the promise that continuing to work will have a 'beneficial effect on their health ... [and] will prevent premature ageing'.[68] Equally important, part-time work is extremely difficult to obtain. Official regulations severely limit the opportunities available to elderly men and women, and factory officials seldom have any interest in experimenting with flexible employment schemes.

In general, working pensioners are employed in those sectors of the economy where they are permitted to retain both their wages and their full pensions. Indeed, legislation aimed at promoting 'the more widespread use in the national economy of the labour of old-age pensioners' directly appeals to the 'material interest'[69] of such individuals by promising such an opportunity, and this approach has met with considerable success. In particular, there has been a dramatic influx of pension-age men and women into jobs in the fields of health care, trade, communications and consumer services – precisely the fields in which they were promised full pension rights, along with their wages.[70]

## IV. CONCLUDING REMARKS

The government's effort to persuade older men and women to remain in the work force after they reach retirement age has met with considerable success. Throughout the country, more and more men reaching 60 and women reaching 55 are deciding to continue working. According to the 1970 census, 12.5 per cent of all pension-age people had jobs.[71] Five years later, the figure had almost doubled,[72] and it now exceeds one-third of all those who are eligible. In the larger industrial cities, whose populations tend to be a good deal older than the national average, the rate of increase has been especially high. Perhaps most strikingly, in recent years, more than 60 per cent of all new pensioners have chosen to work, rather than to retire,[73] so we can expect the total number of working pensioners to rise still further.

In view of the shortage of manpower today, the prospect for more serious difficulties in the near future, declining birthrates, the ageing of the population, and the enormous financial burden brought about by increased social security payments, the Soviet authorities have little room in which to manoeuvre. The monetary factor may well be the most crucial obstacle of all. The continuing slowdown in the country's rate of economic growth, massive expenditures for military expansion and modernization, the increasingly urgent need to improve conditions with respect to agriculture and consumer goods, and the sharp fall in the prices of the USSR's principal exports (oil, natural gas, gold and diamonds), represent a powerful array of economic constraints. The State paid out 21.3 billion rubles for old-age pensions in 1978, and official projections suggest a figure of 67–71 billion rubles by 1990 and 128–45 billion rubles by the end of the century. According to Stephen Sternheimer, total outlays for old-age pensions will rise from 5.1 per cent of Soviet national income in 1980 to 9.6–10.3 per cent in 1985.[74]

If the question of money is troublesome to the regime, it is no less so for the typical pensioner: when asked why they are continuing to work, most people of retirement age cite financial need. Still, almost as many say that they want to retain ties with their fellow workers, to feel that they are doing something useful with their lives, or cite similar motives. Not surprisingly, their reasons vary with their financial status: the higher the per capita income of their family, the less important money is.[75]

Unless the authorities decide to increase pension benefits, financial considerations will probably come to play an increasingly dominant role in the work–retirement decision. Pension levels are inadequate today and, in view of other demands on the State's resources, they may become more inadequate. As two Soviet economists observed at the end of the 1970s, 'in recent years, the income level of non-able-bodied citizens in our country has begun to lag perceptibly behind the standard of living of the population as a whole.' In 1956, they pointed out, 'the hightest old-age pension was more than one and a half times the average wage. Now, the average wage is more than twice as high as the average pension and is higher than the maximum old-age pension.'[76]

In 1980, the average monthly pension for the urban blue- and white-collar workers was 70 rubles, i.e., 41 per cent of the average monthly wage. Official plans call for a doubling of the average pension by the year 1990 and a three-fold increase by 2000. Even if this highly optimistic goal is reached, however, the average old-age pension at the end of the century will still be only 54 per cent of the average monthly wage that will prevail then. The situation of collective farmers is, and will remain throughout the 1980s and 1990s, even worse.[77] Recently announced plans for a retroactive increase in previously calculated pensions will be of marginal help at best. Higher pensions inevitably will deter older people from remaining in or returning to the labour force – hardly an outcome desired by planners who must contend with a manpower shortage.[78] In any event, minimum pension levels are extremely low. For many years, the minimum set for workers and managerial personnel was 50 rubles a month, while that for collective farmers was a mere 28 rubles.[79] On 1 November 1985 a new law went into effect, increasing the minimum old-age pensions for *kolkhozniki* to 40 rubles a month and eliminating the *upper* limit of 60 rubles a month for certain categories of office employees and ordinary workers. (The precise nature of the latter change remains unclear; according to a joint resolution issued by the Party Central Committee, the USSR Council of Ministers and the All-Union Central Council of Trade Unions, pensions for these blue- and white-collar groups will be 'brought closer to the level of the pensions that are currently in force for personnel with similar occupations and skills.'[80] While the increases doubtless were welcomed by especially-needy older people, they continue to be minuscule.

Clearly, the situation of the elderly in the USSR is far from ideal, and it may well get worse before it gets better. As Sternheimer has observed, thus far the real burden of the 'greying' portion of the Soviet population has fallen on the aged themselves.[81] One possible solution to the dilemma – raising the pension age – appears to be acceptable chiefly from the economic point of view, but far less so politically or ideologically.[82] A second suggestion which has received attention in the press involves linking pension benefits more closely to an individual's overall job performance, rather than just to earnings.[83] This approach, should it be implemented, could result in lower pensions; at the same time, however, it would fit in nicely with Mr Gorbachev's emphasis on 'intensification' and discipline.

For the foreseeable future, the prospects for older men and women look rather bleak. It is virtually certain that the typical individual reaching retirement age will continue to work, and will stay on the job as long as possible. Before that day arrives, he or she will have to work much harder; afterward, barring some unexpected and dramatic improvement in public health standards, he or she will be able to work for only a few years. The old Russian saying, '*Starost' ne radost''* (Old age is no joy), is likely to acquire a particularly personal meaning for members of the older generation.

## Notes

1.  Stephen Sternheimer, 'The Graying of the Soviet Union,' *Problems of Communism*, vol. XXXI, no. 5 (September–October, 1982), pp. 81–82; A. G. Novitskii in A. Z. Maikov and A. G. Novitskii, in *Problemy nepolnogo rabochego vremeni i zaniatost' naseleniia* (Moscow, 1975) p. 49.

2.  *Narodnoe khoziaistvo SSSR v 1983 g.* (Moscow, 1984) p. 447.

3.  *Zdravookhranenie Rossiiskoi Federatsii*, 3 (1984) p. 16.

4.  For an effort to assess the impact of Stalin's terror, see Iosif G. Dyadkin, *Unnatural Deaths in the USSR, 1928–1954* (New Brunswick, N.J.: Transaction Books, 1983). For a discussion of urbanization and its consequences, see David E. Powell, 'The Rural Exodus,' *Problems of Communism*, vol. XXIII, no. 6 (November–December, 1974) pp. 1–13, and Novitskii, op. cit., p. 49.

5.  See the statistical annual *Narodnoe khoziaistvo SSSR* for the late 1960s and early 1970s.

6.  Ibid. Western scholars have been engaged in a heated debate, trying to explain whether the increase is real or apparent. According to Feshbach and Davis, official Soviet data reflect a genuine rise in infant mortality. Jones and Grupp have suggested that much of the apparent rise is merely a statistical artifact, reflecting improved data collection and higher birthrates in Central Asia. See Christopher Davis and Murray Feshbach, *Rising Infant Mortality in the USSR in the 1970s*, US Bureau of the Census, Series P-95, no. 74 (Washington, DC: US

Government Printing Office, 1980); Ellen Jones and Fred W. Grupp, 'Infant Mortality Trends in the Soviet Union', *Population and Development Review,* vol. 9, no. 2 (June 1983) pp. 213–46.

7. Murray Feshbach, 'Issues in Soviet Health Problems,' in US Congress, Joint Economic Committee, *Soviet Economy in the 1980s: Problems and Prospects,* Part 2 (Washington, DC, 1983) p. 205.

8. For a discussion of the influence of alcoholism and other factors contributing to the decline in life expectancy, see B. Ts. Urlanis, *Problemy dinamiki naseleniia SSSR* (Moscow, 1974) pp. 187, 188. See also John Dutton, Jr., 'Changes in Soviet Mortality Patterns, 1959–77', *Population and Development Review,* vol. 5, no. 2 (June, 1979).

9. Murray Feshbach, 'Population and Manpower Trends in the USSR', *Occasional Paper no. 34,* Kennan Institute for Advanced Russian Studies (Washington, DC., 1978), p. 92.

10. *Sotsiologicheskie issledovaniia,* no. 1 (1976) p. 102.

11. *Planovoe khoziaistvo,* no. 11 (1973).

12. *Izvestiia,* 6 September, 1974. See also *Kommunist,* no. 9 (1977) and *Sotsialisticheskii trud,* no. 5 (1977).

13. *Materialy XXV s''ezda KPSS* (Moscow, 1976) p. 43.

14. Murray Feshbach and Stephen Rapawy, 'Soviet Population and Manpower Trends and Policies', in US Congress, Joint Economic Committee, *The Soviet Economy in New Perspective* (Washington, DC: US Government Printing Office, 1976).

15. Abram Bergson, 'The Soviet Economic Slowdown', *Challenge,* January–February, 1978, p. 24.

16. Testimony before the Joint Economic Committee, US Congress, Subcommittee on International Trade, Finance, and Security Economics, *Central Intelligence Agency Briefing on the Soviet Economy* (1 December 1982), mimeograph, pp. 20–1.

17. *Literaturnaia gazeta,* 20 August 1975.

18. *Sotsialisticheskii trud,* no. 1 (1978).

19. *Ekonomika i organizatsiia promyshlennogo proizvodstva* (hereafter *EKO*), no. 2 (1978).

20. Allen Kroncher, 'How Can the Soviet Union Increase Its Work Force?', *Radio Liberty Research,* RL 145/78 (28 June 1978).

21. *Ekonomicheskaia gazeta,* no. 4 (1977). See also V. P. Belov (ed.), *Trudosposobnost' pensionerov po starosti: Voprosy stimulirovaniia i organizatsii ikh truda* (Moscow, 1975) p. 140. Hereafter cited as Belov.

22. *Kommunist,* op. cit.

23. *USSR: Some Implications of Demographic Trends for Economic Policies,* Central Intelligence Agency Publication no. ER 7–10012 (January 1977) p. 3.

24. See David E. Powell, 'The Soviet Labour Force', *Current History,* vol. 83, no. 485 (October 1984) p. 330.

25. *Kommunist,* op. cit.

26. Feshbach and Rapawy, op. cit.

27. *Planovoe khoziaistvo,* no. 12 (1978); *Sovetskaia kul'tura,* 10 February 1978, p. 6; *Nedelia,* no. 15 (1979) p. 11; Belov, op. cit., pp. 13 and 145.

28.  *Sotsialisticheskii trud,* no. 10 (1978) p. 135. See also *Materialy XXV s''ezda,* op cit., p. 218.
29.  Soviet sources use the word 'pension' to describe a variety of social security arrangements, including payment to individuals who reach a certain age, people who suffer partially or fully disabling injuries or wounds, and families which have lost their principal breadwinner. I will use the term to describe men and women who are eligible for old-age pensions.
30.  Unless otherwise specified, the following discussion relies on the article by A. A. Kartskhiia in the volume edited by Belov.
31.  In Belov, op. cit., p. 149.
32.  Solomon M. Schwarz, *Labor in the Soviet Union* (New York: Praeger, 1951), p. 329.
33.  *Voprosy truda,* March–April 1929, cited in ibid, p. 331.
34.  Schwarz, op. cit., p. 331.
35.  Belov, op. cit., p. 154.
36.  ᐱFor the text of the law, see *Pravda* and *Izvestiia,* 15 July 1956, pp. 1–2.
37.  For a list of these measures, see Novitskii, op. cit.
38.  For the text of the law, see *Vedomosti Verkhovnogo Soveta SSSR,* no. 29 1964) p. 340.
39.  Lazar Volin, *A Century of Russian Agriculture* (Cambridge, Mass.: Harvard University Press, 1970) p. 428.
40.  Ibid, p. 429.
41.  Novitskii, op. cit., p. 56. For slightly different figures, see M. S. Lantsev, *Sotsial'noe obespechenie v SSSR: Ekonomicheskii aspekt* (Moscow, 1976).
42.  Sternheimer, op. cit., p. 83; William Moskoff, 'Part-Time Employment in the Soviet Union', *Soviet Studies,* vol. XXXIV, no. 2 (April 1982), pp. 277–8; *Sotsial'noe obespechenie,* no. 5 (1984) p. 3.
43.  *Pravda,* 2 October 1979, p. 1.
44.  *Sotsialisticheskaia zakonnost',* no. 11 (1983) pp. 54–5.
45.  Moskoff, op. cit., pp. 279–80. See also A. G. Novitskii and G. V. Mil', *Zaniatost' pensionerov: Sotsial'no-demograficheskii aspekt* (Moscow, 1981) p. 94.
46.  *Sovetskaia kul'tura,* 16 December 1977, p. 3.
47.  Novitskii, op. cit., p. 50; Belov op. cit., p. 141.
48.  *Sotsiologicheskie issledovaniia,* op. cit., p. 102.
49.  Novitskii, op. cit., p. 50.
50.  Cited in ibid, p. 51. See also V. G. Kostakov, *Prognoz zaniatosti naseleniia* (Moscow, 1979) p. 86.
51.  Novitskii, op. cit., p. 50. See also the article by A. Tkachen in D. I. Valentei *et al.* (ed.), *Naselenie i trudovye resursy RSFSR* (Moscow, 1982) p. 78.
52.  See the remarks of Leonid Brezhnev at the 24th Party Congress in 1971, *Pravda,* 31 March 1971. See also the statement of D. Komarova, Minister of Social Security of the Russian Republic, *Sotsial'noe obespechenie,* no. 5 (1984) pp. 3–7.
53.  Novitskii, op. cit., p. 50.
54.  *Sotsiologicheskie issledovaniia,* op. cit., p. 102.

55. Belov, op. cit., pp. 145–6. See also the sources listed in Sternheimer, op. cit., p. 85, footnote 16.
56. Belov, op. cit., pp. 12 and 143.
57. Ibid, p. 6.
58. Ibid, pp. 12–13.
59. See several of the studies presented in ibid., e.g., pp. 16, 18–19, 22, 115, 135 and 144–5.
60. See David E. Powell, 'The Emerging Health Crisis in the Soviet Union', *Current History*, vol. 84, no. 504 (October 1985) pp. 325–8 and 340.
61. *Sotsiologicheskie issledovaniia*, op. cit., p. 112.
62. Novitskii, op. cit., p. 71.
63. Novitskii and Mil', op. cit., p. 177; Novitskii, op cit., p. 60; *Kommunist*, no. 2 (1980) p. 54.
64. A. Novitskii, in *Narodonaselenie: Naselenie i trudovye resursy*, p. 59. Far more part-time positions exist, but few are staffed with pensioners. See *Sovetskoe gosudarstvo i pravo*, no. 10 (1976) pp. 54–61.
65. *Sotsiologicheskie issledovaniia*, op. cit., p. 110.
66. See, *inter alia, Gorodskoe khoziaistvo Moskvy*, no. 2 (1983) pp. 26–7; *Sovetskaia kul'tura*, 26 October 1982, p. 3; *Agitator*, no. 9 (1983) p. 24.
67. *Izvestiia*, 6 January 1976, p. 5.
68. Novitskii, in Maikov and Novitskii, op. cit., p. 52.
69. *Izvestiia*, 17 January 1970, p. 2.
70. *Sovetskaia kul'tura*, 10 February 1978, p. 6.
71. Belov, op. cit., p. 141.
72. Ibid., p. 6.
73. *Izvestiia*, 6 January 1976, p. 5; *Nedelia*, no. 15 (1979) p. 11. Belov, op. cit., p. 143, gives a figure of 57% for 1973.
74. Sternheimer, op. cit., p. 82, footnotes 6 and 7.
75. Belov, op. cit., p. 9.
76. *EKO*, no. 5 (1978) p. 29.
77. Sternheimer, op. cit., pp. 85 and 86.
78. See the joint Party-State Resolution issued on 22 January 1981, in *Spravochnik partiinogo rabotnika*, vol. 22 (Moscow, 1982) pp. 475–6.
79. A. E. Kozlov, *Sotsial'noe obespechenie v SSSR* (Moscow, 1981) pp. 79–80. The law, promulgated on 2 September 1981 by the Presidium of the USSR Supreme Soviet, may be found in *Spravochnik partiinogo rabotnika*, op. cit., pp. 492–3.
80. *Pravda* and *Izvestiia*, 21 May 1985, p. 1.
81. Sternheimer, op. cit., p. 85.
82. For one such suggestion, see *Sovetskoe gosudarstvo i pravo*, no. 1 (1984) p. 57.
83. See *Pravda*, 3 August 1985, p. 2.

# Index

Please note that some, common, items are not indexed at all (e.g. USSR, Poland, GDR and Hungary) and some only selectively (e.g. labour demand, labour market, labour productivity, labour shortage, labour supply).